9/17/03

To Gloria,
Who is our
brothers' keeper

WERE
WE OUR
BROTHERS'
KEEPERS?

Haskel Lookstein

WERE
WE OUR
BROTHERS'
KEEPERS?

*The Public Response of
American Jews to the Holocaust
1938–1944*

HASKEL LOOKSTEIN

VINTAGE BOOKS
A DIVISION OF RANDOM HOUSE
NEW YORK

First Vintage Books Edition, January 1988

Copyright © 1985 by Haskel Lookstein

All rights reserved under International and Pan-American
Copyright Conventions. Published in the
United States by Random House, Inc., New York,
and simultaneously in Canada by Random House
of Canada Limited, Toronto. Originally published,
in hardcover, by Hartmore House, in 1985.

Library of Congress Cataloging-in-Publication Data
Lookstein, Haskel.
Were we our brothers' keepers?
Reprint. Originally published: New York, NY:
Hartmore House, c1985.
Bibliography: p.
Includes index.
1. Jews—United States—Politics and government.
2. Holocaust, Jewish (1939–1945).
3. United States—Ethnic relations.
I. Title.
[E184.J5L76 1988]   940.53′15′03924   87-40114
ISBN 0-394-75598-7 (pbk.)

Manufactured in the United States of America
10 9 8 7 6 5 4 3 2 1

CONTENTS

Foreword   9

Preface   13

Acknowledgments   15

1. A DIFFICULT QUESTION   21
2. KRISTALLNACHT   35
3. THE SADDEST SHIP AFLOAT   81
4. THE FINAL SOLUTION BECOMES PUBLIC KNOWLEDGE   105
5. THE WARSAW GHETTO UPRISING   146
6. THE CAMPAIGN FOR A RESCUE AGENCY   160
7. THE TRAP SHUTS   184
8. WERE WE OUR BROTHERS' KEEPERS?   205

Notes   219

Selected Bibliography   265

Index   275

To Anatoly Scharansky

A dear friend and a
heroic Jew. You taught
us the meaning of the
Biblical command:

"DO NOT STAND IDLY BY WHILE YOUR
BROTHER'S BLOOD IS SPILLED."(*Leviticus,* 19:16)

Thank God we were able to
present to you in Jerusalem a
copy of this book, which you inspired.

FOREWORD

Ask survivors; they will tell you: the indifference of the Allies and friends wounded them as deeply as the cruelty of the enemy. That the Nazis wished them dead, seemed "normal"; besides, the Nazi propaganda hardly sought to hide that fact. But how is one to explain the passivity or the silence of the others?

During the war, the bloodiest of all wars, the victims consoled themselves—or despaired—thinking that their plight was known only to their dark, closed world.

The free world knew nothing about them or it would have put a stop to Auschwitz and Treblinka. That's why messengers risked their lives to escape. To break the walls of silence. To inform humanity of what was happening within the universe of the concentration camp. If the Jews in those organized and efficient camps of suffering and death had known that the leaders of the Allied world were aware of their plight but had chosen to do nothing, I wonder whether they would have had the strength or the desire to cling to life and to hope.

Their despair took place only after the liberation. Little by little, with the passing of years, they began to comprehend their mistake. Documents, discovered by investigators in America and Israel, left no doubt. The Allies, at the highest level, were kept informed of all phases of the Final Solution. In Washington, as in London, in Stockholm as at the Vatican, all aspects of the massacres were well known. The names of Treblinka and Belzec, of Majdanek and Chelmno appeared in the news of the day. The public could not have been unaware of their terrifying meaning. This can be said of the Jewish public as well. Unbelievable but true: the American Jewish community had not responded to the heart-rending cries of their brothers and sisters in nazified Europe. At the very least, not as they should have.

Such strange behavior for a community well known for its solidarity and for its family oriented and humanitarian traditions. Actually, few American Jews did not have close or distant relatives in Poland, in Romania or in Lithuania. How could they not have been moved when they read in their Yiddish or Jewish newspapers what the enemy was inflicting upon them over there? A few years ago, stirred by a need to understand, Arthur Goldberg, a leader of utmost integrity in contemporary American society, convened a group of investigators, representing all factions. This body attempted to examine the role of American Jewry during the Second World War and, in particular, with respect to the Holocaust. Almost all the participants were in agreement: the Jews could have done more.

The report of the Goldberg Commission created a controversy—but not Goldberg himself. This man remains above reproach. This man, whose straight-forwardness, intellectual honesty, and human courage cannot be praised enough, wanted to understand; that's all.

Rabbi Haskel Lookstein, in his well-documented dissertation, filled with painful accuracies, set for himself the very same goal: not to judge those who preceded him but to attempt to understand what it was that had made them overly cautious at a time when they should have been more daring.

Unable to go into all the events in depth, he underscores certain ones. In addition, he concentrates on a few publications. A wise and fruitful decision: the subject is too vast. One can only reach it through detail and example.

Let us take the case of the *St. Louis*. This German ship, with its cargo of a thousand Jewish refugees, hugs the coast of our cities. Everyone knows: if its passengers cannot disembark they will be delivered to the executioner. Days pass, all the same, the screams, the tears as well. The unfortunate refugees drift away and their brothers do not take to the streets to protest, to vent their anger at Roosevelt. They do not go out on strike, sound the alarm, or demonstrate a collective indignation. . . . How is one to explain such an un-Jewish attitude?

Granted, they feared an anti-Semitic reaction. Father Coughlin's evil broadcasts had reached an ever more sympathetic public. Public opinion did not favor a liberal immigration policy. In other words, society at large had its reasons for rejecting those "undesirable" passengers. But what about the Jews?

Didn't they have other reasons for wanting to welcome them, and thus save them? In retrospect, their passivity seems shameful. Even if their protests had been for naught, they should have been heard. This holds all the more true for the serious events yet to come. Lookstein discusses this in a pain-filled and convincing voice. The killers killed, the victims perished, and the world, though at war, did not intercede. Marriages and parties were held, daily prayers were recited, dinners and balls were organized: all this as though no flames were consuming the heavens above a small Polish village named Auschwitz.

Yet in America, they knew. Oh yes, they knew. Lookstein clearly substantiates this with proofs and quotes.

They knew not only at the highest levels of government, but throughout all strata of the general population. They knew that the Warsaw Ghetto was being assaulted by assassins. They knew that the Ghetto was resisting, that it was fighting and that its sons were dying in battle. They knew that the Hungarian Jews were threatened; they knew that their time was coming; they knew what their fate would be. Here and there, certain individuals, certain groups had tried to do what they could to stop the massacres, but . . . but what? For want of a large scale operation? For want of imagination? For want of coordination? Perhaps for lack of compassion? The fact remains that the Jewish community failed to conquer its internal divisions and it failed to overcome its hesitations. It failed to rise to the task incumbent upon itself: to put everything aside in order to save those who could yet be saved.

Lookstein says it well in his concluding words; "The Final Solution may have been unstoppable by American Jewry, but it should have been unbearable for them. And it wasn't."

Too harsh a judgment? Lookstein judges no one. No one has the right to judge. Lookstein can only relate his own pain. It overwhelms us. It reflects a broken heart. But a broken heart is an open heart, open to suffering and to prayer, to anger and to hope, to hope in spite of anger, to faith too, to faith in spite of despair. A heart filled with sorrow and strengthened by the need to overcome sorrow is alone capable of reaching the highest level of the most Jewish of Jewish virtues: the love of the Jewish people, *ahavat Yisrael*.

It is for the sake of *ahavat Yisrael* that Rabbi Haskel Lookstein has written this volume. It is for the sake of *ahavat Yisrael* that you must read it.

Elie Wiesel

Translated from the French by Danièle Gorlin Lassner.

PREFACE

Writing about the American Jewish public response to the Holocaust poses certain problems. The temptation is strong to judge the past by the standards of the present, to expect public reactions and responses in the thirties and forties that would be the norm today and to assume that American Jews of that day understood what was happening to European Jewry and should have been equal to the challenge posed by the cataclysm through which they were living. These judgments, expectations, and assumptions impinge upon the objectivity of the historian and even call into question his standards of fairness.

I have tried to avoid some of the expected pitfalls by following the advice of Professor Jacob Katz in "Was the Holocaust Predictable?" (*Commentary*, May 1975). He suggests a careful reconstruction of the situation as precisely as historical sources will permit, so that one might know what they knew and believed at that time and understand their plight. This is a historian's way of framing the Talmudic aphorism: "Do not judge another until you stand in his place."

I have tried to understand the problems faced by American Jews in the years 1938 through 1944. The more I read in the field, the less judgmental I became. The judgments that have remained in this text are intended in a spirit of love and empathy and are there solely as lessons for the future.

H.L.

New York
Tammuz 17, 5745
July 7, 1985

ACKNOWLEDGMENTS

There are many people to whom I owe a profound debt of gratitude for helping me through an arduous, frustrating, depressing—and yet exhilarating and educational—task. First, my gratitude to my friend and coworker for Soviet Jewry, Jerry Goodman, executive director of the National Conference on Soviet Jewry, who first suggested this topic to me. His idea was to study the difference between the response of American Jews to the Holocaust and their response to the struggle of Soviet Jews for freedom and emigration. I heartily recommend the second half of the topic to some enterprising scholar. To my friend and mentor Elie Wiesel, my profound thanks for helping me to formulate and structure this study, for reading the manuscript, for writing the Foreword and for inspiring me to undertake the depressing research into an unhappy past. My thanks also to my friend and teacher, Dr. Michael Wyschogrod, my sister, Dr. Nathalie Friedman, and my most supportive and enthusiastic congregrant, friend, and uncle, Bernard D. Fischman, for reading the manuscript and making helpful suggestions.

Among the librarians and research specialists who have been most helpful to me, I am pleased to thank Dina Abramowicz and her staff, particularly Zachary Baker, at YIVO for their understanding, patience, and guidance, Cyma M. Horowitz, Marcia Bernstein, Esther Eidensohn, and Judith Levine at the Blaustein Library of the American Jewish Committee for their exceptional cooperation and guidance, and Sylvia Landress, Rebecca Zapinsky Sherman, Esther Togman, Ralph Melnick, and Judith Popick at the Zionist Archives Library for their encouragement of my work and their tolerance in the face of my many requests. My thanks also to Dr. Majer Landau, a chemist by profession but a historian by avocation, for his generous assistance and guidance. I am particularly grateful to Zalman Alpert, a research librarian, for sharing his research expertise with me. I remember also the kindness of the late Mrs. Shoshana Ribalow, who was generous enough to lend me her late husband's bound copies of *Hadoar,* which provided so much insight into the period under review.

Finally, I owe so much to my father, Rabbi Joseph·H. Lookstein, of blessed memory, for everything he taught me, which proved so helpful in this endeavor, and for the unfailing encouragement of him and my mother, Gertrude Lookstein, as well as their prodding me to complete the work. I am grateful to God that my father saw the completed manuscript some months before his passing. My thoughts also turn to my sainted father-in-law, Morris Katz, of blessed memory, who was so supportive of my work and who took so much pride in the first results of my research. I am grateful that my mother-in-law, Esther Katz, shares in the joy of its completion. To Congregation Kehilath Jeshurun and Ramaz School and to all my friends and coworkers there, my gratitude for their patience and forebearance in allowing me to devote so much time to this effort. Among these friends Benjamin Brown, Sandy Eisenstat, and Gregory Katz have been especially supportive.

I have also been greatly encouraged by Ellen and Frederic H. Baumgarten, Roberta and George Baumgarten, Lillian and Samuel Borenstein, Fran Brown, Marilyn and B. Warren Brown, Claire and Fred Deutsch, Arlene and Avrom Doft, Elizabeth and Alan Doft, Suzanne Eisenstat, Caryl and Israel Englander, Hilda Fischman, Frieda and A. Phillip Goldsmith, Rae and Stanley Gurewitsch, Pearl and Zev Hack, Lana and Ben Hauben, Nathalie Herman, Curtis Katz, Carol and Gerald S. Kaufman, Ruth and Lawrence A. Kobrin, Yvonne and Walter Koppel, Wilma and Stephen J. Kule, Lynette and David Levy, Jean and Armand Lindenbaum, Sylvia and David A. Lipton, Hannah and Edward Low, Carol and Melvin D. Newman, Inge and Ira Rennert, Frida and Herman Riederman, Amy and Howard Rubenstein, Trudy and Seymour S. Sadinoff, Audrey and Fredrik J. Schwartzberg, Ruth and Irwin Shapiro, Alice and Burton Usdan.

Gloria Mosesson, my good friend and publisher, took the project in hand and personally saw it through the intricate process of publication. A special word of thanks to Florence Fishel, who typed and retyped the manuscript as an act of commitment and a labor of love. Michael Haber, a student at the Ramaz School, helped me with some important photographic work.

Aharon aharon haviv (last but most important), my loving thanks to Mindy, Debbie, Shira, Joshua, and my son-in-law, Jay Cinnamon, for giving their father a leave of absence and for honoring—usually—the sacredness of his study. I hope that some day one or more of them will follow this same route, with less travail but with no less satisfaction. And to the best wife and friend one could ask for, Audrey—who gave me the kind of selfless support, encouragement, and understanding without which this work would have been impossible—this study is gratefully dedicated.

Blessed is God who has preserved me, sustained me, and enabled me to reach this day.

H.L.

Tammuz 17, 5745
July 17, 1985

WERE
WE OUR
BROTHERS'
KEEPERS?

Chapter one

A DIFFICULT QUESTION

The indifference and insensitivity of those non-Jews who stood by *While Six Million Died,** doing nothing when "They Could Have Been Saved,"† has been exposed and documented. But what did American Jews do in the years of the Holocaust?

The Jewish Spectator
November 1968, p. 8

The question posed by *The Jewish Spectator* is in part an outgrowth of the work of a revisionist school in Holocaust history,[1] which made its appearance a decade and a half ago with the publication of Arthur D. Morse's *While Six Million Died: A Chronicle of American Apathy.*[2] This school of thought suggests that, while the Nazis were the perpetrators of the Holocaust, they were not the only guilty parties. The Western democracies, the Pope, the neutral countries, and the potential refuge nations of South and Central America, because they stood by while 6 million Jews were murdered‡ by Hitler, shared in the guilt and became, in

---

*A reference to Arthur D. Morse, *While Six Million Died: A Chronicle of American Apathy* (New York: Random House, 1967).
†A reference to Reuben Ainsztein's article, "They Could Have Been Saved," *Jewish Spectator,* June 1967.
‡I prefer the word "murdered" to the more generally used term "exterminated." One exterminates insects, rodents, and similar vermin. The Nazis murdered *people*.

a sense, passive accessories to the most terrible crime in human history.

Since the publication of Morse's work, several scholars have published more broadly based studies, which examine the refugee-rescue problem, 1938–1945, and which consider dispassionately the possibilities that existed for resettlement and rescue: David S. Wyman, *Paper Walls: America and the Refugee Crisis 1938–1941*, published in 1968; Henry L. Feingold, *The Politics of Rescue: The Roosevelt Administration and the Holocaust, 1938–1945*, published in 1970; Saul S. Friedman, *No Haven for the Oppressed: United States Policy Toward Jewish Refugees, 1938–1945*, published in 1973; Martin Gilbert, *Auschwitz and the Allies*, published in 1981; and, most recently, a second widely acclaimed volume by Wyman, *The Abandonment of the Jews: America and the Holocaust 1941–1945*, published in 1984. All give some scholarly confirmation to the story told by Morse. These historians, however, join Morse in suggesting that there was an additional group that must share the burden of guilt for the Holocaust. That group was American Jewry. Many American Jews, Morse observed, were "as disinterested as their Christian countrymen" in the plight of European Jewry and thus "became bystanders to genocide."

Jews who occupied high places in the New Deal, in greater numbers than in any previous administration, have been criticized by historians for failing to exert maximum pressure upon a President who might have been more responsive had such pressure been forthcoming. Divisiveness within the American Jewish community, it has been noted, served as an impediment to efforts on behalf of the victims of Nazi persecution. In general, the Jewish community of the Holocaust period has been accused of being too timid in responding to the indifference of America and its Allies and, consequently, of being unequal to the unprecedented human challenge with which it was confronted.[3]

This study is an attempt to shed some light on the validity of these criticisms of American Jewry. It is an analysis of what American Jews were doing *publicly*. It does not touch on initiatives, undertaken in private, by individuals or organizations.[4]*

---

*A specific example of such initiatives is the rescue work of the Vaad Ha-Hatzala, organized through the monumental efforts of Stephen Klein.

Because of the vast area to be covered, this study has focused upon six events from November 1938 through July 1944, two prewar and four during the war. I am indebted to Professor Elie Wiesel for his shared wisdom in advising me as to the choice of events to be studied. Each of these events, and the periods that followed them, presented a challenge to American Jewry that called for a public response. The events and their subsequent periods are as follows:

1. *Kristallnacht* and its aftermath, November 10, 1938, through the end of December 1938. The pogrom of November 10 and the ensuing physical and economic persecutions of German Jews represented a decisive turning point in the tragedy of German Jewry, of which German Jews and American Jews were aware. Gerald Reitlinger considers *Kristallnacht* to be the beginning of the chronology of the Holocaust. Lucy S. Dawidowicz calls *Kristallnacht* the night "the Jewish community of Germany went up in flames."[5] Until *Kristallnacht* Jews were subjected to severe economic restrictions and their legal and political status was undermined. But it was not until November 10, 1938, that the Nazi government launched a campaign of physical brutality toward Jews, a new course of action which led eventually to their annihilation.

2. The voyage of the *St. Louis*, May 13–June 21, 1939. During this thirty-nine-day period a ship filled with German-Jewish refugees sailed to Cuba, was not allowed to land her human cargo, and, after lingering for eleven days in Western Hemisphere waters—several of those days off the coast of Florida—set sail back toward Hamburg, where a terrible fate awaited her frantic passengers.

3. The news of the murder of 2 million Jews and the American Jewish response evoked by that news, November 24, 1942, through March 1943. This was the period during which many American Jews were presented with the facts about the impending genocide of European Jewry. Their response to this disclosure will contribute much to an understanding of American Jewry's public attitude during the Holocaust.

4. The Warsaw ghetto uprising and the public response to it of American Jewry, April 19, 1943, through June 1943.

5. The campaign to create a rescue agency for the relief of European Jews, July 1943 through January 1944, when the War Refugee Board was created. In this period, American Jews were

already committed to a rescue program. Their public response to a concrete proposal for rescue provides insight into Jewish priorities and concerns during the Holocaust.

6. The Nazi occupation of Hungary and the deportation of masses of Hungarian Jews to extermination camps, March 19, 1944, through July 1944.

The public response of American Jews, during each of these periods, to the perilous state of their European brethren can be evaluated by a series of questions, which are applicable to each period. What was publicly known about the Holocaust in general, or the particular event or issues involved, in each of the periods? How was this knowledge interpreted by American Jewry? Were the available facts understood? What implications were drawn from the facts? How did the Jewish press report these events? How much coverage of the events and the issues was offered to the Jewish readers? What was the editorial comment in each of the periods? How did Jewish leaders express themselves publicly in reaction to these events and the issues they raised? Finally, what public action was taken by Jews in response to the events and the issues?

In order to answer these questions, a broad sampling of the Jewish press has been studied for each of the periods. The press has been chosen as a primary source because it reflected well what was known by American Jews and what the different segments of American Jewry were thinking and doing. The Jewish community in the United States, unlike its Catholic counterpart, does not have a hierarchical unity. Nevertheless, it is a community with many organizations, and these, in sum, reflect every major group difference within the total community. The public statements of these organizations may be found in the Anglo-Jewish press, where virtually every periodical serves as the house organ for some specific communal organization. As Henry L. Feingold has concluded: "The opinions of . . . the American Jewish community can best be gleaned from the Anglo-Jewish press."[6]

But the press is a good source for more than opinions and attitudes. It is also an instrument by which to measure what Jews knew about the Holocaust, since it was their primary source for news about Jews around the world. It also enables one to gauge what public activities were carried on during the period under review. The Anglo-Jewish weekly newspapers and periodicals depended almost entirely upon the *Jewish Telegraphic Agency Daily News Bulletin (JTA)* for its news reports about European Jewry, as well as for the world reaction and the response of Jews in America and throughout the world. An analysis of the *JTA,* therefore, should provide a reliable index of the information available to American Jews.[7]

The other major source of Jewish news was the Yiddish press, which provided virtually a measurement of the pulse of the community. No other foreign-language press in America reflected the intimate life of the people it represented so deeply or was so influential in molding the opinions and attitudes of its public. During the Holocaust, the Yiddish press had a circulation of around 400,000 nationally, of which approximately 250,000 was in New York. The readership was probably two to three times higher than the circulation figures. This study has focused on the four major daily Yiddish newspapers in New York, which ranged in viewpoint from conservative to communist.[8]

Besides relying upon the Anglo-Jewish press sampling, the *JTA,* and the four major Yiddish dailies in New York, this study has also included *The New York Times* for each period. The reason for choosing the *Times* is its status as the "paper of record" and the newspaper that is expected to have the most complete and reliable news coverage. It is likely that many New York Jews relied upon the *Times* for their Jewish news and respected the accuracy of the reports found in that newspaper.[9]

For the purposes of this study, the following newspapers and periodicals were read for each of the six periods:

The New York Times.

Jewish Telegraphic Agency Daily News Bulletin.

Jewish Daily Forward—the New York Yiddish daily with the largest circulation. Its viewpoint was socialist, universalist, and unsupportive of Zionism. It was the paper of Jewish labor.

The Day—the most prestigious Yiddish daily in New York because of its columnists. Its editorial stance was mildly liberal and actively Zionist.

Morning Journal—originally the widest read of the daily Yiddish papers, because at first it was the only large morning paper among them. This paper combined a religious outlook with patriotic Americanism. It was politically conservative and supportive of Zionism.

The Freiheit—official communist Yiddish daily.

Congress Bulletin (later *Congress Weekly*)—published weekly by the liberal, activist, and pro-Zionist American Jewish Congress.

National Jewish Monthly—published by B'nai B'rith. A magazine of general Jewish news, editorials, features, and B'nai B'rith news.

Contemporary Jewish Record—published bimonthly by the American Jewish Committee, featuring essays and a chronicle of Jewish news for the preceding two months.

American Jewish Year Book—an annual, published by the American Jewish Committee, containing feature articles, statistical tables, and a comprehensive review of Jewish news for the year.

Reconstructionist—published bimonthly by the liberal-wing Conservative religious group of the same name. It was a Zionist, liberal, and activist magazine. (There was no regular publication of the Conservative religious movement during the Holocaust period.)

Opinion—an independent monthly edited by Stephen S. Wise, liberal, Zionist, and deeply committed to the American democratic tradition as exemplified by Franklin D. Roosevelt.

Jewish Spectator—the only other independent magazine, a monthly, edited for most of the periods by the activist, pro-Zionist Trude WeissvRosmarin.

Jewish Frontier—a Labor Zionist monthly, liberal and activist in its approach to Jewish problems.

The *Answer*—published irregularly by Peter Bergson's activist, Zionist-Revisionist group, beginning in early 1943.

The *Orthodox Union*—published more or less monthly by the Union of Orthodox Jewish Congregations of America and devoted largely to news and essays of concern to modern Orthodox Jews in America.

The *Synagogue* and *Liberal Judaism*—monthly or bimonthly publications of the Reform Jewish movement in America.

Menorah Journal—a liberal literary magazine published quarterly by the Menorah Society.

Jewish Center—published quarterly by the Jewish Welfare Board and devoted to articles of concern to Jewish social and group workers.

Hadoar—the Hebrew language weekly.

Notes and News—published "from time to time" by the Council of Jewish Federations and Welfare Funds and devoted to philanthropic issues and activities.

The *New Palestine*—published weekly and later bimonthly by the Zionist Organization of America, containing news and articles largely devoted to the Zionist cause.

Hadassah Newsletter—published monthly by Hadassah, the women's Zionist organization. It was a parallel publication to *New Palestine*.

Jewish Outlook—a monthly magazine published by Mizrachi, the religious Zionist organization.

Conference Record—a short-lived publication founded in August 1943 to describe the work of the American Jewish Conference.

The Sentinel—a weekly newspaper for the Chicago Jewish community. Chicago was the second largest Jewish city in America, with a Jewish population of 363,000 in 1937. This newspaper is a partial reflection of what Chicago Jews knew about the Jewish tragedy in Europe during this period and what response was forthcoming from the community.

Jewish Exponent—a weekly newspaper published in Philadelphia, the third largest Jewish community in the United States, with a Jewish population of 293,000 in 1937. This newspaper provides information on the public response of Philadelphia Jews during the six periods.

Jewish Advocate—a weekly newspaper published in Boston, the fourth largest Jewish community in the country, with a Jewish population of 118,000 in 1937. (In the late thirties, there were no other Jewish population centers in America with more than 100,000 members.) This newspaper served the same purpose for Boston as the *Jewish Exponent* did for Philadelphia and the *Chicago Jewish Chronicle* did for Chicago.[10]

WHAT WAS THE RESPONSE OF AMERICA AND HER ALLIES?

The public reaction of American Jews to the Holocaust can only be understood against a background of the American and world response. Scholars who have analyzed that response have found it extremely limited, and voices from the period itself testify eloquently to the same indifference. Freda Kirchway, the editor of *The Nation*, writing in March of 1943, summed it up thus:

> In this country, you and I, the President and the Congress and the State Department are accessories to the crime and share Hitler's guilt. If we had behaved like humane and generous people instead of complacent cowardly ones, the two million lying today in the earth of Poland . . . would be alive and safe. We had it in our power to rescue this doomed people and yet we did not lift a hand to do it— or perhaps it would be better to say that we lifted just one cautious hand, encased in a tight-fitting glove of quotas and visas and affidavits and a thick layer of prejudice.[11]*

Kirchway's moral outrage might offend the judgment of more dispassionate historians, but the facts to which she alluded are, by now, a matter of historical record. The United States did not open her doors to refugees fleeing from Hitler. She did not even admit the number of immigrants that her quotas allowed from countries under Nazi Germany. From 1938 to 1941, the restrictionist quotas allowed for 212,000 immigrants from those lands, whereas only 150,000 were actually permitted to enter. This was due to the even more restrictionist visa administration of State Department Undersecretary Breckinridge Long. Even in 1943, when the United States government knew what was happening to European Jews, only 23,775 aliens entered this country, the lowest figure in eighty years.[12] Of course, after January 1942, the issue ceased to be merely hospitality to refugees but a matter of rescuing Jews who were condemned to death by the Nazis. Hitler's machinery of extermination was pitted against the Allied determination to rescue the intended victims. It was no contest. The Allied determination simply did not exist—rescue was to be accomplished through victory. Any departure from that policy was considered criminal.[13]

Does this mean that Roosevelt and Churchill were indifferent to the fate of European Jewry? Scholars disagree on that

---

*It is worthy of note that Kirchway, as early as March of 1943, takes it for granted that her readers knew all about that figure of 2 million dead. The news of that number had been widely disseminated for almost four months.

point. Some dispute the word "indifference" and ascribe the meagre rescue effort to the fact that rescuing European Jews had a low priority with a President and a Prime Minister whose main concerns were with winning the war. Others observe that Roosevelt's State Department actively opposed a large-scale rescue effort and that the British Foreign Office was actually fearful that a serious effort might be successful. This would pose an even more difficult problem: What should be done with all those rescued Jews? In the meantime Hitler's death camps were efficiently ensuring that fewer and fewer Jews would remain to be rescued.[14]

A former adviser to Roosevelt, Benjamin V. Cohen, interviewed twenty-three years after the liberation of Auschwitz, commented on the President's refugee policy as follows:

> When you are in a dirty war, some will suffer more than others. . . . Things ought to have been different, but war is different, and we live in an imperfect world.[15]

It is hard to suppress a sense of despair at this dispassionate, almost callous judgment on the part of a Jew who had the President's ear in those desperate days.

An editorial in the London *New Statesman and Nation,* reprinted in *Jewish Spectator,* April 1943, was not quite as sanguine about the matter. Pondering the Allied failure to rescue and the British determination to bar the entry into Palestine of those few who might escape, the writer concluded bitterly:

> When historians relate this story of extermination, they will find it, from first to last, all but incredible. For Hitler there is the excuse of madness. But this nation is sane.

It is against this background of official indifference, callousness, or simply an inability to inhibit Hitler's war against the Jews, that the American Jewish response to the Holocaust must be understood.

CONDITIONS THAT AFFECTED THE AMERICAN JEWISH RESPONSE

The relatively weak response of the United States and the Western democracies was a source of great anguish to many Jews. But there were other factors during the Holocaust period that both promoted and hindered their response. These factors will be discussed at length in later chapters of this study. It is desirable, however, to present some of them at the beginning in order to gain preliminary insights into what American Jews could and could not do.

In the 1940s, American Jewry was better prepared in some ways than any other hyphenated group for the task of influencing American foreign policy. Its population in the 1936–1937 census was 4,771,000—only 3.69 percent of the country's total population—but 69 percent of that number was concentrated in the eleven largest cities. More than 2 million Jews, for example, lived in New York City where they constituted 28 percent of the population. The potential political power of American Jews therefore was not insignificant. Moreover, they were, on the whole, better informed and educated than other groups, and they were more politically active. They had a rich organizational life, and their recovery from the Depression was more advanced than that of other Americans.[16]

Furthermore, there was a strong Jewish presence in the Roosevelt administration, which had access to the President and could wield power in Congress. Roosevelt's inner circle of advisers included Felix Frankfurter, Bernard M. Baruch, and Henry Morgenthau, Jr. Among his trusted aides and associates were Benjamin V. Cohen, Sidney Hillman, Herbert H. Lehman, David K. Niles, and Samuel Rosenman. Moreover, the chairman of the three major committees in Congress concerned with rescue and refugees were Jewish: Rep. Sol Bloom (House Foreign Affairs Committee), Rep. Samuel Dickstein (House Committee on Immigration and Naturalization), and Rep. Emanuel Celler (House Judiciary Committee).

These advantages, however, were far outweighed by a series of factors that inhibited strong Jewish pressure on American policy. American Jews, in the first place, were sufficiently insecure to feel that they had to be more patriotic than the most chauvinistic of American groups. Consider the statement made by Stephen S. Wise as he addressed the American Jewish Conference in August 1943—a Jewish group meeting on Jewish issues, which was considering a proposal on Palestine and a plan to rescue the remaining 3 million Jews of Europe in the knowledge that the first 3 million had already been exterminated.

> This is an American Conference. We are Americans, first, last, and all the time. Nothing else that we are, whether by faith or race or fate, qualifies our Americanism. Everything else we are and have deepens, enriches and strengthens, if that can be, our Americanism.[17]

Such defensiveness did not encourage Wise or his fellow American Jews to press the government to take the steps necessary to rescue Jews. "Throughout the Second World War," writes Raul Hilberg, "the Jewish people adopted the Allied cause as their own; they shut out many thoughts of their disaster and helped achieve the final victory." Ironically, American Jews did not even get recognition for their patriotism. When Americans were asked between November 1938 and December 1942 whether they thought Jews were as patriotic, more patriotic, or less patriotic than other Americans, only 5 percent answered "more," and between 25 and 30 percent answered "less."[18]

An even more inhibiting factor was the virulent anti-Semitism that was rampant during the Holocaust years. As late as 1944, 24 percent of the respondents in one poll regarded Jews as "a menace to America." A series of surveys taken between 1940 and 1945 indicated that "between 31 and 48 percent of the public throughout the war years would have actively supported a hypothetical anti-Semitic campaign or at least sympathized with it; about 30 percent would have opposed it; and the rest would have taken no stand." As late as 1944, 56 percent in one poll answered "yes" to the question "Do you think Jews have too much power in the United States?"

This kind of national mood was nourished by the blatant and public criticism of Jews by such bigots as Father Charles E. Coughlin, who spoke weekly in 1938–1939 to a radio audience of 3.5 million Americans on a nationwide network. The result was to encourage among Jews, in the closing years of the thirties, what one sociologist called the "sha-sha philosophy . . . which 'sought to turn away wrath with gentle words, to obscure the Jew from public gaze. . . ." The maintenance of a low profile was not conducive to the mounting of a vigorous campaign to pressure an unwilling American leadership to save European Jews.[19]

But American Jewry faced an even more imposing obstacle to effective pressure on the United States: a widespread anti-alien panic in Congress and throughout the country, which militated against making America a haven for the persecuted. Before 1942, this panic was nurtured by three forces: high unemployment, a strong feeling of nativistic nationalism, and widespread anti-Semitism. Once the war began, the antialien tendency was strengthened by a veritable "security psychosis," a fear that the Nazis would plant agents and spies among the refugees. As late as January 1945, a National Opinion Research Poll reported that 46 percent of Americans opposed admitting Jewish refugees to the United States. This figure was down from a high of 77 percent in 1938. It would have required a mighty effort on the part of American Jews to counter such a strong restrictionist sentiment—in a country whose President was particularly sensitive to the public mood.[20]

An example of Roosevelt's sensitivity to public opinion, which also had a negative effect on the Jewish response, was his extreme caution not to refer to a *Jewish* plight. At a time when Berlin was calling all of its enemies Jews—to gain propaganda benefit at home—Roosevelt was calling Jewish victims of Nazi persecution by the bland term "political refugees." He was sensitive to his administration's being labeled "Jew Deal" and did not want to arouse American sentiment against rescue (although some believe that in private the President had a less charitable motive, namely his disinterest in saving Jews qua Jews). But it also tended to conceal the fact that Jews were overwhelmingly the major victims of German persecutions and thus helped the Nazis to "muffle the rumbles of the Final Solution."[21]

This caution about identifying the uniquely Jewish aspect of the Holocaust was to become a pattern, which was not broken until March 1944, by which time 5 million Jews had been murdered. There is no telling how many might have been saved had the predominantly Jewish identity of the victims not remained unacknowledged for almost six years.

Jews themselves caught some of this hush-hush fever. Chaim Weizmann noted in December 1939 that to speak with Jews in America about the Jewish tragedy was to be accused of warmongering. They called it propaganda. Instead of countering President Roosevelt's attempt to mask the problem, they surrendered to his policy of secrecy.[22]

This Jewish surrender to the President may have been part and parcel of another tendency that had a restraining effect. American Jews were in love with a President whom they saw as God's chosen "saviour for America and the rest of the world." This blind adoration even embraced Secretary of State Cordell Hull, who was described by Rep. Sol Bloom as "the most wonderful fellow God ever put on earth." The Jewish faith in Roosevelt's humanitarian leadership had such a paralyzing effect on the community and its leaders that they were neither able nor willing to exert strong pressure on him directly. Without such direct pressure, the only other political weapon the Jews possessed was the ballot box, and this was a weapon they could not bring themselves to use. Jewish support for the President was stronger than that of any other ethnic group, manifesting itself in a general allegiance to the Democratic party. In 1944, Jews who might legitimately have accused their President of inaction and delay in bringing aid and rescue to European Jewry, marched instead to the polls almost as one to express their gratitude to the architect of the impending victory over the Nazi murderers. The one man upon whom pressure had to be brought if European Jews were to be helped was apparently immune to Jewish pressure.[23]

These, then, were some of the factors that inhibited the American Jewish public response to the Holocaust in the six periods under review. Those periods were part of what has been called "an absolute aberration of history." Auschwitz and Treblinka had no historical precedents. Nothing in human experience had prepared the victims for their murder or their American brethren for the responsibility for alleviating this dimension of suffering. The Holocaust was a novum, unassimilable by the mind, unexpressible in any vocabulary.[24]

Nevertheless, historians and Jewish leaders, a generation after the Holocaust, are beginning to lay blame upon an American Jewry, which Shlomo Katz characterized as having been paralyzed in the face of danger. Walter Laqueur, in his recent book about why the news of the Holocaust was neither believed nor acted upon, criticizes Jewish leaders for, on the one hand, a paralyzing fear of facing the truth and, on the other, a reckless optimism about the outcome.

The president of the Hadassah organization, in a November 1977 letter to the editor of *The New York Times*, was even more blunt and damning with her judgment: "The chief lesson of the Holocaust is that we were silent when we should have shouted."[25]

In short, the question posed by the *Jewish Spectator*, "What did American Jews do in the years of the Holocaust?" is now being analyzed and answered. It is hoped that this study of public Jewish activity during the Holocaust will contribute significant information that may help American Jews to answer the question more accurately and with greater insight. An accurate and informed answer is important not alone for the historic record; it has profound implications for Jewish communal life today and tomorrow.

Chapter two

KRISTALLNACHT

The Night of the Broken Glass, or as it was known then, Black Thursday, had its origins in an ordinance promulgated by the Sejm, the Polish Parliament, on March 25, 1938. Apprehensive over reports that Germany might deport its 50,000 Polish Jewish residents, the new Polish law provided that any Polish citizen who spent five years or more in continuous residence outside Poland could be deprived of his citizenship and refused reentry. It was further decreed on October 6, 1938, that any citizen who did not renew his passport by October 29 would lose his citizenship under the provisions of that law.

On the night of October 27 and all day on October 28, the Gestapo rounded up 11,000 to 12,000 Polish Jews who were residents in Germany, deported them to the Polish border, and dropped them there with a maximum of ten marks each in their possession. The Poles refused to accept them, and some 8,000 were interned at the border town of Zbaszyn. From that town, Zindel Grynszpan, one of the deportees, wrote to his son Herschel in Paris about the tragic plight of the family. "Don't write any more letters to Germany," he told the boy, "we are now in Zbaszyn."[1]

On November 7, young Grynszpan, in a state of anxiety and bitterness over the fate of his family, walked into the German Embassy and shot Ernst vom Rath, the third secretary.[2] Vom

Rath's death two days later provided the Nazis with the excuse to launch the operation that came to be known as *Kristallnacht.*

The lead editorial in *The New York Times,* November 11, 1938, described the scene as follows:

> In a day of terror [November 9–10] surpassing anything even the Third Reich has seen, synagogues have been burned, shops sacked and looted, homes raided, a number of citizens beaten and thousands jailed. In Vienna a new wave of suicides swept over a people already broken and terrorized beyond endurance. These victims have never seen Poland or Paris. They were not Poles and Germans. Nor were they set upon by "mobs." The patriots arrived in autombiles, went about the work of destruction with method and precision, wore the boots which go with the uniform of Storm Troopers and other Nazi units. The police looked on until, after fourteen hours of violence, the orgy was officially called off by Dr. Goebbels.
>
> Thus does a great Government take revenge for the act of a maddened boy, a Government which exercises supreme and unquestioned power over 80,000,000 people, boasts of the order it maintains and aspires to spread this order over all of Central Europe. Recently this Government has extended its domain with the consent of the Western Powers, who acquiesced in its bloodless victories as the prelude to European appeasement. Instead they were the prelude to the scenes witnessed yesterday, scenes which no man can look upon without shame for the degradation of his species.

On the night of November 9, and continuing into November 10, Nazi cadres conducted an orgy of violence against the Jews of Germany—so brutal that the *Atlanta Journal* commented that to compare present-day Germany and the Middle Ages "is slandering the Middle Ages." One hundred and ninety-one synagogues were burned out. Over 7,000 Jewish businesses and shops were destroyed and looted. Nearly 100 Jews were killed, and thousands were subjected to wanton violence and sadistic torments. Many homes were devastated. Thirty thousand Jews were interned in Buchenwald, Dachau, and Sachsenhausen. The smashing of glass became the symbol of the destructive force of this pogrom and also gave it its name in history: *Kristallnacht,* the night of the broken glass. The amount of plate glass that was smashed that night equalled the entire annual production of the plate-glass industry of Belgium from which it had been imported.[3]

But more than Jewish store-front plate glass had been destroyed. Jewish life in Germany was smashed ruthlessly that night and in the month that followed. In rapid succession the Nazis instituted a number of severe decrees against German Jewry. A 1 billion mark ($400 million) fine was levied on November 12 against the Jews of Germany. The use of bank accounts was restricted. Jewish retail establishments were closed. Stock holdings were seized. Jews were prohibited from either purchasing or selling real estate. The driving of cars was forbidden to them. Jews were required to live in circumscribed areas (the forerunner of ghettoes). This was all accomplished and reported widely in the American and Jewish press by December 7, 1938.

THE REACTION IN AMERICA

Black Thursday and its even blacker aftermath received extensive treatment in the American news media. From one end of the country to the other, readers of newspapers and magazines and listeners to the radio were kept well informed about developments in Germany.

The New York Times gave the widest publicity to the Nazi program of brutality toward Jews by featuring it on its front page each day from November 10 through November 24, frequently with bold headlines, three and four columns wide. On five of the first six days there were editorials on the tragedy, three of them the lead editorial for the day. By November 15, there were so many items dealing with the crisis that the paper's index assigned a special listing entitled "German Situation." As late as November 25 there were still four citations on the subject listed in that index. On November 17 the *Times* printed three full columns of letters under the heading, "COMMENT ON CURRENT SITUATION IN GERMANY: Public Opinion in This Country, as Indicated by Communications Received by the *Times,* Appears to be Wholly Condemnatory of Recent Actions."[4]

The general theme in the *Times* and throughout the American press ranged from horror to sadness. Black Thursday ranked in horror with the Saint Bartholomew's Day massacre of 1572, wrote the *Washington Post*. The Nazis outdid the Black Hundreds in ferocity, observed the *Plain Dealer* in Cleveland. "A lynching party at its worst," was the description of the *Springfield Republican*.[5]

These could hardly be considered hyperbole if one read the news columns. Two characteristic examples will suffice to convey the kind of horror story that greeted American readers as they sipped their morning coffee. The first is an excerpt from a Berlin dispatch, which appeared on the front page of the *Times* on November 23.

> Unless the democracies evacuate the German Jews at once and at their own expense, they will be starved into crime and then exterminated with "fire and sword." This lurid picture of the fate confronting the Jews, which if it were printed in any foreign publication, would look like a revival of war atrocity-mongering, is splashed all over the front page today by the Schwarze Korps, organ of the Gestapo (secret police) and Hitler Elite Guard, which together dominate the German domestic situation.

The correspondent then proceeded to elaborate upon the above theme in a long frightening article in which he reported that these threats were an authentic reflection of the plans of Nazi Germany.

Further confirmation of these barbaric intentions came from *Time,* the weekly news magazine. It carried the following story in its foreign news section on December 5, 1938, p. 19:

GERMANY AD NAUSEAM

> How 62 prosperous German Jews were forced to run a bloody gauntlet at Sachsenhausen Concentration Camp was reported last week in the liberal *News Chronicle* of London. Two long ranks of Adolf Hitler's personal Schutzstaffel formed the gauntlet, down which the 62 Jews were forced to run. "As they approached between the ranks, a hail of blows fell upon them," said the *News Chronicle*. "As they fell, the Jews were beaten further. The orgy lasted half an hour. . . . Twelve of the 62 were dead with skulls smashed.

All the others were unconscious, some with eyes out and faces flattened in. . . . Police, unable to bear the cries, turned their backs. . . ."

The nauseating atrocity, whether or not the honest *News Chronicle* was correctly informed as to exactly what happened, is undoubtedly the truth in the sense that such atrocities do occur today in many parts of Germany, especially the countryside.

Horror, outrage, disgust, and finally fear for the future, not alone of German Jewry but of all humanity, were the dominant themes in the news. Anne O'Hare McCormick, the premiere columnist for the *Times,* reflected what may have been the general mood of the press and the country when she wrote: "Germany's Black Thursday . . . raises up in the heart of Europe, in a civilized country, a threat to the civilization of the world."[6]

The press both reflected and inspired a deep sense of outrage that came forth immediately and then, in an increasing crescendo, from virtually all segments of the community. On Friday night, November 11, while the fires in Germany still smoldered, former New York Governor Alfred E. Smith and then District Attorney Thomas E. Dewey addressed a nationwide audience over the radio. Dewey's words were illustrative of what was to be expressed by hundreds of political, communal, and religious leaders in the days and weeks to come:

The civilized world stands revolted by a bloody pogrom against a defenseless people. Every instinct in us cries out in protest against the outrages which have taken place in Germany during the past five years and which sank to new depths in the organized frenzies of the past two days. . . .

The outbursts of plundering, looting and arson in leading cities of Germany and Austria all at the same time, are the unmistakable earmarks of an organized plot to crush the Jewish people. . . .

Not since the days of medieval barbarism has the world been forced to look upon a spectacle such as this. Never even in the darkest days of Russia with its bloody pogroms was human cruelty so well organized on a national scale.[7]

Ministers and priests on Sunday, November 13, expressed outrage against the Nazis and encouragement to their oppressed victims. The New York City Board of Estimate was the first governmental body in the country to pass a resolution of condemnation. Students at Hunter, New York University, and other colleges staged protest meetings almost immediately, and thousands attended. Writers, actors, and educators cabled Roosevelt collectively to urge condemnation of the Nazis and to ask for the severance of economic relations.[8]

Some groups were more active in their protests. Some 5,000 persons responded to a call from the New York State Communist Party to picket noisily as the North German Lloyd liner *Bremen* set sail for Europe. The Jewish People's Committee, a communist-front organization, attracted over 20,000 to a Madison Square Garden Rally on November 21.[9]

Saturday and Sunday, November 19 and 20, were days of prayer for the persecuted, observed in synagogues and churches. A special prayer was composed jointly by Rabbi David De Sola Pool, president of the Synagogue Council of America, and Rev. Joseph R. Sizoo, vice president of the Federal Council of Churches of Christ in America. The full text of this lengthy prayer was printed in *The New York Times* on November 18.

There were symbolic protests also. Thirty thousand food and drug stores closed for one to three hours on November 23. One sign over a Whelan's drug store explained the action as follows: "People of America stop Hitler now! This store is closed in protest against barbaric outrages inflicted upon German Jews, Protestants and Catholics by Hitler's mad ruffians. . . ."[10]

One month after *Kristallnacht* the expressions of anger were still in evidence. On December 10, a manifesto was publicized denouncing the outrages in Germany and repudiating "all false and unscientific doctrines, such as the racial nonsense of the Nazis." It was signed by 1,284 American scientists, including three Nobel Prize winners and sixty-four members of the National Academy of Sciences.[11]

In summary, public sentiment was deeply touched by the savage pogrom and the official persecution that followed. The concern in America was not necessarily an expression of love for the Jews. There is reason to believe that the opposite may have been true, as one might conclude from a diary entry of Harold Ickes, Secretary of the Interior, dated November 15, 1938.

The Nazi government during the last two or three days has issued a series of decrees especially aimed at the Jews. . . . Public sentiment in this country has been very much stirred up over this situation despite the growing feeling of anti-Semitism here.[12]

The concern of the American public, therefore, may not have been aroused because of the Jewish plight at all.[13] It may have simply represented a reaction to the blatant brutality of a powerful regime and the ominous turn of events from the peace-through-appeasement in Munich on September 29 to an event that seemingly superseded it six weeks later on November 10.[14] *Kristallnacht* shocked and angered American public opinion. The implications of the shock and anger were not lost on the President of the United States.

THE RESPONSE OF ROOSEVELT

A bold four-column headline on the front page of the November 16 *New York Times* was typical of how the news media of the country viewed the significance of President Roosevelt's first public reaction to *Kristallnacht:* "ROOSEVELT CONDEMNS NAZI OUTBREAK: 'COULD SCARCELY BELIEVE IT,' HE SAYS."

The news followed by one day the recall from Berlin of Hugh R. Wilson, the American ambassador to Germany. The critical nature of the President's statement was reflected in the heading of the article in the lead news column on page 1: "STATEMENT SHARP: Language Is as Strong as a President Ever Used to a Friendly Nation."

Roosevelt's reaction, however, came after some internal agonizing in the State Department. Secretary of State Cordell Hull questioned the recommendation of Undersecretary George Messersmitt, who urged the recall. Hull argued that "it would deprive us of an Ambassador in Berlin at a time when one was needed to keep in close contact with the aims and acts of the German Government and to give weight to any representations we need to make."[15]

Roosevelt apparently sensed that some response was necessary and decided in favor of recall. Hull prepared a statement for the President to read at his press conference. The statement was calculated by Hull to be firm, but neither alarming nor offensive to Germany. The President changed the statement to give it a greater sense of shock and indignation:

> The news of the past few days from Germany has deeply shocked public opinion in the United States. Such news from any part of the world would inevitably produce a similar <u>profound</u> reaction among American people <u>in every part of the nation.</u> [This sentence was intended by Hull to soften the direct verbal attack on Germany. The words added by Roosevelt—underlined in the text—effectively negated that intention.]
> <u>I myself could scarcely believe that such things could occur in a twentieth-century civilization.</u>
> With a view of gaining a firsthand picture of the situation in Germany I asked the Secretary of State to order our Ambassador in Berlin to return <u>at once</u> [Hull's version had the words "return home"] for report and consultation.

The President later implied that Ambassador Wilson would not return to his post unless and until there were positive changes in Germany's policy toward racial and religious minorities.[16]

The media responded with general approval of Roosevelt's condemnation of Germany and the recall of Wilson. Editorials applauded the moral stance of the President. A few isolationist dissents interrupted the chorus of support. Representative of this small minority was the *Lincoln* (Nebraska) *Journal,* which cautioned against the United States becoming "suddenly wrought up over the situation in Germany . . . [as a] result of subjection to propaganda and appeals of various sorts."[17]

The broad approval in the press of the President's response, however, may not have reflected accurately the feelings of Americans. While public opinion polls at the time did report 94 percent disapproval of Germany's treatment of Jews, those same polls reflected a bare 60 percent in support of Roosevelt's recall of Ambassador Wilson. Twenty percent registered opposition to the recall and another 20 percent expressed no opinion.[18]

This significant split in public opinion may well have influenced the President to move cautiously—if at all—on the crucial issue that lay before him: the admission of German-Jewish refugees into the United States. Moreover, on the issue of admitting refugees there was little division of opinion. Seventy-seven percent of Americans polled by Gallup in November 1938, after *Kristallnacht,* opposed an increase in the quota of refugees from Germany who would be allowed to come to the United States.[19]

Considering the reluctance of public opinion to respond generously to the refugee crisis, Roosevelt's response to a question at his news conference on November 15 is understandable politically—if open to question morally. Asked whether he was contemplating a mass transfer of Jews from Germany, he replied: "I have given a great deal of thought to that. . . . The time is not ripe for that." Would he recommend to Congress the relaxation of immigration quotas? "That is not in contemplation; we have the quota system."[20]

At a press conference three days later, the President did take one humanitarian step. He extended the visitor's visas of 15,000 Germans—not just Jews—who were then living in the United States. At the same time, he assured the public once again that he would not recommend to Congress any change in the immigration laws.

By then, the question of what to do with 600,000 potential Jewish refugees from Germany was very much on the world agenda. Great Britain had already intimated a plan—actually announced on November 21—to settle German-Jewish refugees in sparsely settled areas of the world, like Tanganyika (a former German colony), British Guiana, Nyasaland, Northern Rhodesia, and Kenya.[21]

The announcements were greeted with banner three-column headlines on page 1 by the *Times* on November 17 and 21, perhaps because the *Times* had already editorialized that such "resettlement" in open, undeveloped, and underpopulated areas was the only solution. Palestine, it observed, was no solution since it would absorb only "a comparatively small number of Jews."[22]

Great Britain did admit five hundred refugee children herself in a special gesture, but she, together with other European countries, was unwilling to open her doors further to the unfortunate victims of Nazi oppression.[23]

The Jews of Germany thus learned, in the first phase of the Holocaust, that sympathy was not to be equated with hospitality. Economic and political considerations precluded the latter. The refugee was perceived as a danger to the British standard of living. Sympathy, of course, was abundantly felt and nobly expressed. "Dreadful, dreadful are the afflictions of the Jewish people," wrote the London *Daily Express,* but it went on to say that there was no room for them in Britain. Graphically summing up the gap that existed between British sympathy and English hospitality were the words of the London *Evening News:* "Money we will provide if need be, but the law of self-preservation demands that the word 'Enter' be removed from the gate."[24]

The American press tended to be less frank about the issue, preferring instead to express outrage against the oppression and consolation to the victims, but without facing the issue of refugee settlement. Generally opposing larger immigration to America, the press either ignored the refugee question, paid lip service to the wild schemes of resettlement in underdeveloped lands, or (considering the fact that German Jews were a highly cultured group), judged the idea of unloading them in sparsely populated, tropical lands "too impractical for serious consideration."[25]

A few hospitable voices did break through the wall of indifference. Henry Ford, who was not known for his concern for Jews or his antipathy toward Nazi Germany, stated publicly that America should admit as many refugees as possible because they "would constitute a real asset to our country."[26] The *New York Daily News* in editorials on December 4 and December 8 argued persuasively for liberalizing our immigration laws and adding 10 percent (13 million) to the population to invigorate and rejuvenate the market for American goods.

There were other isolated examples of support for admission of refugees, but on the whole the English pattern prevailed: sympathy without hospitality. This pattern drew the specific editorial ire of the *New Republic:*

> There is a masochistic type of pity which merely enjoys feeling the woes of the oppressed or the unfortunate but actually is reluctant to do anything effective to ameliorate the plight of the victims since that would end the possibility of luxuriating in the sorrows of others.[27]

This, then, was the public reaction in the United States to what may have been the best reported event of the Holocaust. The public knew the facts; the leaders reacted in anger against the oppressions and with sympathy for the victims; and the President reflected this twofold sense of outrage and pity. The significance of this life-threatening event for German Jewry was understood to a large extent by the political, communal, and religious leadership in America. In the face of this understanding and sympathy, however, not much was done to relieve the plight of German Jewry.

THE REACTION IN THE JEWISH PRESS

It is now possible, against this background of American and world reactions, to consider the public response of American Jews to the terrifying events of *Kristallnacht*. That response can be seen first from the way in which the tragic episode was treated in the American Jewish press.

The three major Yiddish dailies, *The Day, Morning Journal,* and *Forward,* all reacted with alarm, but with differing degrees of intensity and with varied emphasis on the elements in the plight of German Jewry.

The Day gave the most complete news coverage of the three and editorialized daily on the plight of German Jewry from November 11 through November 26. Day after day, bold headlines on the front page and on several inside pages screamed the highlights of the dreadful story; news reports supplied the grim details, and columnists interpreted the significance of the tragedy.

Most of all, however, the readers were moved by the editorial pen of Samuel Margoshes, the passionate advocate for his people, who empathized with his suffering brethren in Germany and pleaded with his indifferent brethren in America.

> The flames that have destroyed the synagogues and schools make our blood boil, do not give us rest and force us to take to the streets and scream in pain so that the whole world should hear. . . .
> We have been quiet for some time, hoping that the Na-

zis would tire of their murderous ways, believing in quiet diplomacy and being dubious about the efficacy of our own protests. We have been patient. But now our patience is at end!

We can no longer be silent. We cannot rely on private intercessions on our behalf. We are dealing here with an enemy which will not give up our sacrifices . . . which begrudges us life and which misses no opportunity to embitter our existence.[28]

Margoshes continued in this front-page five-column editorial to demand public protest on the part of Jews on a scale higher than the massive demonstrations of March 1933 in New York. He pleaded for this form of reaction on three grounds: first, to awaken ourselves; second, to maintain our own self-respect; third, to scream because America would not understand our silence and would conclude that our brothers' misery did not disturb us and that hence we deserved the beating we were receiving.

Anticipating that certain powerful Jewish leaders would oppose him—an anticipation that proved to be correct when the General Jewish Council (see page 58) met on November 13, 1938, and specifically urged no Jewish public protests of any kind—[29]Margoshes concluded his plea with a ringing challenge:

Let our leaders lead! Let them not delay and postpone. Let the General Jewish Council meet and deliberate immediately. The Jewish masses are waiting to go out into the streets, to close their places of business, to stop all work, to declare a fast and to demonstrate to the entire world that we will no longer allow ourselves to be slaughtered by a barbaric regime.

Time will not stand still. Those who do not deal immediately with this crisis forfeit their right to leadership. The masses are waiting; they will not wait for long.

The General Jewish Council has an opportunity right now to make Jewish history. . . . Will it rise to this historic occasion? We will be watching.

This was the tenor of The Day's treatment of Kristallnacht. For weeks there was nothing to preempt its place as the most important event and developing tragedy of that day. "Tomorrow a fire, a disaster, a trans-Atlantic flight or a divorce scandal, may deflect men's minds from . . . the Nazi outrage," but not if *The Day* could help it.[30]

The *Morning Journal* reflected the same concern and sense of urgency that one could feel in *The Day,* but its emphasis was more spiritual. "BITTER TEARS SHED IN SHULS OVER THE NAZI POGROM" read page 1 double-column Yiddish headline on Sunday, November 13, 1938. Although the entire page was devoted to *Kristallnacht,* this article comparing the tragedy to the *churban* (the destruction of the Temple in 586 B.C.E.), dominated the page. "Woe unto us; what we have lived to see!" was the *Morning Journal*'s quote from the *"shul-*goers." A telegram of appeal to Roosevelt sent by the Young Israel movement, a body of synagogues, was also featured prominently. The *Morning Journal* also gave bold treatment to an important decision of the General Jewish Council: "AMERICAN JEWISH LEADERS CALL FOR A DAY OF PRAYERS AND MOURNING."[31]

The general feeling one gets from the *Morning Journal,* however, is the same as that which emerges from *The Day:* The editors were deeply concerned, single-minded in their mourning over the tragedy, and their feelings accurately reflected the mood that prevailed in their community, especially the religious community.

The *Forward,* representing the labor, socialist segment of American Jewry, presented a significantly different picture. While the news of *Kristallnacht* was given bold and shocking treatment over a period of two weeks, it subsided substantially thereafter. Even at the height of the crisis, the news did not completely absorb the interest and concern of the *Forward.*

For example, on November 11, while front-page headlines were announcing, "MOST TERRIBLE DAY AND NIGHT OF MURDERS OF JEWS IN GERMANY" and subheads asserted that "Wild Murders of Jews Are Worse Than in the Most Terrible Periods of the Middle Ages," four center columns on page 1 were devoted to a headlined story about CIO chief John L. Lewis. Moreover, a box announced the second serialization—"by popular demand"—of the new novel, "The Secret on the Death Bed," a badly timed choice of titles, considering the main news of the day.

This pattern continued. The *Forward*'s front page was never dominated by the Jewish tragedy. Labor news invariably also occupied a central position. Editorials on the crisis were irregular. On the third and fourth day after the pogrom, while the Jewish world was aflame, the *Forward* devoted its only editorials to a general comment on Fascist advances in the world since the end of World War I and an analysis of the International Ladies Garment Workers Union leaving the CIO.

There is a sense from the *Forward*'s editorials and feature writers that the crisis may not have been fully comprehended by the paper. A mood of optimism prevailed despite the horror stories. "We believe the civilized world is regaining its conscience and courage after the initial shock," said one editorial. "America and other countries are not sending refugee aid," the *Forward* explained, "because such aid would play into the hands of the Nazis. The Christian world will find a place of refuge for the Jews. We may have trust in the civilized world."[32]

Such optimism may perhaps explain why the *Forward* was not deflected from its political, social, literary, and general journalistic concerns by the developing tragedy of the Jewish people, then in a state of convulsion. It continued to perform the function that was generally served by the Yiddish press: to be the guide, teacher, and entertainer of New York Jews.[33] It maintained its normal policy of devoting the majority of its space to general reading matter, human interest stories, and serialized novels. And it retained its calm optimistic view. It was characteristic of this view on the part of the *Forward* that one of its columnists, contrasting the "Heroism of Hitler's Murderers" with the "Courage of Jewish Martyrs," assured his readers that this, too, shall pass and concluded his article with *Nachamu, nachamu ami*—"Comfort ye, comfort ye, O my people."[34] A more appropriate quotation for November 18, 1938, would have been *Eicha yashva vadad* ("How doth Jerusalem sit solitary!")—the opening refrain of Lamentations.

The *Jewish Telegraphic Agency Daily News Bulletin (JTA)*, as the main source of news in English for the Anglo-Jewish press, served its function competently in the months of November and December. The German-Jewish tragedy was the main subject for most of the period. Often it took up most of a six- to ten-page issue, expanded from the normal four-page bulletin. In the reportage, however, one could feel the absence of one ingredient: an American-Jewish response. The brutal facts from abroad were covered; the world Jewish response was reported; the American public reaction was recorded; but there was almost no record of a public Jewish response in America.

An interesting aspect of the *JTA*'s reportage was the tendency of the newsletter to bury atrocity stories rather than to give them prominence. The brutal beating of Jews in Sachsenhausen—from which twelve died—reported prominently in *Time* magazine (see pages 38–39), in *The New York Times,* and on page 1 of the *Morning Journal,* was the last item in the *JTA*'s five-page issue on November 25. A terrible threat from *Das Schwarze Korps,* the organ of the Gestapo, that Germany would first render her Jews destitute and then destroy them by fire and sword, was featured by the *Times* on page 1 but it was printed in the *JTA* on page 3.[35]

One can only speculate why the *JTA* gave great prominence to political and economic developments and to public reactions while it assigned less importance—in terms of space and location—to human tragedies. Perhaps there may have been something unnewsworthy about atrocity stories. Perhaps other papers were giving them prominence and hence the *JTA* did not have to feature them. Perhaps the *JTA,* which served opinion makers rather than the public and employed no headlines at all, considered placement of no importance. Whatever the reason, this lack of emphasis upon the individual suffering was characteristic of the *JTA* reportage during the post-*Kristallnacht* period. To some extent, it continued throughout the Holocaust.

THE PERIODICALS

The reactions of Jewish periodicals spanned the spectrum of possible responses from total involvement—as if nothing else in the world mattered—to total indifference—as if *Kristallnacht* were a nonevent.

Congress Bulletin, the weekly organ of the American Jewish Congress, reflected the most comprehensive reaction to the crisis. From November 18 through December 30, its four-page issues were almost entirely devoted to reportage and analysis of the tragedy. In the December 2 issue there was a day-by-day record of events from November 8 through November 30 entitled "A Month in Nazi Germany." This included a lengthy report of the brutal beatings in Sachsenhausen.

The magazine's response was emotional and intellectual. Outrage and indignation, compassion and pity, deep concern and a sense of urgency were all reflected by the editors and evoked in the readers. While no specific way of alleviating the plight of oppressed brothers was suggested, the need to act was clearly enunciated. The entire episode was viewed as the greatest crisis in Jewish history. Not only was German Jewry being destroyed, but it was clear that other Jewries in Europe were also in jeopardy, for other states "seek the solution of their internal problems through a forcible migration and expulsion of Jews" a reference to Poland, Romania, and Hungary.

In this same issue of the *Bulletin* (November 25, 1938) an editorial on page 2 gave one of the first public statements cautioning against too much aid for refugees. It quoted a veiled threat from Polish official circles to the effect that if Germany were "rewarded" for her persecutions by receiving aid in the "transfer" of unwanted Jews, other countries would learn from the German example: "The Jewish problem from an economic point of view was graver in some other countries than it was in Germany."

The frightening implications of *Kristallnacht* were set forth almost prophetically by the *Congress Bulletin* in an editorial on December 16, 1938. Commenting on the spread of Nazism to Poland, Romania, and a proposed "independent Ukraine," the writer asserted that this

> means Nazi domination over a Jewish population of some *six million people*. It means the total ruin of the Jewries of Poland, Ukraine, Rumania [sic] and others—the actual *extermination of European Jewry* [my emphasis].

The *Contemporary Jewish Record* did its usual competent job of recording the event and the reactions and of interpreting the news. Its November 1938 issue contained a special supplement on events in Germany from November 7 through November 14, in addition to reports on world reactions, statements by leading

Americans, and a record of the position taken by the General Jewish Council. The remarkable part about this supplement was that the November issue was normally designed to cover events only from September and October. The publication of this issue was delayed—with apologies—in order to include this urgent material. This was the only periodical that seemed to have held up publication in order to cover this event. The best summary of all the material and the interpretations on *Kristallnacht* and its aftermath was in the January 1939 issue of this bimonthly chronicle.

Stephen Wise's *Opinion* was, like the *Congress Bulletin,* totally absorbed in the crisis. The December 1938 issue featured reactions from Wise himself, two Protestants (Henry Smith Leiper and the frequent contributor, John Haynes Holmes, in his column "Through Gentile Eyes") and a Hindu (Taraknath Das). Wise's article began with a tribute to the American reaction and particularly to President Roosevelt, "the voice of America's conscience." This was a theme that Wise was to sound again and again during the Holocaust. It represented the thinking and judgment of most American Jews at the time.[36]

The *Jewish Frontier,* led by the patriot-polemicist Hayim Greenberg, provided one of the strongest responses to this crisis and, for that matter, to all the news of the Holocaust as it developed. Its lead editorial in the December 1938 issue divided its concern between bemoaning the tragedy and berating Chamberlain for his eschewing Palestine as a refuge for German Jews and for replacing it cynically with "jungle lands, rich in wild animals, poisonous snakes and dangerous insects." "Tanganyika," the writer asserted, "boasts the tsetse fly among its charms." The writer deplored the madness of a world that accepted Germany's right to plunder and expel part of her citizenry and then closed its doors to the victims. There were 600,000 German Jews to be saved. Palestine could take many of them; the civilized world—not East Africa and the jungles of South America—must take the rest.

This issue had five editorials on various aspects of the crisis. In one of them, the writer applauded Roosevelt's statement and recall of Wilson but, he asserted, words were not enough. America must admit refugees from a Germany that "had now become a huge Concentration Camp."

The *Reconstructionist* reflected the crisis editorially, urging a strong American Jewish response. The *National Jewish Monthly* demonstrated concern over the seriousness of *Kristallnacht*. Its December 1938 issue recorded the Christian world's reaction to the event rather than the event itself. Its lead editorial, entitled "The Pogrom," stated: "In all these dreadful years, Jews have been speaking for themselves vainly; now the world was speaking for justice to the Jew."

Any of the newspapers and periodicals discussed thus far would have aroused the reader's emotions and conveyed to him the tragic facts and implications of *Kristallnacht*. There were, however, a number of periodicals from whose contents one could hardly guess that German Jewry was in the process of being destroyed. These periodicals were concerned with many things during the months following November 10, 1938; *Kristallnacht*, however, was not one of them.

The *New Palestine*, a weekly news bulletin published by the Zionist Organization of America, was one of three Zionist organs that did not give significant coverage to the calamitous events taking place in Germany. Not until December 9, the fourth issue after *Kristallnacht*, was there an article that offered details of the tragic events. The refugee question was discussed prominently by the *New Palestine*, beginning with November 18. The emphasis, however, was not on the plight of the refugees but rather on the need to open the doors of Palestine to them. As a matter of fact, the paper's policy seemed to be that Palestine took precedence over the rescue of refugees. "It is necessary to do everything possible to save the Jews," the *New Palestine* quoted Weizmann as saying. "But we must not split our forces nor divert attention from the central solution which is Palestine."[37]

The *New Palestine* maintained consistency in this approach, stressing the role of Palestine as a haven for German Jews rather than emphasizing the plight of the victims themselves. Apparently, this approach elicited some criticism from other quarters, for in its December 9 issue, an editorial in the *New Palestine* affirmed that "immediate relief . . . is of the first importance. . . ." But, the writer added, "in the consideration of immediate relief, no Jew has a right to start with a prejudice against Palestine."

The *New Palestine* was apparently reflecting an inner conflict in its parent organization, the Zionist Organization of America, over the proper allocation of the limited resources and political influence of American Jewry. Given finite funds and energies, where should they be directed: to Zionism or to rescue; to the struggle to open Palestine for Jewish settlement or to the effort to save German Jews whose lives were in danger? What should be the order of priorities for the Jewish people as it faced ominous threats to its existence? This conflict within the Zionist movement was destined to grow and deepen throughout the Holocaust, ultimately with some painful consequences for the rescue effort.

The *New Palestine* also emphasized the necessity of American Jews joining its parent organization as the most appropriate response to the German Jewish tragedy. It reported on page 1 that Dr. Solomon Goldman, president of the Zionist Organization of America, cabled "all Districts throughout the country to launch an unprecedented and extraordinary effort for the strengthening of the Zionist Organization in view of the latest events in Central Europe." After urging that Jews should press for the opening of the doors to Palestine, Dr. Goldman added: "No conscious Jew can fail to join the organized ranks of American Zionism and by this means signify not only his or her continued affiliation with the Zionist Organization, but a determination to support our efforts in securing a haven for our unfortunate brethren from Germany and Austria."

The monthly *Hadassah Newsletter* similarly emphasized its parochial concerns at the expense of educating its readership on the nature or meaning of the events in Germany. Judith K. Epstein used *Kristallnacht* to urge the organization to redouble its efforts to support Palestine as the only realistic haven for the refugees. We must enlarge our health programs, she wrote, intensify our Youth Aliyah, work and buy more land. "Above all, we must nourish that deep abiding faith and that loyalty that has made Hadassah the powerful instrument that it is for the upbuilding of Palestine and for the enrichment of Jewish life in America."[38]

It was not quite the same direct appeal for membership that was made by Dr. Goldman, but the self-serving exploitation of the plight of European Jewry was evident nevertheless. It was to be manifested more directly in later periods of the Holocaust. The newsletter did not convey a sense of the seriousness of *Kristallnacht*. Besides the Epstein article and an editorial in the January 1939 issue, praising Roosevelt's response, there was no discussion of the German-Jewish tragedy in three issues following *Kristallnacht*. Even the lengthy report on the Junior Hadassah Convention, held in late November, contained no direct reference to the catastrophe. It was as if nothing terribly significant had happened.[39]

The *Jewish Outlook,* published monthly by the Mizrachi Organization of America, followed the pattern of its secular Zionist brothers. There was space for everything except *Kristallnacht*. An exception was one brief editorial in the January 1939 issue, condemning Great Britain for refusing to admit 10,000 Jewish children to Palestine in the wake of the persecutions in Germany.

The *Orthodox Union,* published monthly by the Union of Orthodox Jewish Congregations of America, had no reference whatsoever to the plight of German Jewry in the three issues following *Kristallnacht*. Instead, it offered space to such subjects as "Orthodox Union Subsidizes Jewish Education," "Aid to the Temple of Religion at the World's Fair," an elementary Yeshiva established in Capetown, an attempt to blow up a synagogue in Johannesburg, the prohibition of ritual slaughter in Italy, and an appeal to synagogues to honor the memory of George Washington on the 150th anniversary of his inauguration at a Re-Inaugural Dinner at the World's Fair on April 30. For some reason—perhaps the assumption that readers would get the important news elsewhere—there was no room in the *Orthodox Union* for reflection on the mortal threat to German Jewry.

The Reform movement in America was hardly more responsive. Its organ, *The Synagogue,* had an article on the Evian Conference (an unproductive, international conference on refugees held in France in July 1938) in the December issue, but the magazine did not mention the changed status of German or European Jewry after *Kristallnacht*.

Notes and News, an irregularly published organ of the Council of Jewish Federations and Welfare Funds, generated no heat on the misery of German Jewry, although in its December 1938 and February 1939 issues it reflected the concern of the philanthropic community for refugee settlement:

We must be prepared to accept as rational and inescapable the unreasonable demands that would be made upon us for some time to come. . . . A life of unrelenting pressure and crushing burdens is not a passing emergency for a month or two but of a whole period whose exact duration cannot be predicted.[40]

Despite the pressing need to rescue refugees and absorb them properly, one writer cautioned that funds for refugee projects should not come at the expense of local communal needs.[41]

A less concerned response—in fact, no response at all—was recorded by the *Jewish Center*, the quarterly publication of the National Jewish Welfare Board. In its first post-*Kristallnacht* issue, March 1939, the magazine, which was concerned with "Jewish educational, cultural, dramatic, recreational and physical education programs and activities of Jewish Centers,"[42] had no room for even a mention of the catastrophe in Germany. There was not even a suggestion on how Jewish groups might create programs to make the Jewish plight more intelligible to the average American Jew. The issue was so completely ignored that even a digest of Louis Adamic's pamphlet, *America and the Refugees,* was presented without reference to the new, desperate condition of German Jewry, which had created 600,000 potential refugees.

The *Menorah Journal,* in its Spring 1939 issue, editorialized on its front page about anti-Semitism in America, but was completely silent about the brutal situation in Germany. It did, however, carry a fine article explaining *Kristallnacht* and drawing some of the tragic implications for all the Jews of Eastern and Central Europe. A further piece on the subject applauded the generosity of two hundred colleges—beginning with Harvard—which were enabling refugees to attend on scholarships.[43]

One of the most responsive periodicals during the *Kristallnacht* period and throughout the Holocaust was *Hadoar,* the Hebrew weekly. Under the editorship of Menachem Ribalow, who sometimes wrote under the pen name M. Shoshani (taken from his wife's name, Shoshana), *Hadoar* printed articles and editorials on the anguish of German Jewry in every issue from November 18 through December 23. The Nazi pogroms were contrasted with the Kishinev Massacres of 1903—a contrast, the editor concluded, that made Kishinev look like the work of amateurs. The magazine called for a forceful response on the part of American Jewry. Goebbels wants us to accept the slaughter in silence, Shoshani wrote, but we refuse. "With all our strength we shall scream and arouse the world until the world will be stirred from its terrifying indifference." In its first issue after *Kristallnacht,* a front-page editorial of the magazine referred to the event as a *sho'a,* the present-day Hebrew term for the Holocaust.[44]

The three weeklies that represented the three largest American Jewish communities outside New York varied in their reportage and editorial reactions. *The Sentinel* carried the most news of the three papers, usually devoting its two-column news summary on page 1 to news of the crisis. The paper also printed an editorial on the subject for four consecutive issues following *Kristallnacht.*

The *Jewish Exponent* in Philadelphia provided the least news coverage of the three papers. Its first two issues after *Kristallnacht* reported the news, but after that the issue was not deemed newsworthy. Its editorial section, however, remained concerned for three issues. Its first editorial response expressed gratification with the new concern of the world for the plight of the Jew and contrasted this happily with the recent history of indifference. Another editorial took a strong position on admitting refugees to America, expressing the conviction that immigration, far from being a hindrance to America, would prove to be a blessing.[45]

The *Jewish Advocate's* news coverage in Boston was somewhat more extensive than that of the *Jewish Exponent.* Its editorial reaction to *Kristallnacht* was particularly noteworthy. The editor did not focus on the tragic proportions of the event but rather on the extent of the world's response. We must not be disheartened or discouraged, he urged; the wave of public, liberal, Christian protest "should give us renewed courage and faith in the fundamental goodness of mankind." The writer expressed ecstasy over the "magnificent response of enlightened Christendom," and concluded: "That is the lesson which can be drawn from the events of the past week. Courage and new hope grip Jewry everywhere."[46] The lesson proved quickly to be illusory when the "magnificent response" faded into indifference and a reluctance to save Jewish refugees from Nazi control. The momentary happiness of the editor of the *Jewish Advocate,* however, may suggest how lonely the American Jew felt in November 1938 in an unfriendly world and in an unconcerned, sometimes hostile, American society.

PUBLIC PROTEST

The public response of American Jewry to *Kristallnacht* can be seen first in the way the event was treated by the press. Its full extent, however, can only be measured by analyzing what other specific avenues of response were open to American Jews then and by examining which avenues were actually utilized and which were eschewed.

The first method of response available to American Jews in late 1938 was public rallies and protests designed to express a sense of the tragedy, arouse public opinion, and create a climate in which concrete help to alleviate the suffering might be offered. There were ample precedents for such public demonstrations, and one might reasonably have expected that this bloodiest of actions would have produced the most dramatic Jewish protests ever mounted in public. In fact, quite the opposite was the case. Intentionally, purposefully, and by communal consent, the public Jewish response to *Kristallnacht* was repressed. The press spoke loudly, but public action, except for a day of prayer and a few scattered protests, was virtually nonexistent.

The source of this policy of silence was the General Jewish Council, an umbrella group organized in Pittsburgh, June 13, 1938, and comprising the four major Jewish defense organizations of that day: the American Jewish Committee, the American Jewish Congress, B'nai B'rith, and the Jewish Labor Committee. Its purpose was to coordinate activities of the four organizations (and eventually additional groups) that were concerned specifically with safeguarding the equal rights of Jews.[47]

The council had scheduled a regular meeting for Sunday, November 13, in the Waldorf Towers. (It is unclear whether or not the council would otherwise have arranged a special meeting for this crisis. Its next meeting followed its normal six-week interval, being held on December 18, 1938—a rather long wait, considering the turbulence in Jewish life created by *Kristallnacht*.) A significant portion of the meeting was devoted to *Kristallnacht* but many other relatively unimportant items consumed hours of time at this eight-hour session.[48]*

Henry Monsky, president of B'nai B'rith, offered four proposed courses of action in response to the crisis:

> 1. That the General Jewish Council issue a statement addressed to American Jewry and the American people.
>
> 2. That efforts be made through various newspapers, both locally and in smaller communities, to gather and express the opinion of prominent people in regard to the German situation.
>
> 3. That members of the Council should communicate with such non-Jewish agencies as possible to seek their advice and cooperation.
>
> 4. That a day of prayer and intercession be appointed, at which Jews and Gentiles together should gather and express their feelings of sorrow at the present tragedy and suffering of our people.[49]

The day of prayer, already a matter of consultation between the Federated Council of Churches and the National Conference of Jews and Christians, was set for Sunday, November 20.

---

*The meeting began with eulogies and tributes for the late B. Charney Vladeck, chairman of the JLC. It continued with a resolution proposed by Stephen S. Wise in honor of the eighty-second birthday of Justice Louis D. Brandeis. Later in the day the council discussed, among other things, the following topics: Jewish unemployment; the United States census and a proposed religious question in it; the Italian-Jewish situation; the anti-Semitic radio campaign of Father Coughlin; the need for a full-time legal assistant for the Public Relations Committee; the change of the council's name from "The General Council for Jewish Rights of the American Jewish Committee, the American Jewish Congress, B'nai B'rith and the Jewish Labor Committee" to "General Jewish Council" and to change all stationery and publications accordingly; the different methods of community organization; the desirability of accepting new members; use of the Irving Trust Company as the depository of the council; and James Waterman Wise's report on approaches to the problem of anti-Semitism. How significant some of these matters were in the light of the pogrom of three days earlier is difficult to assess from the perspective of almost fifty years, but the reading of these minutes does give one the impression that the American Jewish leaders, assembled at the Waldorf Towers on November 13, may have been fiddling while German Jews were burning.

One course of action was conspicuously absent: protests and demonstrations. This option was discussed and a majority opposed such a course. The following resolution was proposed and seconded:

> Resolved that the General Council was against holding, either under our auspices or under the auspices of any Jewish organization, any public demonstrations or mass meetings in any place other than a place of worship.

Adolph Held of the Jewish Labor Committee requested that consideration of this resolution be postponed until after the luncheon break in order to allow the members of the JLC delegation to discuss the matter among themselves. Late in the day, the JLC delegation agreed—probably reluctantly—to support the following amended resolution, which was carried unanimously:

> Resolved that it is the present sense of the General Jewish Council that there should be no parades, public demonstrations, or protests by Jews.

Instructions were given to pass on this decision to all local branches of the four organizations and to request the cooperation of the Yiddish press. The leadership of American Jewry had decided on a policy of public silence and that the community should make what representations it felt necessary in private.[50]

A public statement of some kind was obviously necessary. The following was approved:

> The world is aghast at the latest news which has come from Germany. In the hour of their oppression we offer our fellow Jews in Germany the assurance of our deepest sympathy and understanding. In the midst of our grief we derive a measure of solace from the fact that the world has come to realize that this barbarism directed against Jews is violence against the whole of humanity. This reaction of the entire world is a recognition that we are here confronted with an issue which goes far beyond the persecution and torture of a particular minority and that today it is civilization itself that is under attack. All Americans— Protestants, Catholics, and Jews alike—have reacted to these hideous accounts from abroad as a national calamity.[51]

The reasons for the decision to keep publicly silent in response to *Kristallnacht* had their roots both in history and in contemporary conditions. Historically, from Hitler's rise to power, there were two schools of thought concerning the method of fighting Hitler. The American Jewish Congress preferred mass meetings, rallies, economic boycotts, and other public responses, visibly Jewish. The American Jewish Committee—and to some extent B'nai B'rith—favored behind-the-scenes work, private representations or *shtadlanut*, as it was known in Europe. Briefs, papers, and statements were prepared for public officials. Public education was carefully fostered by printing pamphlets and establishing sympathetic contacts with the political and educational communities. There was concern that public Jewish protests would make this a Jewish issue, which would mean that other Americans would do nothing and the Nazis would retaliate further against German Jews.[52]

The *shtadlanut* view regarding public protests against Hitler was stated clearly as early as March 20, 1933, when the American Jewish Committee and B'nai B'rith issued a joint statement in opposition to a proposed public protest parade in New York. They warned that public agitation in the form of boycotts and mass demonstrations would "serve only as an ineffectual channel for the release of emotion. They furnish the persecutors with a pretext to justify the wrongs they perpetrate and, on the other hand, distract those who desire to help with more constructive efforts."[53] The "more constructive efforts" refer to the enlisting of non-Jewish support. This view felt that any public expression should be made by groups composed entirely, or at least predominantly, of non-Jews.[54]

Why did the *shtadlanut* view prevail over the activist view so decisively in the *Kristallnacht* period? Why did the American Jewish Congress abdicate to the American Jewish Committee at this critical moment? Several answers suggest themselves. It must be remembered that the General Jewish Council was barely five months old when this crisis developed. The American Jewish Congress had been working for such a coordinating body since 1934. It is unlikely that Stephen S. Wise would have wanted to break the unity that had taken so long to achieve. This concern was implied in an editorial in the *Congress Bulletin,* which virtually apologized for the fact that the congress' normal militancy had been tempered with restraint because of a collective discipline that had to be maintained among all the members of the General Jewish Council. The editorial writer consoled his readers with the thought that the congress had been active quietly and that a conference was being called for 2,000 leaders on November 24 to consider what should be done.[55]

Another reason for Wise's acceptance of a policy of reticence may have been his belief that the outcry among Americans was so impressive that there was no need for Jewish protests. Wise explained his relative silence during the weeks after *Kristallnacht* thus:

> I led the protest [against Hitler] in 1933 and ever since. I led the protest and I spoke because the world was largely silent and the American people seemed to be inert and apathetic to and unconscious of what was happening. At last, at long last, America has spoken and the world has spoken, overwhelmed by the barbarism of nationwide reprisals in recent weeks. . . .[56]

There may have been a third reason for the turn to reticence. There was a growing concern among American Jews over Goebbels' threat of November 11 to retaliate against the Jews of Germany if American Jews stirred up the public media against Germany. "I am trying to keep Jews silent," Wise wrote to his friend John Haynes Holmes, "until after tomorrow's funeral of the victim of the crazed Polish Jewish boy. I have an undefined dread that 'Hitler the madman, and the cripple-minded Goebbels' may call for a widespread massacre. God help us!"[57]

Wise's concern for these innocent hostages should not be dismissed lightly. It is true that conditions were so horrible for Jews in Germany that it was hard to see how they could get much worse. (The *JTA*, November 18, 1938, p. 5, quoted the Foreign Policy Association as urging that Americans not accede to Nazi threats of further oppression: "The Jews in Germany have already been condemned to a living death. Under the circumstances . . . physical death can hold little added horror.") Nevertheless, fear of the unknown horror can paralyze the hardiest of souls. Emanuel Ringelblum records that even in the Warsaw ghetto in June 1942—when conditions were indescribably brutal and the eventual extermination of all residents in the ghetto was well understood by Jewish leaders—these same leaders equivocated over whether to send out a message to the West and demand retribution against Germans in America. Some held "that if we were to demand retribution, this would incite the Germans still further and lead to the complete extermination of the Jews." If the persecuted themselves could not decide to flout the Nazis, can one blame American Jews for timidity in the face of such a threat?[58]

Finally, even the activist Wise could not help but be intimidated by an American public opinion that was increasingly supportive of anti-Semitism. At a time when anti-Jewish feeling was peaking in America, when Father Coughlin, a Detroit priest who was the outstanding spokesman for anti-Semitism in America, was at the height of his popularity, and when 35 percent of Americans answered "yes" to the question "Do you think Jews have too much power in the United States?" it may have been easier and safer for Wise and the American Jewish Congress to accept the "sha sha" philosophy, which sought to obscure the Jew from public gaze, to acquiesce in the *shtadlanut* strategy of the American Jewish Committee, and to encourage quietly the spontaneous indignation and resentment toward Nazi Germany being expressed publicly by Americans of all persuasions.[59]

And yet, despite all of the arguments, Wise's activism was only temporarily suppressed. It wasn't long before he asked editorially in his own magazine, *Opinion,* whether membership in the General Jewish Council was not obtained at too high a price: the dulling of the sense of purpose and militancy of the American Jewish Congress, which was being reduced to the inert level of other Jewish organizations.[60]

In the meantime, however, the Jewish community accepted the policy of public reticence promulgated by the General Jewish Council. American public opinion was expressed freely, but purely Jewish meetings were almost nonexistent. Outside New York this policy was followed without exception. There is no record in the Chicago, Philadelphia, and Boston weeklies of any departure from the policy. In New York City on the other hand, there were a few notable exceptions, most of them organized by communist-front organizations like the Jewish People's Committee, over which the council could exercise no influence.[61]

Some of the public protests that were staged in the weeks following *Kristallnacht* were the following:

A two-hour demonstration of about 150 pickets on November 14, as the German liner *Bremen* docked at 45th Street and the Hudson River. This was staged by the American League for Peace and Democracy, a fellow-traveler organization.[62]

Two "massive demonstrations" in Columbus Circle that were announced in the *Frieheit* under the auspices of the Jewish People's Committee and the American League for Peace and Democracy, but neither of these was reported upon in any other newspaper.[63]

A large protest was called by Fiorello LaGuardia, mayor of New York, in Carnegie Hall on December 7. Sponsored by non-Jews, it was nevertheless actively supported by the Yiddish press and, behind the scenes, by the General Jewish Council. It attracted several thousand listeners both inside and outside the hall.

The United Wholesale and Warehouse Workers Union and the Down-town Dry Goods Jobbers Association closed all dry goods stores for half the day on November 20. Meetings were held during that half-day to plan how to strengthen the anti-Nazi boycott.

The only large demonstration was held under the auspices of the Jewish People's Committee on November 21 in Madison Square Garden. Twenty thousand jammed the Garden, according to *The New York Times,* and an additional 5,000 listened through loudspeakers in the street, according to *The Day.* Addressed by a variety of speakers, mostly—but not all—Communists, the meeting produced a resolution condemning Nazi barbarity, praising Roosevelt's statement, urging a total boycott of German goods, and asking Roosevelt to call an international conference of England, France, and the Soviet Union to solve the refugee problem that had been created.

There is little doubt that the Communists were sensitive to the Jewish public's need to protest. This would explain the large crowd. There is also no question that certain Jewish circles were angry at the seizing of center stage by the Communists through this action. While *The New York Times* gave the rally a full column of coverage on page 6 and *The Day* gave it headlines and extensive reportage on page 1, the *JTA,* acknowledging that the meeting was cosponsored by seventeen governors and a number of senators, buried it on a back page and the *Forward* utilized its entire editorial section to denounce the protest under the title: "The Meeting in Madison Square Garden Should Not Have Taken Place."[64]

The *Forward* charged the sponsors of the meeting with blurring the issue of Nazi brutality against the Jews by bringing in such extraneous issues as England's treatment of the Irish and America's treatment of Negroes. The editorial argued that, although it is easy to fill several Gardens with Jewish protesters, non-Jewish protests are much more effective against the Nazis. Further, this was a self-serving venture, designed by the Communists to make political capital with the Negroes and the Irish: "They were not concerned with enhancing the general protest against Hitlerism. And, therefore, they broke the communal discipline and carried out this shameful undertaking."

Clearly, the *Forward* was stung by the success of the left-wing venture. The Jewish Labor Committee had already issued an urgent call, on page 1 in the *Forward* of November 18, for a meeting of representatives of all labor and folk groups at Manhattan Center on November 29. But this was not to be a mass protest. It couldn't be under the terms of the policy of the General Jewish Council. Nevertheless, that meeting was used as an outlet for the emotions of the Jewish masses. Apologies were expressed for the lack of public demonstrations by Jews. "it's not that we didn't care," the assemblage was told; "it's that we didn't want to drown out the general, non-Jewish protest. The recall of our ambassador from Berlin is more expressive than all of the Jewish protests would have been." One day's labor was pledged at that meeting by the Jewish labor groups, the proceeds to be given to aid Jewish refugees. David Dubinsky, president of the International Ladies Garment Workers Union, pledged $1 million from the clothing industry through a special charge for every label.[65]

It was a well-attended meeting, 2,236 delegates from 528 unions and other groups, but it was far from a mass protest. The only mass protest was the one staged by the outcasts of the Jewish community—the Communists. The rest of the community held firm.

But holding firm did not necessarily signify agreement. Some observers, despite their best instincts, agreed to be silent only reluctantly and only for the moment. World demonstrations by non-Jews are better than a *Yiddisher krechtz* (Jewish sigh), commented the *Morning Journal* editorially. The Nazis may be forced to retreat from their brutality by the general population's reaction. We will hold our fire for the moment, editorialized *The Day:*

> Let America speak for us; let the Christian world protest for us; let the American government negotiate for us and then—
> And then—*if it will be necessary* [their emphasis] we will mount our own mass demonstrations to make certain that the voice of protest will be maintained further. . . .[66]

Not everyone, however, accepted patience and communal discipline. A strong segment of Jewish opinion was in favor of public protests.[67] Jacob Glatstein, a prominent columnist in *The Day,* reflected their disillusionment with the Jewish establishment when he argued that, while Christian protests may be more effective, our enforced silence has lulled us into a deep lethargy that has undermined our sense of responsibility toward our own flesh and blood. It was this same Glatstein who, three days after *Kristallnacht,* had called for a one-day general strike, a Yom Kippur in the middle of the week, and a rabbinic march on foot to Washington to the steps of the White House.[68]

The last proposal may or may not have been practical, but the deep anguish felt by Glatstein—and, presumably, by many other Jews—needed an outlet. B. Z. Goldberg articulated this when he asked:

> How can one sit quietly when one's flesh and blood is beaten? . . . Aren't [Jews] people too? Aren't they also Americans? Can't they also scream of their pain.[69]

Words like these must have been on the mind of many a repressed American Jewish soul in the aftermath of *Kristallnacht* as its instinctive cry was stifled by community fiat.

Nevertheless, despite what one senses was a significant amount of disapproval of the General Jewish Council's policy of silence, only one responsible Jewish organ openly attacked the council's decision. The *Reconstructionist,* in an editorial in its December 2

issue, berated the council for confining its public response to
Kristallnacht to the public statement cited previously. Charging
the council with a policy of "centralized *shtadlanut*" as opposed
to the former factional variety of the American Jewish Committee, the *Reconstructionist* applauded the efforts of the leftist
Jewish People's Committee, which "has taken the lead in rallying the masses to public demonstrations . . . in picketing Nazi
steamers, in spreading the Nazi boycott and in urging that the
government impose a trade embargo on Nazi Germany." The
editorial warned that if the council continued to prove incapa-
ble of publicly meeting the challenge of the times, "a realign-
ment ought to be undertaken by those elements in the General
Jewish Council who would rather unite with the Jewish People's
Committee in fighting anti-Semitism and fascism on the economic and political front."[70]

This, however, was the only official Jewish dissent from the
council's communal policy. Jewish unity, for perhaps the first
time in America, was almost perfect. However, whereas on many
previous occasions, a disunity stemming from organizational rivalries prevented an effective communal response, in this case
quite the opposite was true. It was Jewish unity that made possible Jewish silence.

PRESSURE FOR THE RESCUE OF REFUGEES

Public protest was but one avenue of response open to
American Jewry in the wake of *Kristallnacht*. Another avenue,
of greater practical significance, was pressure to solve the refugee problem in its new dimensions.

The dimensions were new and without precedent. By November 29, 1938, the United States consulate in Berlin reported 160,000 applications for American visas. Short of new
legislation, there was no way for these people to receive permits
for three years, according to the acting consul general there. That
same official had been told on November 17 that the 35,000 to
50,000 Jews who had been thrown into jail in the wake of *Kristallnacht* would be released if they received immigration permits
to other countries. The challenge to America and her allies was
clear and compelling. Flight was both necessary and possible in

the weeks and months following the terror of November 10, 1938. It remained so through 1941. The world was aware of this necessity and possibility. What could not be fully foreseen, however, was the future—the human price that would be paid after 1941 for the failure of the world to open its doors while there was still time.[71]

America was in no mood to take the lead in accepting refugees, despite the good intentions expressed rhetorically by the President and the State Department. While the United States had a glorious tradition of offering asylum to the oppressed, this tradition had been abandoned by the country with the passage of the Johnson Immigration Act in 1924, which instituted a strict quota system, resulting in a substantial reduction in immigration. The new restrictionist policy was strengthened further by the Great Depression. Moreover, at the time of *Kristallnacht*, the country was living through a recession marked by grim statistics of 10 million unemployed and staggering relief burdens. That recession did not ease appreciably until America's entry into the war.

Another factor militated against any liberalizing of the immigration law in favor of Jews fleeing from the Nazis. In 1938 there were many alien-haters and Jew-baiters in America, who were well represented in Congress and who opposed enlarging the quotas for German refugees on both alien and Jewish grounds. Public opinion polls taken after *Kristallnacht* showed that, despite the widespread horror over the Nazi persecutions, between 71 percent and 83 percent opposed any increase in the German quota for immigration to this country.[72]

Confronted with strong congressional opposition on the one hand and an absence of public support on the other, President Roosevelt made no attempt to enlarge the quotas. His only humanitarian gesture was to grant long-term asylum to 15,000 Germans who were visiting in the United States in November 1938. Even that minor gesture drew sharp criticism from the restrictionists in Congress.[73]

It is not surprising, therefore, that American Jews were of two minds over whether or not to press for enlarging the immigration quotas. The negative factors seem to have outweighed the possibly positive results, for, in fact, no pressure was exerted.[74]

What were these negative factors that inhibited the Jewish response on the matter of immigration? The first was economic. There was concern in the native Jewish community over the scarcity of jobs at the time. "Much has been done for the refugees," a twenty-five-year-old Jew from New Jersey wrote in the lead letter to the editor of the *National Jewish Monthly,* "but the American Jewish youth is left to look out for his own future. . . . There are probably a million like me in this land of ours, but nobody seems to worry about what happens to us. . . ."[75]

Closely associated with the economic issue was the concern about the capacity of Jewish philanthropy to care adequately for a mass of penniless, jobless people.[76] There was also fear that greater anti-Semitism would be aroused by the general belief that America would be admitting more Jews than could be properly absorbed by the country.[77]

Overriding all of these concerns, which were endemic to the 1930s in general, was another fear unique to 1938–1939: Germany was not the only country with a Jewish problem. Poland and Romania were also anxious to force their Jews to emigrate.[78] Moreover, the Poles made no secret of their intentions. In late November, the Polish press and radio hinted quite clearly that Poland might emulate German methods as the most efficient way of getting rid of her Jews. These hints were well publicized in the Jewish community[79] and beyond. It was not by coincidence that, on November 30, Frances Perkins, Secretary of Labor, spoke about the impossibility of the United States accepting a wholesale influx of Jews from Germany, because it would encourage other countries to "solve" their Jewish problem by torturing Jews, thereby inducing them to emigrate.[80]

This American apprehension clearly troubled Jewish leaders, who found themselves suspended between the humanitarian regard for their fellow German Jews on the one hand and the fear of creating a European floodtide of expelled Jews on the other. The dilemma was reflected in the minutes of the General Jewish Council as it grappled with the formulation of a statement on refugees:

> Although it was felt that on humanitarian grounds mass immigration of German Jews could not be opposed, it was

felt with equal force that other countries, with far more semblance of right than Germany (overcrowded Poland?), might demand a similar solution for very genuine population problems. Though efforts were made to reconcile these opposing desires by acquiescing in German mass immigration because of the imperative necessity, while at the same time stressing the fundamental wrong in such a policy, no satisfying solution was found. . . . It was finally determined that, at least for the time being, nothing should be done with regard to this matter.[81]

One might add, if Jewish leaders could not agree to take the risks involved in rescuing refugees, how could one expect world leaders to have made the humanitarian decision? One can appreciate the difficult dilemma facing the leaders of the council, but one still wonders how they could have decided on a policy of "sit tight and do nothing" while German Jews were facing oblivion. In this case, doing nothing amounted to doing something. By their inaction, American Jewish leaders became passive accomplices to a policy that closed the door on the Jews of Germany at a time when escape was still possible.

Moreover, as individuals, some of those leaders were in a position of influence and used their position to strengthen the restrictionist tendencies of Roosevelt and the State Department. Bernard Baruch, one of fourteen members of Roosevelt's Advisory Committee on Refugees, opposed the idea of letting more refugees come here.[82] Perhaps it was that kind of opposition from Baruch or from other influential Jews that encouraged U.S. Undersecretary of State Sumner Welles to reject a British offer, following *Kristallnacht*, to assign 65,000 of its places in American immigration quotas to Jewish refugees. Welles said in reply that it was his "very strong impression that the responsible leaders among American Jews would be the first to urge that no change in the present quota for German Jews be made."[83]

Judge Samuel I. Rosenman, a member of Roosevelt's inner circle and an American Jewish Committee leader, played a similarly crucial—and, as it turned out, costly—role. When, after *Kristallnacht*, Myron C. Taylor, head of the Intergovernmental Committee for Political Refugees, asked him whether the quota system ought to be liberalized somewhat, Rosenman replied, "I do not believe it either desirable or practicable to recommend any change in the quota provision of our immigration law."[84] Two days after this negative recommendation, Taylor delivered a radio address in which he spoke of the increased urgency to find settlement opportunities for German Jews because hopes for long-range emigration were dimming. But, he added, the Intergovernmental Committee did not plan to ask for changes in existing immigration laws.[85]

Another factor in the failure of American Jews to press the government to admit additional refugees was the excessive faith and trust they placed in Roosevelt. When the President spoke out against Hitler, recalled Ambassador Wilson, and extended the visas of 15,000 German visitors, American Jews drank *l'chaim* in their synagogues and recited special prayers for the welfare of the President—"with tears in their eyes and choked with emotion."[86]

Rabbi J. Konvitz, the president of the Agudat Ha-Rabanim (the organization of Orthodox rabbis, mostly European-born), speaking before his organization, expressed his trust in Roosevelt this way:

> The greatest friend we have, who lights up the darkness of the world, is our President, Franklin D. Roosevelt. His words are like balm for the broken Jewish hearts. . . . Traditional Jewry will engrave, with the blood of our holy martyrs, the names of our President and his people in the annals of Jewish history for generations to come.[87]

Such an attitude was not conducive to mounting a campaign to pressure the President into changing the immigration law. The President had spoken generously, and American Jews responded with gratitude, love, and acceptance of a bitter status quo. Few presumed to expect Roosevelt to do more.[88]

As was the case in the matter of public protest, there were few voices raised in opposition to the generally silent policy with respect to America's accepting additional refugees. One such dissenting voice was Margoshes in *The Day*. He criticized America's role as a promoter of solutions overseas while she maintained her strict quotas at home. "America, like other countries, must learn that one cannot get by with nice words alone. . . . Specific help must be given and the sooner the better." Such help meant opening the doors wide. The fear that such an influx of Jewish refugees might arouse latent anti-Semitism must be considered, but this should not paralyze our undertaking. The plight of European Jewry was far more serious than any possible anti-Semitism here. Therefore, we must press for an open-door policy. This must become part of the Jewish political platform, and this must be done not alone for German Jewry but also for refugee Jews from all over Europe.[89]

Only the *Jewish Frontier* joined *The Day* in an unequivocal call for open doors.[90] Were they both naive or were they the only realists? Were they blind to the restrictionist forces in Congress and the country or did they feel that the fact that Jews were 28 percent of the New York City population gave special weight to their demands?[91] Were they unaware of Roosevelt's cautious approach on changing quotas or did they feel that, if American Jews sounded the alarm, public opinion would change sufficiently to enable the President to use any of the many options open to him to accept refugees?[92]

Whatever moved *The Day* and the *Jewish Frontier,* they were two lonely voices crying in a wilderness, a wilderness on the eastern side of the Atlantic from which Jews were desperately trying to flee and a wilderness on the western side of the same ocean where Jews were paralyzed in silent inaction.

There was one area of political activity on which most of American Jewry agreed: pressure to force Great Britain to open the doors of Palestine. Substantial sums of money were raised—or pledged—for such settlement. Petitions were gathered. Many articles and editorials were written. All of American Jewry could seemingly agree that German Jews should go to Palestine. There was little concern about the effect on Polish or Romanian Jews. There was no fear that Jewish philanthropy would be unequal to the task. Many of the obstacles that blocked immigration to America melted away when the emigrants' destination was changed to Palestine.[93]

PRAYER

If American Jews were largely silent politically, they did express themselves in prayer and fasting, both traditional Jewish responses to crisis and tragedy. Here, too, however, the response was a little late in developing, and it did not quite match the intensity and breadth of the response in other lands.

The Yishuv in Palestine, for example, reacted immediately with a day of prayer and shofar blowing on November 14. The communitywide response was led by Chief Rabbi Isaac Halevi Herzog.* Under the leadership of the Polish Union of Rabbis, Polish Jewry began a month of mourning (Sh'loshim) on November 20, during which all Jewish entertainment and celebration were banned—except for marriages already scheduled. Special prayers and psalms were to be recited throughout the month, and charity for German Jews was to be collected in the synagogue. A general fast was called by Rabbi Chaim Ozer Grodzinski of Vilna for November 23. The São Paulo Jewish community in Brazil launched a similar month of mourning on November 20, with broad communal support. Chief Rabbi Joseph H. Hertz of Great Britain proclaimed Sunday, November 20, as a day of humiliation and prayer for Jewish congregations throughout the British Empire. Canadian Jewry responded accordingly and also scheduled protest meetings for that day in order to give Jews an opportunity "to give expression to their grief over the tragedy of German Jewry."[94]

The American Jewish prayer response was confined to two occasions. The first was the interfaith prayer day of November 20, referred to above. The second was a much more expressive day of fasting and prayer announced by the Agudat Ha-Rabanim on November 21, to take place one week later on November 28. The announcement itself took place at a meeting that The Day described as filled with tears for the murdered Jews. How extensive the observance of the day itself was is hard to judge. The Morning Journal, which had been urging its readers all week, through front-page pleas, to join in, described the day itself as a veritable Yom Kippur eve, with crowds gathered in their synagogues to pray and wail. The Day's description spoke similarly of tens of thousands of young and old, men and women, who crowded the synagogues and shteiblach. The kosher restaurants were empty all day. There was a particularly poignant gathering at Yeshiva College, where the president, Dr. Bernard Revel, brought an audience of over 1,000 students to tears and weeping.

*Whose son Chaim was later to become President of the State of Israel.

Outside New York it is not clear how many American Jews were actually involved in the day of prayer and fasting. There was no mention of it at all in *The Sentinel,* nor did the *Philadelphia Jewish Exponent* support it or report any observance of it. In Boston, on the other hand, the *Jewish Advocate* reported that 5,000 participated in a November 20 service that had been promoted by the Conservative, Reform, and secular Jewish groups, while thousands more fasted under Orthodox Jewish auspices on November 28. Hundreds of businesses were closed, and Rabbi Joseph B. Soloveitchik* addressed a gathering of 3,000 in Roxbury, Massachusetts, that day, urging them to devote the Hebrew month of Kislev to giving charity in behalf of the persecuted Jews of Germany.[95]

The religious response of American Jewry to *Kristallnacht* was impressive, but it was late in coming. Seventeen days went by before the day of prayer and fasting. By that time, other Jewish communities around the world, in less secure surroundings than those in America, had responded more intensively and extensively.[96] Even the medium of prayer and mourning seemed to have been tempered by the general policy of silence on the part of the community.

FUND-RAISING

The most effective avenue of response pursued by the American Jewish community following *Kristallnacht* was fundraising.

The crisis seems to have stimulated a natural reaction on the part of the Jewish community. If they could do nothing else, they could at least give charity. The different fund-raising organizations provided immediate opportunities for the expression of this philanthropic response. The United Palestine Appeal embarked upon a $10 million drive, of which half was to be raised by the Jewish National Fund. In Philadelphia, Rochester, and Cincinnati, unprecedented success was recorded in the Joint Distribution Committee drives for overseas needs. Hadassah launched a $250,000 drive for settling refugee children in

---

*In later years regarded as the dean of the Orthodox rabbinate of the United States— if not the world.

Palestine. A $2 million drive was begun in Chicago to aid European Jews. All reported phenomenal success.[97]

In addition to raising huge sums, there was one other development in the area of community coalescence. In December 1938, as a direct response to *Kristallnacht* and its aftermath, the United Jewish Appeal was founded. It combined into one organization the overseas relief efforts of the American Jewish Joint Distribution Committee (JDC), the United Palestine Appeal (UPA), and the refugee relief and settlement programs in America of the National Coordinating Committee (NCC). The new organization was named the United Jewish Appeal for Refugee and Overseas Needs, and it was to affect favorably the character of Jewish fund-raising for the indefinite future. As of 1938–1939, approximately 50 percent of its funds were to be allocated to the JDC.[98]

A united campaign and distribution organization had been suggested earlier in 1938. Some of the anti-Zionist, JDC stalwarts, notably James N. Rosenberg and Rabbi Jonah Wise, had argued, however, that a united campaign would force a charitable Jew, wanting to alleviate the plight of Europe's Jews, to contribute to something he did not approve of—Palestine. Jonah Wise was rather blunt about the matter: "If helping the Jews of Europe meant imposing Zionism on American Jewry, he might rather not help."[99]

Until November 9, 1938, the Rosenberg-Wise view prevailed, and unity talks broke off. *Kristallnacht* changed the Jewish world irrevocably, and with that change, partisan positions were quickly subordinated to the new needs of world Jewry. "You can no longer separate the problems of Palestine and Europe," Rabbi Abba Hillel Silver told the leaders of the JDC. And they agreed; even James Rosenberg agreed. *Kristallnacht* accomplished what the Zionist idealogues could not. It made Palestine acceptable as a philanthropic partner.[100]

The philanthropic response went beyond organized charity and manifested itself among individuals and groups at the grassroots level. The cloak-and-suit industry agreed that the member firms would raise $270,000 for the refugees through a two thirds of a cent tax on each garment. The Agudat Ha-Rabanim called upon each Jew to give one dollar for each member of his family, to be sent to the JDC as an act of personal charity (*kofer nefesh*). A football game was held on Saturday, December 3, between the New York College All-Stars and the Brooklyn Dodgers football team, the proceeds of which went to the victims of Nazi persecution. The painting and interior-decorating industry—labor and management—pledged overtime work to raise $100,000. The Modzitser Rabbi, a great Hassidic leader, called upon Sabbath-observing Jews to eat Sabbath meals of black bread and herring and send the money that they thus saved to relief agencies.[101]

It was inevitable that this widespread readiness to contribute money should generate several unorthodox schemes. Many may have been well meant, but they tended to divide the Jewish community. One group, calling itself the International Jewish Colonization Society, developed almost overnight through the efforts of a young Chicago industrialist and a Dutch philanthropist and announced a plan to "centralize and coordinate the efforts of Jewish societies all over the world." Its stated purpose was to resettle European Jewish refugees, and it reported initial contributions of $2 million.[102]

Such solo efforts drew cautious criticism from the JDC, the American Jewish Congress, and other established Jewish communal organizations. The established groups were best prepared to deal with the crisis, they said. By contributing to them, the donor could be sure that his donation was being properly used.[103]*

BOYCOTT

A final avenue of response to *Kristallnacht* was one which had been traveled since 1933: the boycott of German goods. The anti-

---

*The effort on the part of the established philanthropic organizations to prevent diversion of desperately needed funds into inexperienced hands led unintentionally to a revealing glimpse into Jewish life in late 1938. On November 18, 1938, there appeared in the Yiddish press a large advertisement entitled "The Tragedy." Framed in black borders, the advertisement mourned the pogrom and its consequences, and it cautioned donors to give only to established charities. The ad was jointly sponsored by the JDC, United Palestine Appeal, Committee for Catholic Refugees from Germany, and the American Committee for Christian German Refugees. In the *Forward* this mournful advertisement was placed on the radio and theater page with its full entertainment listing. In *The Day* it was placed adjacent to ads inviting the public to enjoy the Thanksgiving holiday weekend in Lakewood and to reserve early for New Year's Eve in Atlantic City. This bizarre juxtaposition is a disturbing indication that *Kristallnacht* probably did not interfere much with the parties and holiday celebrations of many New York Jews that year.

Nazi boycott originated with the establishment of a boycott committee by the Jewish War Veterans in March 1933. In May of that year, the American League for the Defense of Human Rights was founded. It eventually became the Non-Sectarian Anti-Nazi League. The specifically Jewish boycott movement was organized by the American Jewish Congress in August 1933. This was expanded into the Joint Boycott Council in 1936 with the participation of the newly created Jewish Labor Committee. The boycott was able to gain the cooperation of every large department store in New York beginning with Macy's in March 1934 and ending with Sears in October 1937. Its effect on German trade with the United States was attested to by the Reich Foreign Ministry in a government report that showed a steep decline in exports to—and imports from—the United States from 1932 to 1937.[104]

Kristallnacht served as a stimulus to broaden community participation in the boycott beyond the American Jewish Congress and the Jewish Labor Committee. The severity of the Nazi persecution resulted in far wider support for anti-Nazi activity among Americans in general and Jews in particular. A page 1 report in the *Morning Journal* was headlined as follows: "REPORT PRESIDENT ROOSEVELT SERIOUSLY CONSIDERS BOYCOTT AGAINST GERMANY. FROM ALL SIDES COME REQUESTS TO PRESIDENT THAT OUR COUNTRY SHOULD DISCONTINUE ALL BUSINESS WITH NAZI BARBARIANS."[105]

Among organizations dominated by Jews there was a flurry of boycott activity. To cite a few examples: The Greater New York Dry Goods Association called upon its national counterpart, the National Federation of Small Businessmen, to join the boycott. The national commander of the Jewish War Veterans called on all Americans to exercise a "rigid boycott" on all German goods and services. Margoshes, in his English column, issued a strong appeal to the government to break off all trade relations with the Nazis as America did with Czarist Russia at the turn of the century. We should campaign for this in Congress, he wrote, on the basis of our Declaration of Independence. "It is entirely incongruous and irreconcilable for us to continue commercial and diplomatic relations with a land controlled by barbarians." J. Fishman, in his daily column in the *Morning Journal,* reported enthusiastically on a proposal, publicized by the *Herald Tribune*, that Congress tax all bank accounts and stock holdings of noncitizens or corporations from countries who persecute people for religion or race. The results would include money which could be used to help refugees and to create pressure by the investors upon their government to cease the persecution.[106]

The strong proboycott position of the community following *Kristallnacht* forestalled favorable consideration by American Jewry of the so-called Schacht Proposal for ransoming 150,000 German-Jewish wage earners and their dependents. Hjalmar Schacht, head of the *Reichsbank*, proposed that the emigration of those Jews would be financed by a 1.5 billion *Reichsmark* bond issue to be financed in foreign currency ($600 million) by "international Jewry."[107]

The plan was designed to improve Germany's foreign exchange position and to increase exports. The bond issue would be amortized only if exports increased. American Jews, for the most part, condemned the proposal as blackmail, coming on top of the expropriation of Jewish assets in Germany. Nine hundred representatives of Jewish organizations met on December 18 at the Hotel Astor under the auspices of the Joint Boycott Council and rejected the proposal out of hand. We would be ready to pay a ransom in order to save Jews, editorialized the *Jewish Frontier*, but this plan called upon us to serve as agents for the sale of Nazi merchandise and to strengthen the Nazi economy. Moreover, few Jews would be saved by the plan. Therefore, it deserved to be rejected. This view, widely held by American Jews, was consistent with their economic fight against Germany at this time. Had American Jews known then that the Final Solution would soon replace forced emigration as Germany's tactic for ridding itself of Jews, the reaction to the Schacht Proposal might have been more favorable.[108]

A RESPONSE SOTTO VOCE

Black Thursday and the cold pogrom of legislation[109] that followed it produced a crescendo of response in America and through much of the Western world. The reaction of American

Jewry, however, was more diminuendo in character. Its intensity varied inversely with that of the non-Jewish world.

There was ample precedent for a vigorous response with far less external stimulus. In 1903, a short report in *The New York Times* on April 20 about a pogrom in Kishinev, which claimed around one hundred lives, produced a loud and enduring Jewish response. And that, in turn, triggered an American public, economic, and diplomatic reaction. Mass meetings were held under Jewish auspices almost daily for three months. Editorials, sermons, urgings in the Yiddish press, and massive collections of funds through Jewish collection agencies, all testified to an aroused community.[110]

Why was the response to *Kristallnacht* relatively weak by comparison? To answer the question one must try to re-create the conditions that existed in the American-Jewish world of 1938. Only in this way can one feel the impulses that moved the Jews of that day.

American Jews in 1938 were an insecure, hyphenated group, unsure of their own place in American society and fearful of creating a Jewish issue and problem for America. There was already a widespread accusation that American Jews were using their influence to bring America to war against Germany.[111]

Anti-Semitism was at a peak in the country in late 1938. Fifteen million listeners heard Father Coughlin occasionally while 3.5 million listened "religiously" every Sunday to the anti-Semitic diatribes of a man of the cloth who was backed by a fund of $1.5 million.[112] The Yiddish and Anglo-Jewish press was obsessed with what Coughlin was saying and the impact he was having. The subject frequently eclipsed the suffering of German Jews. It was a difficult time in which to stand up and be counted as a Jew.

Social Justice, Coughlin's weekly magazine, serialized in 1938 the notorious forgery known as the "Protocols of the Elders of Zion." The last installment appeared at the height of the *Kristallancht* reaction, November 21, 1938.[113] Was it easy to promote Jewish protests and pressure on the government in a public way against a backdrop of such scurrilous accusations? Is it surprising that many Jewish leaders wanted Jewish power to be exerted only in private?

It was not at all an easy time in which to go public. It was a time in which negative stereotypes about the Jew were so deeply rooted that although 88 percent of Americans disapproved of Hitler's treatment of the Jews in 1938, more than 60 percent considered it entirely or partly the fault of the Jews.[114] Some of this, moreover, was expressed quite openly by such as British author H. G. Wells, writing in *Liberty* magazine.[115] Much more, however, lay beneath the surface, harbored there by the best and worst elements in American society. Even the President was not immune. In 1942 he was to remark to the French resident-general in Rabat, Morocco, after its liberation, that after the war the number of Jews in the professions should be limited in accordance with their percentage in the population of North Africa. "This plan," he observed, "would eliminate the specific and understandable complaints which the Germans bore towards the Jews in Germany, namely, that while they represented a small part of the population, over fifty percent of the lawyers, doctors, school teachers and college professors, etc., in Germany were Jews."[116]

American Jews could not have known what Roosevelt felt then—and perhaps it was better that way—but they were well aware of the existence of such views among the best in America. A Harold Ickes would urge them to stand up like men. A Heywood Broun would endorse this confident approach.[117] But the American Jew of late 1938 could not stand up proudly and publicly like an exclamation point; his natural posture was bowed and bent, more like a questionmark.

There were, as we have seen, other factors that militated against a public response. Some Jewish leaders considered the hard-won unity of 1938 too precious to tax even for a crisis like *Kristallnacht*. Some were so trusting of Roosevelt and world democracy as to be sure that somehow, in some way, things would work out. And so they waited with muted voices, for the assistance that never came.

Some observers saw in the restrained response of the General Jewish Council an act of reprehensible cowardice. An entry of Harold Ickes in his diary put it this way:

> I spoke to him [Brandeis] of the cowardice on the part of the rich Jews of America. I said that I would like to get two or three hundred of them together in a room and tell

them that they couldn't hope to save their money by meekly accepting whatever humiliations others chose to impose upon them. [Ickes added that they must be more aggressive and active in defense of Jews as the Catholics were.] Justice Brandeis agreed with me completely. He said there was a certain type of rich Jew who was a coward. According to him, these are German Jews and he spoke of them with the same contempt that I feel for them.[118]

Was the Jewish response appropriate for the times and the deepening crisis? Was private *shtadlanut* combined with prayer, fund-raising, and boycotts a sufficient reaction, given the threat to Jewish lives? Had the community mounted massive protests and exerted public pressure on the President, the State Department, and public opinion, would the quotas have been enlarged? Would the restrictionists in Congress have been defeated by Jewish "power"? Would Roosevelt have matched humanitarian rhetoric with humanitarian action if Jews who were close to him had urged such a course?

And even if public protests and pressure had produced nothing, would they have been worthwhile at least as a precedent for the future? Did the sotto voce response to *Kristallnacht* set a pattern for similar reticence in future crises?

Only the last question has a definitive answer. A precedent *was* set in November 1938 for American Jewry and America. No real efforts for rescue were exerted until some five years later. By that time, 5 million Jews had been murdered and another million were about to be annihilated. By then American Jewry had gone public, and the American government had begun to act. But the hour was already late.

Had American Jewry known in 1938 what the future held in store for German Jewry, would its reaction to *Kristallnacht* have been substantially different?

The next chapter may provide a clue to an answer, for it discusses the plight of 930 German-Jewish refugees aboard a Hamburg-America ocean liner bound for a Cuban port that was closed to them. Their fate, if they were returned to Hamburg, was frighteningly clear to all. How did America's Jews respond to the ill-fated *St. Louis* and its human cargo?

Chapter three

THE SADDEST SHIP AFLOAT

On May 13, 1939, the *St. Louis,* a luxurious cruise ship of the Hamburg-America line, set sail from Hamburg, bound for Havana, Cuba, with 936 passengers. All but six of them were Jewish refugees fleeing from the Nazis. The inability of the *St. Louis* to discharge its passengers in Cuba or in any other Western Hemisphere port offers an interesting case study in how the American Jewish community responded to the refugee-rescue crisis at an early stage, a time when flight from the Nazis was still possible.[1]

The refugees aboard the *St. Louis* were part of a stream of emigrants from Austria and Germany, who had fled in increasing numbers following the *Anschluss* (Hitler's annexation of Austria, March 12, 1938), *Kristallnacht,* and the severe restrictions upon Jews that were enacted in late 1938. Approximately 140,000 departed within a year. Only a minority of that group was able to flee beyond the borders of Europe: 20,000 to South America, approximately 30,000 to the United States, and 12,000 to Palestine. The rest went to so-called transit countries in Western Europe to await their turn for entry into the United States, Palestine, or some other country overseas. By the spring of 1938, the wait promised to be an extended one. The visa quota for the United States was filled for from four to six years. The British White Paper, limiting Jewish immigration to Palestine to

10,000 a year from 1939 to 1944, had gone into effect on May 17 despite vigorous Jewish protests. The transit countries—England, France, Holland, Belgium, and Switzerland—which were bursting with refugees en route to places that were for all practical purposes closed to them, began to close their frontiers as well.[2]

In early 1939, when the receiving countries could no longer accommodate refugees in transit, German steamship companies and Latin American officials collaborated in the sale of illegal visas, which would enable the refugees to leave Germany but which did not always guarantee them a destination—a risk of which the refugees were often ignorant. The Gestapo, which controlled emigration at that time and which was anxious to promote the exodus of Jews from Germany "by every possible means,"[3] connived with the companies and the officials to allow the sale of such visas at rates between $150 and $300 per visa, depending upon supply and demand. Cuban visas were particularly valuable, for Jewish refugees considered Cuba an ideal transit country in which to wait for entry into the United States.[4]

The refugees aboard the *St. Louis* had spent an average of $150 on Cuban landing certificates. These had been sold wholesale by Colonel Manuel Benites, Cuba's director-general of immigration, to the Hamburg-America Line, which in turn resold them to the passengers. When the ship weighed anchor at Hamburg on May 13, the happy passengers were unaware of a tragic fact: On May 5, President Federico Laredo Bru of Cuba had signed Decree No. 93, invalidating all landing certificates. (This decree was well known to the Hamburg-America Line before the sailing, although not to the extraordinary commander of the *St. Louis*, Captain Gustav Schroeder.) Henceforth refugees would be admitted to Cuba only upon presentation of a visa approved by the Cuban State, Labor, and Treasury Departments. The papers in the hands of all but twenty-two of the refugees aboard the *St. Louis* were worthless; 907 people were on a voyage to nowhere. As they sailed down the Florida coast on Friday afternoon, May 26, less than twenty-four hours before the ship was due to dock in Havana, many of the passengers used their last "shipboard money" (a sum allowed by Germany to be taken aboard but which had to be used at sea) to send joyful telegrams to waiting friends and relatives in Cuba and the United States. "More than one message contained only the words: 'Arrived safely.' "[5]

The liner did arrive safely in the port of Havana on the following day, May 27, but the 907 refugees who held only the landing certificates were not allowed ashore. The reason given by Cuban officials for this refusal was that the landing certificates had been sold illegally and that, in any event, the decree of May 5 had rendered them invalid. The intransigence of the Cubans on this matter, however, suggested that there were other compelling reasons shaping the government's policy toward the *St. Louis* refugees. Cuba had already admitted a greater number of refugees proportionately than had many of the richer nations. These refugees were causing problems for the economy, which suffered from stagnation in any case. Moreover, the Nationalist Fascists, the strongest opposition party in the government, were then mounting a strong campaign against admitting more Jews. They urged, on the contrary, that some of the Jewish refugees already in Cuba should be expelled. In the days just prior to the arrival of the *St. Louis,* the reactionary Cuban press raised a cry against admitting its passengers. This climate of opinion made President Bru reluctant to act compassionately with regard to this boatload of hapless and deceived fugitives from Nazi persecution.[6]

The Joint Distribution Committee sent Lawrence Berenson, a prominent New York attorney, to Cuba to negotiate landing rights for the refugees. Berenson had headed the Cuban Chamber of Commerce in the United States and had developed a personal friendship with Fulgencio Batista, chief of staff of the Cuban Army. The lawyer's negotiations with the Cubans were backed by the readiness of the JDC to post a $500 bond for each of the refugees on the *St. Louis* and for each of ninety-eight refugees aboard the French liner *Flandre* and 154 aboard the British steamer *Orduna,* both of which had also been turned away by the Cuban authorities. The Chase National Bank in Havana was authorized to pay these funds, and in addition the Joint Distribution Committee guaranteed "that none of these refugees will become a public charge to the Cuban government."[7]

The negotiations were marked by cordiality on both sides. The Cuban government was careful to demonstrate its friendship for the JDC, its compassion for the plight of the refugees, and its record of "hospitality to persecuted people." James N. Rosenberg, acting chairman of the JDC, telegraphed President Bru that despite his disappointment over the *St. Louis* case, he was "mindful and appreciative of the traditional hospitality of Cuba to the refugees who have found a haven" in Bru's country. The spirit of amity prevailed during several days of discussions following the enforced departure of the *St. Louis* from Havana harbor on June 2. The ship sailed slowly up and down the Florida coast, while negotiations with Cuba continued, with hopes alternately rising and falling as Cuban positions alternately softened and hardened.[8]

The distress of the passengers became front-page news in the United States.[9] *The New York Times* featured the story on its front page on June 2, 5, 6, 7, and 8. It editorialized sympathetically on June 8 about "the saddest ship afloat today," laden with her "cargo of despair," cruising off the coast of Miami whose shimmering towers were, for these passengers, "only the embattlements of another forbidden city." These unfortunates, who were rejected by everyone, will be welcomed home by "Germany, with all the hospitality of its concentration camps."[10] On June 9, the *Times* editorialized:

> We can only hope that some hearts will soften somewhere and some refuge be found. The cruise of the *St. Louis* cries high to heaven of man's inhumanity to man.

The *Times* was not alone in noting the significance of the ship's proximity to Miami, but it failed to ask why the *St. Louis* refugees were not offered asylum in the United States. There is some speculation that the JDC had privately asked Washington to offer a temporary haven at least for the 734 passengers who already had numbers on the American quota list, but the offer was "rebuffed unqualifiedly."[11] James Cannon, Jr., Episcopal bishop of Richmond, Virginia, in a letter to the *Richmond Times-Dispatch*, asked the question that may have troubled other Americans:

> Why did not the President, Secretary of State, Secretary of the Treasury, Secretary of Labor and other officials . . . arrange for the landing of these refugees who had been

caught in this maelstrom of distress and agony through no fault of their own?[12]

When it became clear that Cuba's doors were irrevocably closed to the *St. Louis* refugees, the JDC launched a search for a friendly European destination for this tragic voyage. Morris Troper, the JDC's European chairman, began working from Paris to find a haven for the passengers who, he was warned by the New York office, were "doomed once they reach German soil." The first rumor of some success in the search for a haven was a report on June 12 that France was suggesting Morocco as a potential refuge for five hundred of the passengers. On June 13, Troper reported that the Netherlands had agreed to receive some refugees. This was followed, a day later, by Belgium, England, and France who agreed to divide the remaining passengers among them.[13]

The New York Times applauded the "noble banner" raised by the four countries in their acceptance of the refugees. Thus a problem was solved, it said,

> which was not even dreamed of a generation ago, when in three successive years more than a million immigrants came into the United States. Those days will not return, for mass migrations are no longer the simple solutions of economic difficulties.

The *Times* avoided the question that troubles the historian as he looks back at the *St. Louis* episode. Why did not America open her doors to the refugees on that hapless ship? Why didn't the *Times* suggest refuge in the United States? Morse notes with chagrin that nowhere "in the archives of the United States government is there a suggestion that the refugees be sheltered temporarily within the capacious boundaries of the United States." Morris Troper encountered difficulties in his negotiations with the Europeans because of this restrictive policy. It seems a pity, the head of the Sûreté Nationale in Paris said to him, "that our American friends were not able to direct them to one of their own ports instead of urging them upon us."[14]

Bishop James Cannon, Jr., in the letter to the *Richmond Times-Dispatch* quoted above, charged that the American failure to assist the Jewish refugees on the *St. Louis* "was one of the most disgraceful things which has happened in American history and leaves a stain and brand of shame upon the record of our nation."[15] Was this assessment a fair judgment of American policy concerning this tragic episode? What were the factors that militated against the United States admitting these refugees? And what was the reaction of the Jews in America to the plight of their brethren on the *St. Louis*? How did the Jewish press report the story and what response was forthcoming from the Jewish community? Did the Jews of America acquiese in their country's closed-door policy or did they endeavor to open the doors for the *St. Louis* refugees?

THE RESPONSE OF THE JEWISH COMMUNITY

The Yiddish press in New York reacted vigorously to the plight of the *St. Louis* passengers. *The Day*, the *Morning Journal*, the *Forward*, the *Freiheit*, and the *JTA* all gave front-page coverage to the voyage from the beginning of June until the end of the voyage. As early in the crisis as June 2, the *Forward* printed a headline at the top of page 1 stating: "BEWILDERED REFUGEES CABLE *FORWARD* FOR HELP." The cable read:

> We appeal to world Jewry. We are being sent back. How can you be peaceful? How can you be silent? Help! Do everything you can! Some on the ship have committed suicide. Help! Do not allow the ship to go back to Germany!*

The other papers printed similar cries of anguish from the ship and provided details of the rising and falling fortunes of the passengers. *The Sentinel* and the *Boston Advocate* gave news of the event in their issues of June 9 and 16. The *Jewish Exponent* did not mention the *St. Louis* until it printed an editorial on the denouement in its June 23 issue.

One periodical, the *Congress Bulletin*, in its June 9 issue,

---

*Strangely, on that day when the *Forward* highlighted this painful cry from the *St. Louis*, its only editorials were devoted to a speech by a Soviet leader and the opening of the Czech pavilion at the World's Fair in New York.

printed the only direct call to the United States for permission to land and find refuge there.

> The 907 refugees aboard the *St. Louis* . . . prayed for divine intervention today to find them a place of refuge. Sunday morning is the deadline. Unless a decision is made by then it will be impossible, for technical reasons, for the *St. Louis* to turn back. . . . [By Sunday, June 11, the *St. Louis* would have been halfway back to Germany and could not return.] As the ship continues toward Hamburg uneasiness increases. A panic would be almost inevitable if the Sunday deadline passed without hope. . . .
>
> There was great excitement when the wonderful Florida coast was sighted and hope rose that we might be able to enter that beautiful land. Please help us . . . to end this tortuous journey and avoid disaster. With trust in God and the proved magnanimity of powerful America we await our deliverance hourly.

If we are to judge from the Jewish press, American Jews and their organizations did not respond to the plea in this telegram. The *Contemporary Jewish Record,* which chronicled the activities of the American Jewish community during May and June, did not list a single activity, program, resolution, or discussion on the *St. Louis* crisis except for the vital work of the JDC. The Yiddish papers and the three out-of-town weeklies did not record any communal reaction or response. The Central Conference of American Rabbis, representing the Reform rabbinate of America, held its fiftieth annual convention in Washington, D.C., beginning on June 13. The press did not report any reference to the *St. Louis* throughout this five-day conclave.[16] The subject was not even mentioned in the resolutions as reported on by the *JTA.* Moreover, from *The New York Times* advertisements of rabbis' sermons for the Sabbaths of June 3, 10, 17, and 24, and from the reports that appeared on the following Sundays, there appears to have been only one sermon during the entire period that highlighted the plight of the refugees aboard the *St. Louis.*[17] The response of American Jews to the *St. Louis,* like their response to *Kristallnacht,* appears to have been muted, though in this latter case, unlike the former, there was no conscious communal decision producing the muted response.

Some organs of the Jewish press reacted strongly to the silence of the Jewish community. Writing about the sad specter of a "ship of destiny without destination," the *New Palestine* asked: What had happened to Jewish leadership? Where were they? Where was their guidance and counsel? The secretaries and executive directors of our relief and refugee organizations had given assurances that much was being done.

> But at such a time we would expect the *g'dolei ha'am*, the elders of our people [to be] at the helm . . . giving every measure of encouragement to their subordinates. Why have not the eminent leaders and spokesmen been heard from? . . . Has everything now been relegated to the judgment and discretion of the social workers?
>
> In "Ships That Pass in the Night" . . . Beatrice Harraden symbolizes the isolation of individuals who, though moving in the same sphere, remain unconscious of each other's thoughts and wishes. The tragic voyage of the *St. Louis* and the strange silence of our leaders, lend acute poignance to the moral of that story.[18]

The Day was even more insistent about the failure of B'nai B'rith, the American Jewish Congress, the Jewish Labor Committee, the General Jewish Council, and other organizations to act in behalf of the passengers on the *St. Louis*. It argued that Jewish influence could be brought upon Cuban authorities, particularly Colonel Batista, who had many Jewish friends in the United States. Why was nothing being done? "The Jewish leadership owes us an immediate explanation. If they cannot do anything, let them make room for new, energetic Jewish leadership."[19]

The American Jewish Congress, stung by the harshness of *The Day*'s criticism of Jewish leadership, nevertheless embellished the charge by accusing Jewish leaders of harboring too many doubts and questions and of nurturing rivalries and their own egotistic ambitions.[20] Evidence of the validity of this last complaint is found in a running battle of words among the *Freiheit, The Day,* and the *Forward* on the degree of responsiveness of each to the anguish of the refugees. The *Freiheit* condemned *The Day* for its failure to organize the community to deal with the refugee crisis. It charged the JDC and its defender, the *Forward,* with a reluctance to deal with a progressive government in Mexico, which it claimed was anxious to develop organized Jewish settlements. And it deprecated American Jewish leadership in general for its failure to lead with initiative and strength. The only quarter that was spared the vituperation was Cuba because, the *Freiheit* argued, condemnation of Cuba would hurt the local Jewish population and would also strengthen the Fascist forces there. The reference to progressive forces in Mexico and Fascist groups in Cuba were part of the political egotism of the *Freiheit.* The paper may have been influenced also by the strong opposition of the Cuban Communist Party to the landing of the *St. Louis* passengers in Cuba.[21]

The *New Palestine, The Day, Congress Bulletin,* and the *Freiheit,* representing various segments of the community, were nevertheless in agreement that Jewish leadership in America did not respond effectively to the plight of the 907 passengers aboard the *St. Louis.* The *Forward* demurred. "We are swimming to our death," the *Forward* quoted the passengers pleading, "and you are helping us sink." Who was "you"? asked the *Forward.* If the passengers were referring to American Jews, then—although their desperation is understandable—their blame is misplaced. The guilt lies at the door of the leaders of the nations of the world.[22]

What was there for American Jews to do in response to the *St. Louis* crisis? Aside from expressing sympathy for refugees, outrage at the Nazis, and disappointment with the closed-door policy of Cuba and other nations, their one course of action was to urge that the United States receive the passengers, 734 of whom were on American visa lists already. A number of guarded statements suggesting such a humanitarian gesture were made by Yiddish papers. The *Morning Journal* criticized the United States for its coldness toward the homeless wanderers. "We don't even want to think about the possibility of bringing the refugees here."[23] *The Day* remarked hopelessly that the United States was not likely to be more hospitable than Cuba. In a depressing editorial, "'Auf Widersehn' Pitiful Brothers and Sisters," the *Forward* lamented the demise of the spirit of cooperation and concern fashioned by President Roosevelt:

> The ship came close to Florida, close to the shores of the United States; they called for our help to save them. "Save

us, free, good America." Yet the ship had to continue on its journey.[24]

Most of the Jewish press did not even hint at the desirability of bringing the refugees to the United States. *The Sentinel* called for a solution to the refugee problem but the United States was not mentioned as part of the solution.[25] M. Shoshani in *Hadoar* bitterly assailed a world in which not even one country could open her gates to people on the brink of annihilation:

> The image of this wandering vessel, with hundreds of men, women and children who call for help and were not answered, will be engraved as a "mark of Cain" on the forehead of the world.[26]

But nowhere did Shoshani suggest that the United States specifically might save the *St. Louis* passengers. The same hesitancy was demonstrated by the *Jewish Exponent,* which deplored the indifference of the world and which quoted *The New York Times* editorial about the passengers watching the "shimmering towers of Miami," but which never suggested that the United States might dissociate itself from the world's indifference by providing a haven for the refugees. This possibility was apparently so remote that the *Jewish Exponent*'s editor did not seem to appreciate the irony of an analogy he offered from history. The discovery of America, he wrote, was timed by Providence to synchronize with the cruel expulsion of the Jews from Spain. Is there no other continent to be discovered where the exiles from a more ruthless and barbarous land could find relief?[27]

UNDERSTANDING THE JEWISH RESPONSE TO THE ST. LOUIS CRISIS

Why was the communal response of American Jewry so muted in this crisis? Why was there no clear call on the part of the Jewish press and the leadership of the Jewish community for the United States to offer refuge to these 907 souls. Two factors may shed some light on these questions: the anti-Semitic climate of the times and the perception that American Jews held concerning restrictionism and antialienism in the United States.

The extent of public anti-Semitic words and behavior in the spring of 1939 may have been sufficient by itself to explain Jewish timidity on the *St. Louis* issue. David S. Wyman's judgment that "the years from 1938 through 1945 saw anti-Semitism in America reach a peak,"[28] was shared by Americans living during that period: 45 percent of them felt in March 1939 that anti-Semitism was on the rise in America; 19 percent expected a widespread campaign to be launched in this country against Jews, and 40 percent of Americans would either have supported, or at least sympathized with, such a campaign.[29] These results of public opinion surveys were available to Jewish leaders, but one did not need opinion surveys to detect the hatred of Jews that filled the atmosphere in America in early 1939. These feelings were perhaps most virulent in New York City, the city with the heaviest concentration of Jews in the country.

This study has already noted the powerful influence of Father Charles Coughlin upon the atmosphere of hate that existed in 1938–1939. The Detroit priest was not speaking officially for the Catholic Church, but he was sufficiently popular not to be criticized in public. The most the Church would do was deny the truth of his statements. One such refutation—of a Coughlin charge that Jews were responsible for the communist revolutions—was made by George N. Shuster, who subsequently became president of Hunter College but was then special editor of *Commonweal*, a prominent Catholic journal. Shuster virtually apologized for his defense of the Jews in his concluding sentence: "I have set it down here, not to whitewash anybody but because I believe that unfair assertions are calumnies, however well-intentioned they may be."[30]

New York was the center of Coughlin's Christian Front Organization. Platoons of twenty-five members joined together there for street meetings—an average of fifty to seventy were held each week during the spring and summer of 1939—and incited their audiences to violence against communistic Jews despoiling the country. For fear of treading on Catholic toes, the press ignored the frequent street incidents that were provoked by the Christian Front. Nor were the police helpful. The New York Police Department contained 407 members of the Front, and as a consequence, the police were not inclined to arrest the hate-mongers. Indeed, they sometimes arrested bystanders for protesting against the vituperative rhetoric.[31]

Coughlin and his Christian Front were only the best known of a very large contingent of anti-Semitic leaders and organizations. Coughlin was known by close to 90 percent of Americans and approved of by more than a third of the population—thus he must have reflected what a large percentage of Americans were thinking, whether or not they were among his followers. Fritz Kuhn, leader of the German-American Bund, was known by 70 percent of the American public by 1940. The Bund had seventy-one locals throughout the country with 40 percent of its membership in New York City. On February 20, 1939, the Bund held a tumultuous meeting in Madison Square Garden, attended by 20,000 followers. Hitler was "heiled," Roosevelt was booed, and the mention of Coughlin's name brought thunderous applause. At one point in the proceedings, fifty uniformed storm troopers attempted to throw Dorothy Thompson out of the meeting. Press comment across the nation was generally critical of the meeting—and some felt that the Bund was not even entitled to the right of free speech—but the entire occasion demonstrated the extent of the support for this extreme brand of hatemongering. The fact that a meeting of such magnitude could have taken place at all was viewed by Jews as an ominous sign.[32]

One student of anti-Semitism estimated that 121 anti-Semitic organizations arose between 1933 and 1940. Their development was enhanced by economic privation and the frustration that attended it. Their ideology was influenced by the fear of some Americans that a revolutionary movement was growing in America, of which the liberalism of the New Deal was a dangerous example. These organizations published hate literature, purchased network time on radio, conducted public meetings, and created an atmosphere of hostility that must have contributed to the insecurity of the American Jew.[33]

Even the outspoken and self-possessed Stephen S. Wise was shaken by the poisoned atmosphere. On May 26, the day before the *St. Louis* docked in Havana, he wrote to his friend and relative, Rosemary Krensky, a member of a leading Jewish family in Chicago:

What with the tragic Palestine situation [the White Paper had been promulgated nine days before] and the really rising tide of anti-Semitism everywhere, I do not know what to do! . . . Last night, after Carnegie Hall was refused to the so-called Christian Front, made up of Coughlinites, they marched up and down 57th Street, shouting: "Hang Rabbi Wise to a flagpole! Lynch Rabbi Wise"!—Thousands of them and the police didn't even interfere.[34]

Wise's perplexity and the extent to which he was intimidated by rabid anti-Semitism may well have been shared by other Jewish leaders. At the very least the anti-Semitic climate must have distracted Jewish spokesmen from other pressing matters, the *St. Louis* among them. At the most critical juncture in that tragic voyage, on June 13 and 14, the *Morning Journal* editorials were concerned with Coughlin and anti-Semitic attacks in Baltimore.[35] On June 18, when *The New York Times* celebrated on page 1 the landing in Antwerp of the first contingent of *St. Louis* passengers, the report of the rabbis' sermons from the day before carried no mention of the ill-fated vessel. The major headline was "RABBIS SPEAK ON CHRISTIAN AID IN COMBATING ANTI-SEMITISM."

Looking back on the *St. Louis* episode, the editor of *Opinion* may have addressed himself to the natural fears and apprehensions of many Jews when he urged his readers: "Let us not fear accusations of international intrigue from the Coughlinites *et al.* Our action must be determined not by fear of libel but by the courage of men and the heart of the Jews."[36]

THE *ST. LOUIS* AND AMERICAN
RESTRICTIONS ON IMMIGRATION

In addition to the anti-Semitic atmosphere that prevailed in America in the spring of 1939, another issue may have had a significant effect upon the Jewish response to the *St. Louis* crisis: restrictionism. The policy of maintaining strict limits upon immigration to America, in the face of a burgeoning refugee population in the world, created serious problems for American Jews. They saw their German coreligionists desperately trying to escape from a land of tyranny, but unable to reach the land of the free, because it was kept inaccessible to all but a strictly regulated few.[37]

Restriction of refugee immigration had its legislative origin in the Johnson Immigration Act of 1924, which established the national-origins quota system, by means of which immigration from European countries was regulated. In 1930 President Hoover issued an executive order instructing American consular officials to enforce all regulations strictly, in order to inhibit immigration as much as possible. Special attention was to be given to the requirement that the immigrant demonstrate that he is not likely to become a public charge. The results of this Hoover order (endorsed by Roosevelt in the presidential campaign of 1932) was to reduce total immigration from 241,700 in 1930 to 35,576 in 1932. Of that number, only 2,755 were Jews.[38]

American Jews formed part of the national consensus that approved the restrictive policy. Even after Hitler's rise to power, they were careful not to challenge that consensus. They did urge a liberalization of *procedures* in order to allow for greater immigration of German Jews, but they opposed special *legislation* on their behalf, and they explicitly endorsed the executive order of 1930, declaring it to be "a salutary thing."[39] This policy of leaning over backward resulted in a slight rise in Jewish immigration from 2,372 in 1933 to 4,137 in 1934 and 4,837 in 1935.[40] American Jewish organizations felt that to press for more might backfire. In 1938 the *American Jewish Year Book* concluded,

> No one who knows the situation can have much hope that the immigration policy of the United States will become less restrictive than it is now. On the contrary, the tendency is for more restriction, and it is likely that the next few years will see further restrictive legislation.[41]

The United States, observed one contemporary Jewish scholar in 1939, had entered a period of consolidation rather than absorption. The United States' role as "the asylum of mankind" and "the hope of all who suffer" had ended.[42] Such an observation did not offer much encouragement to an American Jewish campaign to help the suffering passengers of the *St. Louis*.

Moreover, economic conditions, which had improved slightly

in the middle thirties, dipped sharply once more, beginning in the summer of 1937, just at the time that Hitler's persecution of German Jews was intensifying. The so-called Roosevelt Recession reversed the trend toward lower unemployment. The jobless count, which had dropped from 15 million in 1930 to 7.5 million in 1937, now began to rise and averaged between 8 and 10 million through 1938 and most of 1939. Although proponents of increased immigration argued that the influx would not significantly affect the unemployment picture—that, on the contrary, the new consumers would actually help the economy—most Americans firmly believed that every new refugee would eventually cost some American his precious job.

Accusations were leveled against Jewish-owned department stores, charging that they were favoring refugees for job openings over native Americans. Denials were forthcoming from such stores as Macy's (owned by the Straus family), Abraham and Straus, and Stern Brothers. Bloomingdale's even swore out an affidavit stating that, during a three-year period, it had employed only eleven refugees out of a working force of about 2,500.[43]

But more than economic forces were at work to restrict the admission of refugees into the United States. In the twenties and thirties there prevailed, especially among patriotic and veterans groups, an attitude of nativist-nationalism, manifested by pride in everything that was 100 percent American, and by rejection of everything alien. A fear developed that American society was becoming adulterated by foreign influences. "Let us stop immigration completely for a while," wrote the editors of *Defender Magazine* in May of 1938, "and give our present alien population an opportunity to become Americanized first before they foreignize us."[44]

This threat of alien domination was given scholarly credence in May of 1939 by a book entitled *Conquest by Immigration*. Authored by Dr. Harry Laughlin of the Eugenics Record Office of the prestigious Carnegie Institute of Washington and published by the New York State Chamber of Commerce, it purported to show that, just as a foreign power can conquer a country by invasion and occupation, so can a country be conquered by peaceful immigration—another form of "occupation." The Laughlin study, which was discussed in a front-page story in *Congress Bulletin* on June 9, 1939 (while the *St. Louis* was steaming slowly back toward Hamburg), supplied scholarly support for the traditional antialien stereotypes: their disproportionately large incidence of mental disease, their greater tendency toward criminality, their indolence and the resultant enlargement of relief rolls, their competition with native Americans for jobs that were already scarce.[45] The organ of the American Jewish Congress told its readers of Laughlin's conclusion that "a wise country will suspend all immigration during each major lull in employment." A final racial slur was reported in this review essay. Any new blood that might be added, the antialien author advised, now that "the basic seed stock of the country has been established . . . should be definitely better than the average already established here, else it should not be admitted at all." Who would be bold enough at such a time to guarantee the superior blood of 907 refugees aboard a ship sailing slowly back to Hamburg?

The fear of "occupation" by foreigners prompted a concern about great numbers of illegal aliens who might be slipping into the United States, "vast waves of human flotsam" from Europe, which would pollute American shores.[46] The extent of this fear is evident from the care with which Secretary of Labor Frances Perkins dealt with the subject in her *Annual Report* for the fiscal year ended June 30, 1939. Citing the very small rise in the number of nonimmigrants (visitors) during the year, Perkins argued that this should refute the sensational and groundless reports about floods of alien visitors.[47]

The atmosphere on Capitol Hill was influenced by this strong restrictionist sentiments. The twin concerns of unemployment and nativism combined to create a legislative mood in Washington in which widening the immigration quotas was an unrealistic goal. Indeed the closing of *all* doors was a distinct and ominous possibility.[48]

The man who led the restrictionist forces and who syncretized all of the alien phobias, fascist sympathies, and Jew-hatred in the country, was Democratic Senator Robert Reynolds of North Carolina. He was assisted by Democrats John Rankin of Mississippi, Martin Dies of Texas, Joe Starnes of Alabama, and Republican Senator Rufus Holman of Oregon. Reynolds and Starnes cosponsored a bill on which hearings were held March

21–23, 1939, to reduce all immigration quotas by 90 percent, halt permanent immigration for ten years or until unemployment dropped to 3 million, fingerprint and register all aliens, and deport those aliens who were on public relief or whose presence was inimical to the public interest. The CIO and AFL opposed parts of the bill; the Labor Department opposed it in its entirety. But groups that were friendly to refugees scarcely dared speak up for fear that their testimony would inspire a propaganda barrage against them and the refugees themselves.[49]

The Reynolds-Starnes bill did not pass, but the bitter debate it engendered and the restrictionist power it revealed were both reflective of public opinion at the time, as reported in *Fortune* April 1939. Its quarterly survey showed that the percentage of Americans opposed to changing the immigration laws had actually risen from 67.4 percent in 1938 to 83 percent in 1939. Considering that 94 percent of Americans expressed disapproval of the Nazis' persecution of the Jews after *Kristallnacht,* one historian concludes that the public reaction to the pogrom "seemed to represent no more than a strong spectator sympathy for the underdog."[50]

The *Fortune* survey also illuminated the effect on American Jews of this hostile national mood by a startling statistic: Only slightly more than 30 percent of Jews expressed themselves as opposed to changes in the immigration laws to admit a larger number of European refugees. Both Representatives Emanuel Celler and Samuel Dickstein, the latter chairman of the House Immigration Committee, offered bills to widen the quotas—but only temporarily. Celler's bill called for a temporary change in the quotas in order to meet the emergency created by the Austrian *Anschluss.* Dickstein's bill, proposed right after *Kristallnacht,* provided for an emergency quota of 120,000 a year, to admit refugees under the *unused quotas* of other countries. Cautious and limited as both bills were, they were nevertheless withdrawn from consideration in February 1939. Their sponsors feared that their introduction to the House would stimulate passage of quota *reduction* bills instead.

The Washington correspondent of the *Forward* informed his readers, in June 1939, that the best advice on Capitol Hill was for Jews to ask only for the attainable, to accept what was offered, and not to rock the boat. On the question of easing immigration restrictions, he wrote, "Our best friends in Congress advise against starting such a campaign." A colleague of his expressed similar despair at the height of the *St. Louis* drama. Our Jewish leaders, he wrote, sat quietly by, when common sense told us that the solution lay in Washington's pressuring Cuba to admit the refugees. But, he added, the United States would not urge Cuba to do this because the Cubans would respond: "Why don't you, the United States, allow them in?" There would be no answer because "the United States is immovable on the issue of changing immigration laws."[51]

This view was apparently so widely held by Jews and other prorefugee groups that they expended their greatest effort not toward widening the quotas but rather toward preventing the antialien forces from reducing the quotas or eliminating them entirely. The strategy seems to have been to mute the refugee issue as much as possible, a strategy which was extended to include emergencies like that which occurred when the *St. Louis* steamed slowly up and down the coast of Florida.

A further example of how intimidating the anti-Jewish atmosphere was during the *St. Louis* period was provided by the ill-fated Wagner-Rogers Act, a bill that proposed the admission of 20,000 German refugee children over a two-year period in 1939 and 1940. Introduced on February 9, 1939, in the Senate by Robert F. Wagner of New York and in the House by Edith Rogers of Massachusetts, the bill had broad bipartisan support in Congress, in organized labor, and among leading Catholic and Protestant clergy. It was endorsed by outstanding Americans like Eleanor Roosevelt, Harold Ickes, Frances Perkins, Attorney General Francis Biddle, former President Herbert Hoover, and Alf Landon, Republican standard bearer in 1936. It was supported editorially by eighty-five newspapers in thirty states, including twenty-six newspapers in the South, representing every southern state with the exception of Arkansas and Mississippi. Clarence E. Picket, executive secretary of the American Friends Service Committee, headed a Nonsectarian Committee for German Refugee Children, whose job it was to push the bills through Congress.[52]

The opposition consisted of an association of superpatriotic groups led by Senator Reynolds. Hearings were held in late April and May and early June. Despite the strong support in Congress and in the community, the bills could not be reported out of committee. Finally, the Senate committee reported it out on June 30, but only after amending it to death by including the children as first priority in the normal quotas. This drew Wagner's opposition on the grounds that the compassion for the children would result in cruelty to adults who were already on the list and who now would be supplanted by the children.[53] The success of the opposition probably reflected more accurately the mood of the country than did the impressive body of supporters. A Cincinnati poll among housewives in late May 1939 indicated that 77.3 percent opposed the admission of "a considerable number of European refugee children outside the quota limits"; 21.4 percent approved, and only 1.3 percent did not answer, indicating that this was an issue that touched sensitive nerves. In January, when the memories of *Kristallnacht* were still fresh, the percentage was only slightly better: 66 percent opposed the admission of German refugee children.[54]

In summarizing all the sessions of the immigration committees of both houses of Congress in 1939, James L. Houghteling, Roosevelt's commissioner of immigration and naturalization, reported, "The tendency of a considerable part of Congress was toward the reduction of existing immigration quotas; the chance of any liberalizing legislation seemed negligible."[55]

The Jewish community remained largely silent on the issue. Stephen S. Wise labored behind the scenes to rally support, but he maintained a public silence as did the principal spokesmen of other major Jewish organizations.[56] The normally assertive *Congress Bulletin* demonstrated in an editorial just how intimidated the Jewish community must have felt on the issue of restrictionism even in the face of a clearly humanitarian proposal:

> There was a great deal of necessary caution exercised on the part of the responsible Jewish organizations while a committee of the United States Congress was studying the Wagner-Rogers Bill. . . . Now the committee has recommended the adoption of the Bill and it seems that the cautious restraint on the part of liberal and Jewish groups may be eased in order to help the passing of the Bill in the House.[57]

But a strong campaign was never mounted for fear that it might result in quota reduction.[58] Unfortunately, the lack of a campaign was used by the nativist opposition as an argument against the bill. If the Jews did not feel strongly about it, they reasoned, why should American Christians act for them?[59] One American Christian did not act for them. Sensing the popular opposition, noting the muted Jewish support, hearing the strong restrictionist voices in Congress, President Roosevelt refused to take any position on the matter.[60]

Senator Wagner spoke to the nation on the radio on June 7, in a last-ditch effort to save his children-rescue program. But the bill died. It was killed by the same antialien national mood, the same hesitance in Congress and the administration, and the same muted Jewish voices that could not help to save the refugees on the *St. Louis*.[61]

SUMMING UP THE RESPONSE TO THE *ST. LOUIS* CRISIS

The New York Times reported on one Jewish attempt to land the *St. Louis* refugees in the United States. Bernard H. Sandler, an attorney, announced on June 6, that he had promised to raise a $50,000 bond to indemnify the Hamburg-America Line if the *St. Louis* would drop anchor in New York harbor while he appealed to the President and the Congress to grant the refugees emergency asylum as an international goodwill gesture on the eve of the visit here of the British King and Queen. It was a gallant gesture, but apparently Captain Schroeder was in no position to change course on the basis of a promise from a man unknown to him or the company.[62]

Aside from Sandler's gesture, there were no other offers to help land the refugees in the United States. The major Jewish effort in this crisis was maintained by the JDC. It represented a vigorous and successful response from this philanthropic arm of the American Jewish community.

Faced with an inhospitable world on the one hand and what the JDC considered to be a boatload of doomed passengers on the other, the Joint brought the passengers to various ports in the Netherlands, Belgium, France, and England. Many of the refugees later fell into the hands of the Nazis once again and were murdered, but this prospect could not have been anticipated in June 1939.

The Joint acted forcefully despite a policy dilemma of considerable proportions, which it chose to face only after the fact. The cost for posting bonds for the refugees exceeded $500,000. Had Cuba accepted the refugees, the cost might have been $1 million.[63] With many such refugee ships at sea already, and with the prospect for more such voyages, the Joint could easily spend more than its $8 million income for 1939 on refugee ships alone. The JDC, therefore, issued a statement through its executive director, Joseph C. Hyman, following the successful completion of the *St. Louis* voyage, indicating that this kind of crisis was beyond the capacity of private philanthropy and that the Joint

> cannot regard its action in behalf of the *St. Louis* passengers, and the enormous sacrifices it has made in the financial commitments undertaken for this relatively small number of persons, as constituting a precedent for any similar action. . . . The *St. Louis* incident must be regarded, as in fact it was, as a special problem that required special treatment. . . .[64]

The harshness of this position must be viewed with due regard for the philanthropic capabilities of the JDC, the readiness of the Nazis to dump refugees on the world, and the increasing resistance of the world to accept them. On the other hand, one cannot help wondering whether such a statement did not stiffen America's resolve against setting precedents itself by accepting refugees in crisis situations. Furthermore, if there were Jews to be saved, was it not the duty of the JDC and the newly formed UJA to raise the necessary funds? Regrettably, the need for rescue in 1939 appeared to be only to improve conditions of life for Jews then under Nazi rule. The Herculean measures required for that rescue were not forthcoming. By the time rescue had become a matter of life or death in late 1941, fund-raising was no longer the answer. A potentially life-saving two-year period had been lost.

In 1939, the JDC provided the major response of the American Jewish community to the *St. Louis* crisis. The rest of the community did not react to it at all. The press covered the event comprehensively. Compassionate editorials were written. But, for reasons which have been given, no response was forthcoming from American Jewish leaders or their organizations.

Jews knew how to mount pressure upon government officials. They had just completed an arduous campaign against the British White Paper in May, when this new crisis burst upon them. Somehow, however, the press, which had been so forceful and demanding with respect to Great Britain and Palestine, turned timid and docile when confronted with a ship off the coast of Florida. In 1939, it was safe to attack England; it was dangerous and perhaps futile to assault American immigration laws. The Western World was condemned for its heartlessness in the face of these hopeless people, but the demand that the United States open her doors was never made.[65]

In addition, perhaps because of the tragic conditions of Jewry in Europe and the hostile climate toward Jews in America, the Jew of that day was given to despair. "All Jews are on the *St. Louis* and we are all surrounded. . . . Jews have no safe place in this world," bemoaned one journalist.[66] "The world is full of wickedness, cried another, "and no help can be expected from it."[67] In this mood of pessimism the Jewish community did not react quickly to the plight of the *St. Louis* refugees. Looking back on the lost opportunity, one writer observed:

> It did not even occur to Jews to appeal to the American government to find a way of saving the hapless passengers of the *St. Louis*. . . . [We are] showing increasing signs of becoming spiritually and morally reconciled to accept the ghetto and almost voluntarily to surrender the positions won by the Emancipation. Our own depression and demoralization are immeasurably more dangerous to ourselves than the blows of our enemies.[68]

Hitler, Coughlin, Reynolds, and the British White Paper must have had a depressing effect on American Jews by June of 1939. Perhaps the Nazis had demonstrated how weak and vulnerable the Jewish enterprise really was.[69]

Whether or not vigorous political activity might have helped to open America's doors to the *St. Louis* refugees cannot be known for sure. What is clear is that a pattern of muted response by American Jews, which was set in reaction to *Kristallnacht,* was maintained in this crisis, though not entirely for the same reasons. What also became clear through this episode was a grim fact stated boastfully in the Nazi journal *Der Weltkampf:* "We are saying openly that we do not want the Jews while the democracies keep on claiming that they are willing to receive them—and then leave them out in the cold. Aren't we savages better men after all?"[70]

The lesson was not entirely lost on Americans either. In its April 1939 issue, *Fortune* discussed the meaning of the 83 percent negative opinion on widening the quotas for refugees. "Would Herr Hitler and his German American Bund," *Fortune* asked, "be safe in the joyful conclusion from this that Americans don't like Jews much better than do the Nazis?"

During the next three years Hitler's war was expanded to include virtually the entire world. Simultaneously, his war against the Jews was escalated from a policy of persecution and physical brutality to mass murder. By the time the information about this new dimension of cruelty became available, the options that were open to American Jewry to help their beleaguered brethren in Europe were severely restricted. The need for a response could not have been greater, but the avenues for assistance were now limited. How did American Jews react to the news of the planned murder of European Jewry?

EPILOGUE

Events in history tend to repeat themselves and frequently the mistakes are repeated as well. In the case of the *St. Louis* episode, it is noteworthy that while the event has recurred—most recently in the case of the Boat People of South Vietnam and other benighted lands of Southeast Asia—the lessons of history have not been ignored. The United States and other countries have admitted hundreds of thousands of these refugees.

In a remarkable twist of history, Israel was the first to open its doors to the Boat People. On June 21, 1977, the day Menachem Begin took office as Prime Minister, his first official act was to grant asylum to sixty-six Vietnamese, who had been picked up by an Israeli freighter and rejected at several Far Eastern ports. The date, by coincidence, was exactly thirty-eight years—to the day—from that when the last of the *St. Louis* refugees disembarked in Southhampton, England: June 21, 1939.

Chapter four

THE FINAL SOLUTION BECOMES PUBLIC KNOWLEDGE

On December 17, 1942, it was announced to the world that Hitler had decided to achieve the Final Solution to the Jewish Problem through the physical extermination of Europe's Jews.[1] Hitherto, rumors of this infamous move had been leaked abroad but had been dismissed as propaganda. But now the truth had come out.

It was officially condemned by the eleven governments (or governments-in-exile) of Belgium, Czechoslovakia, Greece, Luxembourg, the Netherlands, Norway, Poland, the Soviet Union, the United Kingdom, and the United States, together with the French national committee. Their joint statement, which was front-page news in *The New York Times*, alerted the Allied peoples to the fact that Nazi atrocities were not simply isolated acts of brutality but part of a master plan to exterminate all the Jews under Nazi control.

The eleven-nation statement said in part:

> The German authorities . . . are now carrying into effect
> Hitler's oft-repeated intention to exterminate the Jewish
> people in Europe.
>
> From all the occupied countries Jews are being trans-
> ported in conditions of appalling horror and brutality to
> Eastern Europe. . . . None of those taken away are ever
> heard of again. The able-bodied are slowly worked to death
> in labor camps. The infirm are left to die of exposure and
> starvation or are deliberately massacred in mass execu-
> tions. The number of victims of these bloody cruelties is
> reckoned in many hundreds of thousands of entirely in-
> nocent men, women and children.
>
> The above mentioned governments . . . condemn in the
> strongest possible terms this bestial policy of cold-blooded
> extermination. . . . They reaffirm their solemn resolution
> to insure that those responsible for these crimes shall not
> escape retribution and to press on with the necessary
> practical measures to this end.[2]

This statement was the climax of events which began on August 1, 1942, in Lausanne, Switzerland, when Gerhard Riegner,
the representative of the World Jewish Congress in Switzerland, was informed by a leading German industrialist of the existence of a plan, ordered by Hitler, to exterminate all of the
Jews in Europe, a plan which came to be known as the Final
Solution.[3]

This was not the first report that Riegner had received about
the mass murder of millions of Jews. It was only the latest example of a series of reports and pieces of evidence all of which
pointed clearly to an unprecedented plan for the slaughter of
millions. In May of 1942 Riegner received a report from the
Bund, the Jewish Socialist Party in Poland, which opened with
the stark observation that the Germans have "embarked on the
physical extermination of the Jewish population on Polish soil."
The Bund report, released in June 1942, estimated that 700,000
Jews had already been killed. This information, well publicized
in England and the United States, was given additional credence through its endorsement by the two Jewish representatives of the Polish National Council in London, Shmuel Zygel-

boym of the Bund and Ignacy Schwartzbart of the Zionist Organization.[4]*

Moreover, the British section of the World Jewish Congress had held a press conference on June 29, 1942, in which the facts of the systematic destruction of European Jewry were presented. More than 1 million had been murdered already, the press was told,[5] and Eastern Europe had been transformed into a "vast slaughterhouse for Jews."

The Bund report and the World Jewish Congress press conference, coming on top of many isolated reports of Nazi atrocities in Eastern Europe, stimulated a mass rally in Madison Square Garden on July 21, 1942, sponsored by the American Jewish Congress, B'nai B'rith, and the Jewish Labor Committee, among others. Twenty thousand participants heard a message of support sent to the meeting by President Roosevelt, who promised that the American people would hold the perpetrators of these crimes to strict accountability on the day of reckoning.[6]

On August 1, therefore, Riegner was inclined to accord credibility to this new report from the German industrialist, which added a unique and ominous dimension to all the other evidence he had amassed: the existence of a specific order for the deportation of Jews, their concentration in Eastern Europe, and ultimately their total extermination. After deliberating and investigating for a week and after analyzing numerous current reports of mass deportations of Jews from Belgium, Holland, and France and the beginning of the "resettlement" of the Jews

---

*In an April 1968 article in *Midstream,* entitled "When Did They Know?" Professor Yehuda Bauer argues persuasively that the Bund report was so alarming in its detail and scope that it should have stimulated a strong Jewish response immediately. There was no reason to wait for more evidence. In a more recent study, *The Terrible Secret,* Walter Laqueur supports this view and charges Jewish leadership with either blindness or irresponsibility for failing to act upon the information that was already available in May and June of 1942.

It is, therefore, instructive to read a rejoinder to Bauer's article by one of the most passionate pleaders for European Jewry during the Holocaust, Marie Syrkin, who was a member of the editorial board of the *Jewish Frontier* in the 1940s. Writing in *Midstream,* May 1968, Professor Syrkin explains that she and Hayim Greenberg, the fiery editor of the *Jewish Frontier,* rejected the report "as the macabre phantasy of a lunatic sadist." This recollection probably reproduces quite accurately the attitude of disbelief that prevailed at that time even among the most responsible Jewish leaders and journalists. Ironically, the editors, who could not dismiss the report entirely for fear that it may have had some elements of truth in it, elected to print it in small type in the back of the September 1942 issue. There it can be read today, Syrkin admits, "as a monument to our gross stupidity."

left in the Warsaw ghetto, Riegner sent the following cable to Rabbi Stephen S. Wise in New York and Sydney Silverman, Labour M.P. and chairman of the British Section of the World Jewish Congress in London, using the American and British consulates in Geneva as conduits:

> RECEIVED ALARMING REPORT THAT IN FÜHRER'S HEADQUARTERS PLAN DISCUSSED AND UNDER CONSIDERATION ACCORDING TO WHICH ALL JEWS IN COUNTRIES OCCUPIED OR CONTROLLED GERMANY NUMBERING 3½–4 MILLIONS SHOULD AFTER DEPORTATION AND CONCENTRATION IN EAST BE EXTERMINATED AT ONE BLOW TO RESOLVE ONCE AND FOR ALL JEWISH QUESTION IN EUROPE STOP THE ACTION REPORTED PLANNED FOR AUTUMN METHODS UNDER DISCUSSION INCLUDING PRUSSIC ACID STOP WE TRANSMIT INFORMATION WITH ALL RESERVATION AS EXACTITUDE CANNOT BE CONFIRMED STOP INFORMANT STATED TO HAVE CLOSE CONNECTIONS WITH THE HIGHEST GERMAN AUTHORITIES GENERALLY SPEAKING RELIABLE.[7]

The American cable was suppressed by the State Department's Division of European Affairs on the grounds that its contents were at best unsubstantiated and at worst fantasy. One official in Bern regarded it as a "wild rumor inspired by Jewish fears."[8] Rabbi Wise finally received the cable through Silverman in London—the British had not suppressed his cable—on August 28, the latter having been urged by Riegner, perhaps as a precaution, to "inform and consult New York."[9]

Wise immediately contacted Sumner Welles,[10] Undersecretary of State, "then, as always, deeply understanding and sympathetic."[11] Welles asked Wise not to release the information until the State Department had been able to confirm it. The rabbi agreed. It was an agreement that was to delay the publication of the Riegner report for almost three months from the time Wise first received it, a period that, according to one historian, corresponded to the bloodiest months experienced by Polish Jewry.[12]

September, October, and November of 1942 were months of agonizing and anguish for Stephen S. Wise. In letters to Felix Frankfurter and John Haynes Holmes, he reveals the terrible conflict that raged within him. On the one hand, he was almost "demented over [his] people's grief" because of news of the master plan for extermination and a report that 100,000 Warsaw Jews had been massacred and their corpses used to make soaps and fertilizers; on the other, his hope was revived by a Polish Government-in-Exile report that the 100,000 were not massacred, but were rather sent to build fortifications on the Russian front. At one time Wise was ready to ask Henry Morgenthau, Secretary of the Treasury in Roosevelt's cabinet, to "show the reports to the Chief. . . ." Somehow one feels that the foremost and finest figure in the political world today should know about this. On another occasion, he admitted to guilt over taking an opposite position. He felt he was becoming a *Hofjude* (a court Jew) spending much of his time explaining why America could not do all that was asked or expected of it.[13]

"How could he [Wise] pledge secrecy when millions of lives were involved," asked Elie Wiesel, twenty-five years later. "How was he not driven mad by the secret?"[14] An historical echo of Professor Wiesel's plaintive question can be heard in the words of Rabbi Isaac Lewin, a leader in Agudat Israel in the 1940s, who knew of the decision to suppress the contents of the cable and who was obviously troubled by it. Writing in the November 1942 issue of *Idisheh Shtimeh,* he asked: Where was the storm of protest from Jewish leadership over atrocities which had no parallel in our history? The alarm must be sounded. The "voice of Jacob" must be heard. And then he pointedly added: "We ask the leaders of American Jewish organizations: What will you answer on the day of judgment? What will you say when you will some day be called to account for what you have done while the blood of your brothers was flowing like a river?"[15]

At this late date, one cannot sit in judgment on Wise's readiness to withhold publication of the report until he received confirmation from the State Department. But there are some factors that may explain his decision. Perhaps he, too, was beset by doubts about the credibility of so incredible a report. There was some contrary evidence, as exemplified by the Polish Government-in-Exile report, and in addition, Wise was no doubt familiar with the contention of recent historians that Americans had been skillfully manipulated into entering World War I by British atrocity propaganda. This awareness might well have made him reluctant to announce publicly a mass murder program, the use of prussic acid, and the manufacture of soap from Jewish corpses, without some official verification.[16] There is also a possibility that Wise, like most Americans, was deflected from the tragic plight of the Jews of Europe by a more general concern with the discouraging war news. In September of 1942 the German army had reached the gates of Stalingrad, General Rommel's forces in North Africa were heading toward Alexandria and Cairo, and the Marines were pinned down at Guadalcanal. Perhaps President Roosevelt's friend did not feel that the time was opportune to defy the Chief's State Department and go public without approval.

Scholars can now debate the motives, wisdom, courage, and statesmanship of this American Jewish leader. What is unfortunately not debatable is that the three months during which the Riegner report was being "checked out" saw the murder of close to 1 million Jews in Poland. The leisurely pace of American fact-finding contrasted adversely with the humming efficiency of the Nazi machinery of death.[17]

In November, Welles called Wise to his office in Washington and gravely informed him of the accuracy of Riegner's information. He handed Wise the confirming documents and said: "For reasons you will understand, I cannot give these to the press, but there is no reason why you should not. It might even help if you did."[18]

On November 24, 1942, Wise released the Riegner information to the press in Washington.[19] His release coincided with a similar statement by the Polish Government-in-Exile in London.[20] It followed by one day an announcement of a similar nature by the Jewish Agency in Jerusalem.[21] Speaking for "the American Jewish Committee, the American Jewish Congress, the American Jewish Labor Committee, Agudath Ha-rabanim, B'nai B'rith, Synagogue Council of America and the World Jewish Congress," Wise told the press that all of "the organizations were convinced of the authenticity of a rumored Hitler order for the immediate extirpation of all Jews in German-controlled Europe."[22] He gave figures for all of the countries, showing their Jewish population before the war and contrasting it with the number of Jews currently alive in those countries. The figures demonstrated that of 3,230,000 Jews in ten European countries in December 1939, only 1,412,000 remained at the end of 1942.

Of the missing 1,818,000 some escaped as refugees; most were exterminated:[23]

	December 1939	November 1942
Germany	200,000	40,000
Austria	45,000	15,000
Bohemia-Moravia	80,000	15,000
Poland	2,000,000	1,000,000
Belgium	85,000	8,000
Netherlands	180,000	69,000
France	300,000	235,000
Slovakia	90,000	20,000
Latvia	100,000	4,000
Lithuania	150,000	6,000
	3,230,000	1,412,000

The news shocked the Jewish world. Newspapers in Palestine appeared with a black-bordered front page for a week as part of a generally observed period of mourning for the slain Jews. Wednesday, December 2, was observed as a day of mourning and prayer by Jews in the United States and in twenty-nine countries. On that day the Yiddish papers in New York appeared with a black-bordered front page. The proclamation calling upon Jews to express themselves in prayer indicated clearly that at last American Jewry understood the crisis they faced:

> The greatest calamity in Jewish history since the destruction of the Temple has befallen all Jewish communities in the European lands occupied by the enemy. His deliberate and Satanic purpose to destroy Jewish life wherever his power reaches has now been exposed to the world. Nearly two million Jews have already cruelly been done to death and the remaining millions live in the shadow of impending doom.
>
> In the hour of their unspeakable grief and travail, the Jews of America in the spirit of an ancient and invincible faith turn once again to Him who has been the Guide and Guardian of Israel throughout all generations.[24]

Reflecting the accuracy of the figures and the extent of the calamity and danger, *The New York Times* covered the day of prayer in its news columns on December 2 and discussed in an editorial the figures of 2 million dead and 5 million imperiled.

On December 8, President Roosevelt received a delegation of American Jewish leaders headed by Wise and including Maurice Wertheim, president of the American Jewish Committee, Adolph Held, president of the Jewish Labor Committee, Israel Goldstein, president of the Synagogue Council of America, Henry Monsky, president of B'nai B'rith, and Rabbi Israel Rosenberg, chairman of the Union of Orthodox Rabbis of the United States. The delegation presented the President with a memorandum detailing the extermination facts and urging Roosevelt to speak out for the Jews of Europe, to warn the Nazis that they would be held accountable for their crimes, to appoint a commission to receive and publicize evidence of the crimes, and to enlist the United Nations in this effort. The President expressed shock at the fact of 2 million dead and assured the delegation that while "the mills of the gods grind slowly . . . they grind exceedingly small. We are doing everything possible to ascertain who are personally guilty."[25]

The climax of this reaction came nine days later, December 17, in the official declaration of the eleven Allied governments. Some writers maintain that the declaration was not an American initiative, but the result of English pressure and the work of British Jewry.[26] The British Parliament demonstrated a dramatic response to the announcement. Following its reading in the House of Commons, the entire House rose for a moment of silence in memory of the massacred Jews—a form of tribute normally demonstrated only when a British sovereign dies.[27] In New York, the *Times* editorialized on December 18:

> Despite all that has been written about Nazi persecution of the Jews, the facts in the joint statement issued yesterday in Washington, London and Moscow in the name of the United Nations[28] will come as a shock to all civilized people who have preserved a modicum of human decency. For this statement is not an outcry of the victims themselves to which many thought it possible to close their ears on the ground that it might be a special plea, subject to doubt. It is the official statement of their own Governments, based on officially established facts; it is an official indictment of the Nazi rulers and their satellites; and it is

the pledge of the United Nations that just retribution shall
be visited upon all those responsible for what one member
of the British Parliament rightly calls the "greatest single
horror in all of its history. . . ."

The Final Solution was no longer a secret. Jewish leadership, Raul Hilberg writes, "was now confronted with the facts."[29]
There is some controversy among scholars as to just how early
the leadership actually did receive the news, but most agree that
the Wise disclosures, the day of prayer, the delegation to the
President, and finally the United Nations' declaration opened a
new chapter in the history of the Holocaust. The information
was now available and authenticated. How were these terrible
facts to be presented to American Jews and how did they respond to them?[30]

THE AMERICAN JEWISH PRESS REACTS

In trying to measure the response of American Jews to this
new and qualitatively different development in the Holocaust
years, one should begin with an analysis of the Jewish press and
its reactions. Such an analysis will demonstrate how much was
known by American Jews about the Final Solution, how they felt
about the program of extermination, and what avenues of response were considered. The potential for responding assumed
a new urgency in this period that it did not have in the two prewar periods previously discussed. The humanitarian problem in
1938–1939 was one of alleviating the misery of Jews under Nazi
rule. In the winter of 1942–1943, however, the issue became
one of life or death for the remainder of Europe's 6 million Jews.

The *JTA Daily News Bulletin* reliably recorded the reports from
Europe and from the world capitals. Much of each issue from
November 24, 1942, through mid-March 1943 was devoted to
the extermination reports and the reaction of Jews and non-Jews
around the world. From the pages of this bulletin, written factually and without editorial embellishment, one gets a clear picture of the response of the organized Jewish community in
America.

The initial revelations on November 23 and November 24

inspired immediate activity: the day of prayer and fasting on December 2[31] and the delegation to Washington on December 8.[32] Thereafter, there was very little indication of an organized community response until late February when the giant rally scheduled for Madison Square Garden on March 1 was announced. During the intervening months, the *JTA* reported news of continuing exterminations and some organized protests in England and Palestine, but there was little evidence of public protests, rallies, mourning, political action, or formulation of rescue proposals on the part of American Jews.

This absence of a profound and enduring response was bemoaned by Samuel Margoshes in *The Day:* "We must stop being happy . . . we must mourn." The American press, he wrote, had buried the latest news in contrast to its bold treatment of *Kristallnacht* and the pogroms that followed it. The Catholic Church had been silent:

> And what about the Government of the United States? The Senate and the House of Representatives? Why hasn't a single voice been lifted in advocacy of the rescue of millions of Jews . . . by a mass migration to the United States [a bold and unique suggestion at that time]?[33]
>
> But maybe before we jump to conclusions, we should ask ourselves another question . . . why, oh why have the Jews of America not reacted as fully, as instinctively, as emotionally, as hysterically, if you please, to the alarm that millions of Jews are being murdered in Europe? Do they lack belief or imagination? And where are the mammoth demonstrations we've talked about? We've fasted, that is some of us did, but is that all we can do for the Jews in Hitler-land as they walk in the valley of shadows?[34]

The Day favored public protests on a large scale in order to awaken American public opinion. It argued that these protests had borne fruit in the past and should therefore be continued. Furthermore, even if they did not succeed in promoting the safety of even one Jew, they would have a value for American Jews internally in that they would help to dispel feelings of despair.[35]

The Day had its own feelings of despair to fight off. "What can be done to stop the murderous hand?" asked Margoshes as he reviewed the ghastly new revelations. "I do not know. Today no one seems to know anything."[36] This reaction was perhaps prompted by a realistic appraisal of how difficult it would be to stop the Nazi exterminations. Such an appraisal was reflected in the *Times* editorial of December 18, 1942: "The most tragic aspect of the situation is the world's helplessness to stop the horror while the war is going on. The most it can do is to denounce the perpetrators and promise them individual and separate retribution."

The Day briefly noted this view immediately after the Wise news conference, when it editorialized that "the only way [to save the Jews of Europe] is to beat the Nazis on the battlefield," but it refused to ignore more direct efforts. It suggested retaliatory bombing of German cities. "The Nazis must be aware of imminent retribution." It is not sufficient to threaten punishment after the conclusion of hostilities. "This is a separate and distinct battlefront which until recently was ignored by the Allies." As we had countered the enemy's blitz on other fronts, we must do so on this one as well. It was not enough simply to fight the war on the other battlefronts.[37]

The Day's desire for strong public protests remained unrequited until the mammoth "Stop Hitler Now" rally at Madison Square Garden on March 1, 1943. As would be expected, *The Day* promoted this rally for almost a week with front-page articles and pleas for participation.

The *Morning Journal* also supported the rally strongly. American Jews had not responded adequately until now, it editorialized on the day of the rally. Now they had a chance to react and, in so doing, perhaps to arouse the conscience of the world.[38]

The *Morning Journal's* earlier reactions to the Wise revelations, however, had been rather limited. The week between November 25 and December 2 was filled with news, editorial response, and a spirited promotion of the day of prayer. The attention given to the latter was extensive. Black-bordered boxes with psalms and excerpts from Lamentations appeared for several days in advance. It would have been very difficult for a regular reader of the paper to be a nonparticipant on that day. But after the fast, the subject disappeared from the paper until

December 8 and 9, when the Roosevelt meeting was covered. The next treatment of the subject was on December 18 when the United Nations statement was covered well. Thereafter the crisis was largely ignored until the days before March 1.

The *Forward* was more consistent than the *Morning Journal* in its coverage of the news following the Wise revelations. Its editorial policy, however, underwent a striking change within a matter of weeks. During the first week of this period, the *Forward* expressed horror at the revelations and sympathy for the victims, but it consistently concluded that the only way to help the Jews was to win the war as rapidly as possible. That would be the best form of protest.[39] On December 10, following the Roosevelt meeting, the *Forward* praised the President for "meeting all of our demands." Suddenly, however, the attitude changed. On December 11, a *Forward* columnist accused the President of not going far enough. "Waiting for the war's end is a long time off."[40] Four days later an editorial, entitled "Revenge Later; Rescue Now," accused the Allies of postponing a solution and criticized the American press for not giving sufficient attention to the massacres of Jews.[41] This position was only partially softened after the United Nations declaration on December 17. The paper still insisted that something be done for Jews *now*. The *Forward* was sufficiently disturbed by events so that, contrary to its normal policy, it criticized liberal American institutions. It stopped short, however, of *The Day's* demand that America open her doors.

Outside New York, the local papers treated the terrible revelations in differing degrees. Chicago Jewry received extensive reportage from *The Sentinel*. Beginning with a full report of Wise's disclosures in its December 4 issue and an editorial, "Murder, Unlimited," the paper devoted its front-page news summary for two months to the agony of European Jewry. Readers were able to find excerpts from *The New York Times* editorial presenting the grim figures of 2 million dead and 5 million threatened, and on December 11 the *Times* editorial of December 2 was reprinted by *The Sentinel* on its front page. The paper supported the day of prayer and mourning, which took place on December 2, but strangely, there was no later mention in the paper of how or if that day was observed by Chicago Jews.[42]

Several months passed before *The Sentinel,* noting the rallies in New York in March, asked: "Why can't Chicago, the second largest city in the country, do something similar? It can be done and should be done."[43] But, in fact, it wasn't done.

The *Jewish Advocate* in Boston, in contrast to the Chicago weekly, offered its readers a very limited view of the newly comprehended tragedy. The Wise revelations, which might have merited attention in the December 4 issue, were superseded by the Cocoanut Grove nightclub fire in Boston that claimed the lives of nearly five hundred people: "Nothing in our memory has so severely shocked and so completely stunned, bewildered and confused the whole community as [this] great calamity. . . . Even the tragedy of the global war cannot obscure the horror of the local catastrophe which has plunged hundreds of homes into sudden mourning."[44]

The fire was indeed a grotesque and shocking event, and one can understand how grief close to home might temporarily obscure a tragedy that was taking place across the sea. But what is more difficult to comprehend is a total eclipse, from a Jewish paper, of news about the European Jewish catastrophe. And why did the *Advocate* devote only a small editorial comment to the Wise disclosures—a comment that followed seven editorials on a variety of subjects of considerably less importance?* The plight of European Jews continued to be eclipsed in the *Jewish Advocate* by another local event, the death of an elderly communal leader, Louis E. Kirstein, whose demise also "plunged the entire community into mourning."[45] Not until December 25, in reaction to the United Nations declaration, did the paper direct the full attention of its readers to the Nazis' murder of Europe's Jews. The lead story on page 1 reported on the declaration. A page 3 story described a planned mass meeting of Polish Jews to be held on December 27 (the event drew a crowd of 1,500).[46] An editorial praised the declaration but insisted that words would

---

*The seven editorials were on the following subjects: a Hadassah Donor Luncheon, Victory Loan (war bonds), Writing to Soldiers, Chanukah, Our Women and Bonds, What We Are (concerning a Department of Justice ruling that Jews constitute a race), and a memorial to Professor Nathan Isaacs, prominent teacher and scholar, on the eve of the unveiling of his gravestone.

not suffice; action was needed. The fact that the editorial was placed fifth on the page hardly added significance to the *Jewish Advocate*'s plea for action.*

The *Jewish Exponent* did not provide comprehensive news to the Philadelphia community during this period. Its news columns continued to be devoted to local matters, in keeping with its normal pattern. However, the paper did give front-page publicity to a mass demonstration (which ultimately drew 1,500 people) at the Benjamin Franklin Hotel to be held on December 13.[47] Its editorials, moreover, called for a vigorous response from the world to the terrible crisis. In answer to the United Nations declaration, it published an editorial entitled "Only Sympathy?" It urged that Jewish anger and grief not be assuaged by nice words even when spoken by the President of the United States. Will twenty out of the thirty United Nations "accept immediately 20,000 Jews—well, then 10,000—well, then 5,000: without regard to certificates, visas, regulations?"[48]

The *Jewish Exponent*, however, reserved its strongest urgings and criticisms for American Jewry. Through its editorials one gets the sense that there was an absence of both agony and activity among American Jews in the winter of 1943. In an editorial entitled "Still Silence," the *Jewish Exponent* lamented that, if the governments of the world were silent in the face of the murder of Jews, then

> the Jews of America must also confess their part in the conspiracy. The so-called "reputable" national organizations pursue their ordinary ways. They carry on their trivial business as usual. . . .[49]

The silence of American Jewry, the paper said, was due to the failure of Jewish leadership to arouse the rank and file. American Jews needed guidance and inspiration, courage, and stamina—"flaming indictments" rather than "polite phrases."

---

*The editorial followed a tribute to Albert A. Ginzberg, a communal leader, on his sixty-fifth birthday, congratulations to a David A. Watchmaker, a Bostonian, who was elected to the executive council of the JDC, a tribute by Chicago to Haym Salomon (a heroic Jewish leader in the American Revolution), and a plea to purchase Christmas Seals. Boston Jewry's paper remained concerned primarily with local matters throughout this period.

> Our leaders have not dared publicly to ask the American government to open the doors for refugees—regardless of the response of Congress. . . . We have made fear for our own skins the touchstone of our action on behalf of our bleeding people.[50]

Accusing American Jewish leaders of conducting an ineffective "backstairs diplomacy," a modern version of *shtadlanut,* the paper criticized them for behaving obsequiously before the known anti-Semites in the State Department, who have done all in their power to frustrate the rescue of European Jewry.

> Sure, the Jews of America are "indifferent." What else can they be when there is no course of action mapped out for them that can translate their deep uncertainty and sorrow into a weapon of constructive action?[51]

Congress Weekly was one of the most expressive organs in describing the catastrophe, detailing the atrocities, and promoting concern and compassion among its readers. The issue of December 4, 1942, featured on its front cover a drawing of a burning candle on a black background, with only the Hebrew words from Lamentations 3:48: "Rivers of tears flow from my eyes over the destruction of my people." That issue plus the four that followed were devoted almost entirely to the new facts of the Holocaust and the world's reaction to them. At first it expressed approval of Roosevelt's encouraging response and the United Nations declaration, but by December 25 the tone began to change. Why was there no program of action? "The practical steps taken to implement the declaration must envisage not only the thought of apprehending the guilty . . . but also means of rescue."[52]

In February, the magazine began to write more militantly, as it became clear that the American Jewish community was not itself aroused and was therefore not able to activate government officials to ease the plight of European Jewry to whatever extent possible. In an editorial on February 5, entitled "Why is America Silent?" *Congress Weekly* contrasted the strong response of British public opinion with the relatively weak reaction in America. In italic type, for emphasis, it asked:

> Has the intervening distance of several thousand miles ab-
> sorbed the agonizing cry of those who are dying with the
> hope that one day this great Democracy will come to their
> rescue? Is America less humane than England? Is public
> opinion in this country as indifferent to the fate of the
> murdered millions as its comparative silence would seem
> to indicate?

It was this kind of perception about American indifference that
prompted the call for the March 1 rally.

The *Jewish Frontier* took a position on rescue that was slightly
stronger than that of *Congress Weekly*. As early as November 1942
its editors felt it was time to sound the alarm for American Jews,
and it devoted that entire issue to "Jews Under the Axis: 1939–
1942," an issue that took two months to prepare, causing the
entire omission of the October issue, and was very impressive
in its form and reportage. It appeared *before* the Wise revelations. Like the *Weekly,* it also lamented the weak response in
America as compared with that of Sweden, Great Britain, and
the Central and South American countries. But even demonstrations are not the answer, said the *Jewish Frontier*. Rescue efforts for the remaining 5 million must be launched. "The world
knows. The evidence is in. The question now is what can be done
to save the millions still alive."[53]

The *Jewish Spectator,* at the time under the new managing
editorship of Trude Weiss Rosmarin, spoke even more bitingly.
She was not ungrateful for the United Nations declaration, she
wrote, but neither was she impressed. Ten years ago—even four
years ago—such a declaration might have saved millions of lives,
she wrote. Today the words do not help. "The millions of tortured Jews in Europe . . . whose numbers are declining steadily,
day by day . . . need deeds and action—speedy and drastic action." When the action was not forthcoming, Rosmarin bitterly
characterized the U.N. declaration as "a mere scrap of paper
with eleven important signatures."[54]

The *Jewish Spectator,* however, saved its strongest rebuke for
American Jews, for their tendency to carry on their organizational business as usual, contenting themselves with one day of
mourning while thousands of their brothers and sisters were
dying daily. In its March issue the magazine editorialized:

It is, therefore, shocking and—why mince words—revolting that at a time like this our organizations, large and small, national and local, continue "business as usual" and sponsor gala affairs, such as sumptuous banquets, luncheons, fashion teas, and what not. . . .

It would require the fiery pen of Jeremiah or of a Bialik to find adequate expression of condemnation for the abysmal indifference and heartlessness flaunted by Jewish men and women who can bring themselves to sit down at banquet tables, resplendent in evening clothes, while on the very same evening hundreds of Jews expire in the agonies of hunger, gas poisoning, mass electrocutions—and what other forms of death fiendish sadists can invent. . . .

We are mindful of Rabbi Joshua's sane admonition to the ascetics who, after the destruction of the Temple, refrained from eating meat and drinking wine as a sign of mourning. "To sorrow overmuch is impossible," Rabbi Joshua told them. But he preceded this statement with the touching exclamation: "Not to sorrow at all is impossible!"

The *Reconstructionist* opened its December 11, 1942, issue with a black-bordered box entitled *Yizkor* (a memorial) and recorded the numbers of Jews already murdered in the various countries. In later issues it questioned the value of fasting and praying without creating concrete programs of action—but it offered none itself—and it applauded the Jewish National Fund's program to purchase 2 million dunams of land in Palestine (about 500,000 acres): "one dunam for each of the 2 million Jews who have been exterminated by the Nazis . . . a truly creative form of retribution." The magazine also questioned why Congress' response was so weak in comparison with that of Parliament in Britain. "Is it perhaps that American Jews have not done all in their power to bring the situation to their [the Congressmen's] attention?"[55]

Among the most moving journalistic reactions to the Wise disclosures was found in *Hadoar*, the influential Hebrew weekly. "The news was enough to drive one insane," the editor exclaimed. "A hand that writes Hebrew cannot reproduce the brutal atrocities which human beasts are perpetrating upon the men, women and children of our people." Some would not believe the reports, he wrote. Those who were born and raised in

America had never witnessed atrocities of this nature. But Jews who had lived through crusades, pogroms, and murders knew that the reports were true:

> And so we call meetings, we fast, we rend our garments, we sit *shiva* [mourning] . . . our heads bowed in sadness, our hands useless, our knees weak. . . . Because over and above the pain we see the weakness, the total inability to rescue or save the victims. . . .

The absence of a conscience in the world, the gravity of the crime, and the helplessness of the onlookers all deepened the despair. But despair should not be an excuse for inaction. *Hadoar* urged Jews to fast, to protest, to awaken the world, and not to remain silent. "If we do not succeed today, [then] we will tomorrow."[56]

The magazine offered specific proposals to ameliorate the plight of European Jewry. It called upon the United Nations to consider liberating Europe immediately instead of postponing an invasion. It urged the Allies to bombard the German people day and night by radio and leaflets, informing them of the atrocities and warning them of the collective guilt and punishment. It proposed to all Christians—Catholics and Protestants—that they announce the excommunication of all those who support the Nazis and that such an announcement be conveyed to the Germans day and night.[57]

Opinion magazine, under the leadership of Rabbi Wise, reacted with sensitivity and vigor to the new disclosures. Almost its entire issue of February 1943, thirty pages out of a thirty-six-page issue, was devoted to a symposium on "Ten Years of Hitler." It featured the brief comments of an impressive array of political, academic, communal, and religious leaders—mostly non-Jews—on the meaning of this catastrophe and the obligations of America and the free world.

Vice President Henry A. Wallace, Secretary of State Cordell Hull, Governor Thomas E. Dewey of New York, Mayor Fiorello LaGuardia, Episcopal Bishop William Thomas Manning, Pearl S. Buck, Ludwig Lewisohn, Alfred E. Smith, Herbert H. Lehman, Professor Irwin Edman, Max Lerner, Thomas Mann, and John Haynes Holmes, to mention but a few, excoriated Hitler and Hitlerism, expressed sympathy for the Jewish people, encouraged the belief that, with the changing tide of the battle, the war would soon end and addressed themselves to the humane, free, and tolerant world that must be fashioned after the war. Only one observer out of fifty-two, Dr. Henry A. Atkinson, called for "rescue work [to] be carried out at once" in order to save the 4 million or more Jews who were then in "imminent danger."[58] Atkinson even urged the United States to alter its quota system in order to admit those who might be rescued. No one else mentioned the word "rescue." Israel Goldstein, then president of the Synagogue Council of America, flirted with the need for rescue when, in anticipation of the defeat of Hitler within a year, he wrote: "How many Jews in Europe will live to see that day? Apprehension gnaws at the heart. With prayer we turn toward the future."[59]

Unfortunately, more than prayer was needed in order to provide a future for 4 million potential victims, but, except for Dr. Atkinson, none of the prestigious opinion makers assembled by Rabbi Wise thought in terms of rescue. There may have been plausible reasons for the omission. The antirefugee attitude in America had been strengthened by America's entry into the war, which brought exaggerated fears of infiltration by foreign spies. Every refugee was a potential foreign agent and the State Department made that potential threat to American security quite clear.[60] Furthermore, most avenues of rescue—including negotiating with Germany through neutrals, sending food to Jews under Nazi control, providing asylum for refugees in the United States, using Allied shipping to transport refugees, and retaliatory bombing—could all be challenged as interfering with the war effort. Jews did not want to be suspected of such interference,[61] and apparently the non-Jews represented in *Opinion*'s symposium were similarly disinclined. Moreover, Jews, like all Americans, had fathers, sons, and brothers who were fighting in the war. The thought of doing anything which could possibly prolong the conflict would therefore not only be unpatriotic but also dangerous to close relatives. The State Department's slogan, therefore, "rescue through victory," was accepted with but one dissent: Henry A. Atkinson's. The Atkinson view, however, was shortly to become Wise's position as well. The major thrust of the March 1 rally was to be rescue.

The *National Jewish Monthly* provided extensive news coverage for the terrible statistics of death that reached American Jews from November 1942 through March 1943.

> In two thousand years of Jewish history the Jewish world has never seen anything like the universal outpouring of grief and protest against the present Nazi extermination of an entire people, five million men, women and children. . . . Let us continue to make our protests heard throughout the world, that history may record that the voice of justice and decency was not silent in 1943.

The magazine, however, which addressed the B'nai B'rith constituency, a well-integrated group in American life, added a word of caution, consistent with the official State Department position noted above:

> But let us not permit that to divert our energies one whit from the immediate task at hand. . . . There is only one way to stop the Nazi massacres, and that is by crushing the Nazis in battle, wholly, completely and irrevocably. . . . Everything for victory![62]

The *National Jewish Monthly* maintained this position firmly throughout this period. Win the war; exact retribution after the war; and make a better world for Jews in fashioning peace.[63] Only in reporting on the March 1 rally did the magazine modify its position: "It took a long time, but important sections of public opinion are at last aroused in favor of doing something to save the Jews of Europe who are rapidly being exterminated by the Nazis."[64] Among the "sections of public opinion" newly aroused by the rally was the *National Jewish Monthly*.

The *New Palestine* was more agitated about the Wise revelations than it was following *Kristallnacht*. The news columns described the reports of the exterminations and world reaction to the plight of European Jewry. It applauded the reaction of the JNF in launching a program for reclaiming 2 million dunams of land and hailed the optimistic mood at the JNF convention in Detroit (December 25–27, 1942) where participants felt that rescue was a realizable goal. Editorially, however, the *New Palestine* took the same position as the *National Jewish Monthly*.

Commenting on the December 2 day of prayer, the magazine viewed it as necessary if only for a "spiritual catharsis," but the main task is "doggedly, grimly, resolutely, defiantly . . . [to] turn our full attention to the task of crushing the enemy." Following the United Nations declaration, the editor expressed thanks but agreed, with resignation, that nothing could "be done in the immediate present for the living remainder, except the prosecution of the war to a speedy and victorious conclusion." He added, however, that after the war, justice should be done to the Jew by keeping the promise of Palestine.[65]

The *Hadassah Newsletter*'s first reaction to the extermination story came in its February 1943 issue, in the president's column, in which she described how the board met at Hadassah headquarters for prayers following news of the 2 million slain Jews. A program of action followed in the form of the establishment of a postwar reconstruction and rehabilitation fund. Hadassah apparently was also reluctant to consider immediate plans for rescue. This reluctance disappeared in the wake of the March 1 rally. Hadassah's March issue urged immediate implementation of the "reasonable" and "practical" program of the Madison Square Garden meeting. This sense of urgency was even more apparent in the April issue.[66]

A disturbing note was introduced into an otherwise sensitively written message, "Liquidation." Describing poignantly the murder of 2 million and inquiring "What about the living?" the writer asserted that the only hope for the living is Palestine and therefore "your job, immediate and imperative, is to *enroll more members* [her emphasis] in Hadassah and Junior Hadassah."[67] A similar tendency to increase membership by relating it to the plight of "our unfortunate brethren" was manifested, though not as directly, by the *New Palestine* on the back page of its March 1943 issue. An even more blatant exploitation of Jewish suffering was reflected in the *Jewish Outlook*, which did not even mention the tragedy of European Jewry from December 1942 through April 1943 except for an editorial in the February issue, which used the crisis to urge attendance at the twenty-fifth annual convention of the American Mizrachi:

> At the coming convention . . . there will rise a cry of distress that must touch every heart that is yet complacent.

. . . At the Mizrachi Convention the grief of Israel will be displayed in all its fulsomeness. . . . For this reason alone it would have been essential that the present gathering be called together. Here Jewry's feelings will be sounded on the proper plane, and the problems of solving the bloody dilemma of Europe's Jewish population will most surely encounter due consideration and judgment.[68]

The Synagogue gave its Reform Jewish readers little appreciation of the new disaster that faced world Jewry. In four issues from December 1942 through March of 1943, there was only one serious attempt to grapple with the crisis.[69] Reflecting the low profile of this subject in the community, *The Synagogue* reported on a five-part discussion series in its adult education section on the general subject "How Can Jews Survive the Present Crisis?"[70] Judging from the five subheadings (economic survival, Jewish rights in America, Christian-Jewish understanding, Jewish family life, and Jewish civic life in America) the "present crisis" did not include 2 million killed and 4 million in jeopardy.

The Orthodox Union was even less responsive to the changed condition of world Jewry. In its December and February issues, there was only one oblique mention of European Jewry. In a survey of salient news about Jews and Judaism, the author wrote: "Jewish news of the past month, except for war atrocities and the death of prominent leaders, centered about discussion rather than achievement."[71] The author then described some of the discussions, none of which he related to the European Jewish tragedy. The remainder of this gaily covered Purim issue was devoted to parochial subjects like activating the synagogue, revitalizing Orthodoxy, conducting a junior Sabbath service, and the problem of Jewish youth.

One might explain the omission of the plight of European Jewry from this magazine on the ground that it was an organ with limited religious concerns. On the other hand, one cannot help but feel that the murder of one third of Europe's Jews and the clear peril to the lives of the remaining two thirds should have been a serious issue for religious Jews. Indeed, Purim, with its Haman story, ought to have provided an ideal religious context from which to discuss the terrible developments and to consider appropriate religious responses to the unprecedented threat to Jewish lives. It should be noted, by contrast, that the Jewish Council in Palestine canceled the Purim street carnivals and all festivities in 1943, "in view of the tragic situation of the Jews in Nazi Europe."[72]

Notes and News had nothing in its January 5 issue, but in its February 19 issue, it published a review of the Council of Jewish Federations and Welfare Funds' General Assembly of January 16–18 that revealed the low priority in which the European tragedy was held by the philanthropic community: "More and more the annual General Assembly of the CJFWF is becoming a vital forum for the discussion of vital Jewish community problems and for the determination of national Jewish policy concerning them."[73] But apparently this "vital forum" did not discuss Europe's Jews and their plight, except in the closing session when proposals for the postwar period were discussed. These included refugee aid and the opening of the doors to Palestine and South America for East European Jews, who would not be able to return to their homes after the war.[74] Perhaps, however, the CJFWF felt that nothing could be done for European Jewry. In mid-January 1943, this was a general feeling among Jewish leaders. With but a few exceptions, rescue was not mentioned until the American Jewish Congress began to plan the March 1 rally.

The *Menorah Journal* also surrendered the present and began to plan the postwar reconstruction of Jewish life.[75] In addition, however, it presented one view of acculturated American Jews who may have felt that their perspective was being distorted by excessive preoccupation with overseas massacres. Henry Hurwitz, editor of the magazine, wrote:

> There is a strong pull, for the faithful, to regard Jewish life and interests as being always in the center of the world. To be sure, our enemies have been doing their cruelest to make them so. . . . Yet, as free men and women, our vital concerns with national and world politics, with social and economic problems, with science, literature, art and music, transcend—however intensely they include—our Jewish devotions. *There must be a sense of proportion.* . . . [My emphasis.]

The sufferings of the Jews, inordinate and compounded as they are, constitute but part of the suffering of all the victims of savagery today. Whatever can be done immediately must be done to assuage the sufferings of all. In effect, the safety and freedom of Jews can be assured only with the safety and freedom of all men.[76]

AMERICAN JEWRY RESPONDS TO THE NEWS OF THE FINAL SOLUTION

The editor of the *Menorah Journal* may have been unduly concerned. If one may gauge from the comments of the Jewish press and the statements of Jewish leaders, American Jewry did not "lose its sense of proportion." Its response—at least until the major rally of March 1—was a limited one, in keeping with a limited crisis. An editorialist in *Opinion* wrote, "So far the conscience of American Jews hasn't been aroused to resolute action. . . . British Jews have bitterly commented on American Jewry's unconcern. . . . If Jews themselves aren't deeply moved, how can they expect to move the United Nations?"[77]

American Jews could not claim to have been ignorant of the facts about the annihilation of European Jewry. During the winter of 1942–1943, the figure of 5 to 7 million Jews, who had either been liquidated already or who were candidates for annihilation, was frequently cited. Anyone who read a daily newspaper in a large city, a Yiddish paper, or an Anglo-Jewish periodical could not fail to know these figures. They were to be found readily in news stories, editorials, and advertisements.[78] The newspapers also carried reports about letters written to Jews in Poland and the Baltic countries being returned to the sender with a special German stamp that read: "Died in the course of the liquidation of the Jewish problem."[79]

The failure of American Jewry to "lose its sense of proportion" stimulated a bitter statement from a committee of students of the Jewish Theological Seminary in New York, which was published by the *Reconstructionist*. The students accused the Jewish community of not confronting "the immensity of the tragedy." Rabbis have not aroused "themselves and their com-

The New York Times.

Copyright, 1938, by The New York Times Company.

Entered as Second-Class Matter,
Post Office, New York, N. Y.   NEW YORK, FRIDAY, NOVEMBER 11, 1938.   P

NAZIS SMASH, LOOT AND BURN JEWISH SHOPS AND TEMPLES UNTIL GOEBBELS CALLS HALT

All Vienna's Synagogues Attacked; Fires and Bombs Wreck 18 of 21

Jews Are Beaten, Furniture and Goods Flung From Homes and Shops — 15,000 Are Jailed During Day—20 Are Suicides

Wireless to THE NEW YORK TIMES.

VIENNA, Nov. 10.—In a surge of revenge for the murder of a German diplomat in Paris by a young Polish Jew, all Vienna's twenty-one synagogues were attacked today and eighteen were wholly or partly destroyed by fires and bomb explosions.

Anti-Jewish activities under the direction of Storm Troopers and Nazi party members in uniform began early this morning. In the earlier stages Jews were attacked and beaten. Many Jews awaiting admittance to the British Consulate-General were arrested, and according to reliable reports others who stood in line before the United States Consulate were severely beaten and also arrested.

Apartments were raided and searched and gradually some 15,000 arrested Jews were assembled at police stations. Some were released during the day. Tonight arrests were continuing.

Many of those arrested were sent to prisons and concentration camps in buses. Mobs of raiders penetrated Jewish residences and shops, flinging furniture and merchandise from the windows and destroying wantonly.

In their panic and misery about fifty Jews, men and women, were reported to have attempted suicide; about twenty succeeded.

Scores of bombs were placed in synagogues, blowing out windows and in many cases damaging walls. Floors that had been soaked with kerosene readily caught fire.

Fire brigades were summoned to fight fires in eighteen synagogues, and the fire engines remained in their neighborhood all day. Two of the synagogues were not being used for religious purposes.

Those wholly or partly destroyed were the synagogues in Schiffamtsgasse, Steingasse, Muellnergasse, Neue Welt-Gasse, Tempelgasse, Franz Hochedlinger-Gasse, Stumpergasse, Unter Viadukt-Gasse, Hubergasse, Schmalzhofgasse, Siebenbrunnengasse, Kluckegasse, Turnergasse, Neudeggergasse, Palnamitengasse, Schmelzgasse, Schopenhauerstrasse and Humboldtplatz.

At 9 A. M. the first fires broke out in the Hernalser and Hietzinger synagogues. The Hietzinger synagogue, which was in Moorish style and was the largest and finest synagogue in Vienna, was gutted.

At 11:30 A. M. several explosions took place in the Second District, and a number of synagogues were

Continued on Page Two

BANDS ROVE CITIES

Thousands Arrested for 'Protection' as Gangs Avenge Paris Death

EXPULSIONS ARE IN VIEW

Plunderers Trail Wreckers in Berlin—Police Stand Idle —Two Deaths Reported

By OTTO D. TOLISCHUS
Wireless to THE NEW YORK TIMES.

BERLIN, Nov. 10.—A wave of destruction, looting and incendiarism unparalleled in Germany since the Thirty Years War and in Europe generally since the Bolshevist revolution, swept over Great Germany today as National Socialist cohorts took vengeance on Jewish shops, offices and synagogues for the murder by a young Polish Jew of Ernst vom Rath, third secretary of the German Embassy in Paris.

Beginning systematically in the early morning hours in almost every town and city in the country, the wrecking, looting and burning continued all day. Huge but mostly silent crowds looked on and the police confined themselves to regulating traffic and making wholesale arrests of Jews "for their own protection."

All day the main shopping districts as well as the side streets of Berlin and innumerable other places resounded to the shattering of shop windows falling to the pavement, the dull thuds of furniture and fittings being pounded to pieces and the clamor of fire brigades rushing to burning shops and synagogues. Although shop fires were quickly extinguished, synagogue fires were merely kept from spreading to adjoining buildings.

Two Deaths Reported

As far as could be ascertained the violence was mainly confined to

BATISTA SEES HULL AND TOURS CAPITAL

Tells Press Cuba Will Soon Adopt a Constitution and Elect a President

ITALY INTENSIFIES CURBS UPON JEWS

Cabinet Decrees Exclude Them From Official Employment, Limit Property Holdings

Part of the front page of THE NEW YORK TIMES, *November 11, 1938, the morning after* KRISTALLNACHT.

The New York Times.

LATE CITY EDITION
Partly cloudy, little change in temperature today. Tomorrow showers, temperature unchanged.
Temperature Yesterday—Max. 82; Min. 61

Entered as Second-Class Matter, Postoffice, New York, N. Y.

Copyright, 1939, by The New York Times Company.

NEW YORK, FRIDAY, JUNE 2, 1939.

P P P

THREE CENTS NEW YORK CITY Elsewhere Except and Vicinity | in 7th and 8th Postal Zones

of its finance com-
by Councilman Jo-
, Bronx Democrat.

alled "Extravagance"
:tions by the Council
: economy but extrava-
worst kind," the Mayor
his covering message.
ry item reduced by
Council would cause
·mage to the city.
. not economy. It is
politics. In at least
luctions were made
·ovisions of law.
.hese items should
h argument.

·oval which follows
. distinct and separ-
items it covers and
s therein stated."

: for the year 1939-40
/ prepared and very
. studiously considered
:tor of the Budget be-
ting the departmental
nd ils report to the
: c·vering message de-
le Mayor in turn gave
·ry item very careful
, and, keeping in mind
ources and revenues,
get within that limit.
present budget every
:tion was made and
that could be saved
·irector of the Budget

I appreciate the ef-
Council in attempting
: budget. It was cut to
·efore it reached the

:tions Left Intact

cil reductions left in-
or La Guardia included
of $1,200 to cover the
counsel to the Public
r for Kings County
· the post of Director

ite veto messages the
on Page Eighteen

rives Here;

CUBA ORDERS LINER AND REFUGEES TO GO

Navy to Escort St. Louis With 917 Aboard Unless She Obeys —Compromise Reported

By R. HART PHILLIPS
Wireless to THE NEW YORK TIMES.

HAVANA, June 1.—President Federico Laredo Bru today signed a decree ordering the Hamburg-American liner St. Louis to depart immediately with 917 Jewish refugees from Germany who have been held aboard the ship since Saturday awaiting permission to enter Cuba.

The decree provides, in case of non-compliance, that "the Secretary of the Treasury shall seek the aid of the constitutional navy and shall proceed to conduct the ship St. Louis, with passengers on board, outside the jurisdictional waters of Cuba." It is stipulated also that any member of the crew who may have debarked illegally shall be seized and conducted to the vessel.

The Treasury Department is directed to investigate the entire matter, including responsibility for bringing the refugees to Cuba.

To Leave at 10 A. M. Today

Captain Gustav Shroeder of the St. Louis tonight posted the following notice on the ship's bulletin boards:

"The Cuban Government requires us to leave the harbor but has allowed us to remain until tomorrow morning. So we shall sail definitely at 10 A. M.

"The shipping company is going to remain in touch with various
and offi

SENATE RES' A $50,000,(

Balks Roosevelt Mc Outlay on Flood W $305,188,154

By CHARLES W
Special to THE NEW Y

WASHINGTON, J·
ony received anothe
Congress late today
ate, avoiding a rec
rode its Appropriat
and restored $50,0(
committee had cu
bill appropriating
the civil functions
War Department.

This bill finances
and harbor improve
control work. It
noted as the reposit
barrel" projects w
sentatives and Senato
the most convenient]
individually directed

Passage of the bill
an extraordinary atn
companied by circums
placed the President a
position of a leadin·
technical "economy,"
dividual who probabl;
Senate spending sta
parallel spending pro:

He sent word to
through Senator]
majority leader, that
would uphold the cut
committee he propos·
an equivalent sum of
on projects contained
Instead of stopping t.
propriation, this word
the Senate on to over
mittee, apparently in t
·: the money was to b

The ST. LOUIS *story on page 1 of* THE NEW YORK TIMES, *June 2, 1939.*

The New York Times

Reg. U. S. Pat. Off.
"All the News That's Fit to Print."
ADOLPH S. OCHS, Publisher 1896-1935.

Published Every Day in the Year by
THE NEW YORK TIMES COMPANY.

ARTHUR HAYS SULZBERGER,
President and Publisher.
JULIUS OCHS ADLER,
Vice President and General Manager.
GODFREY N. NELSON, Secretary.

WEDNESDAY, DECEMBER 2, 1942.

THE FIRST TO SUFFER

In every country where Hitler's edicts run, every day is a day of mourning for Jews. Today has been set aside, by action of the chief Rabbinate of Palestine, supported by the leading Jewish organizations of the United States, as a day of mourning, prayer and fasting among the Jews throughout the free countries of the world. So prayers will go up on both sides of the Nazi line— from helpless victims in the shadow of death and from those who appeal on their behalf to the good-will of humanity and the divine justice.

The homicidal mania of the Nazis has reached its peak, according to evidence in the hands of the State Department, in an order of Adolf Hitler demanding the extermination of all Jews in all territory controlled by Germany. The fact that the Nazis are desperate for manpower may delay this projected massacre. What has already happened proves that no other consideration will delay it.

Of Germany's 200,000 Jews in 1939 all but 40,000 have been deported or have perished; of Austria's 75,000 all but 15,000, at most; of the 80,000 in Bohemia and Moravia all but 15,000. In Poland more than 600,000 have died. In the Netherlands 60,000 remain out of 180,000; in Yugoslavia 96,000 out of 100,000 are dead, deported or imprisoned; in Greece all between the ages of 18 and 45 have been enslaved and an unknown number are dead; in France 35,000 out of 300,000 have been deported; of Rumania's 900,000 all but 270,000 are imprisoned, enslaved, deported or dead; Bulgaria has enslaved 8,500 out of 50,000; Slovakia has deported 70,000 out of 90,000; of Latvia's 100,000 one-fourth are reported massacred, the others enslaved or starving in ghettos.

To sum up this horrible story, it is believed that 2,000,000 European Jews have perished and that 5,000,000 are in danger of extermination. This is the work of Adolf Hitler and his New Order.

Why has this unrealizable crime been committed? The Jew was a tiny minority in Germany, a small minority in every European country. The key to his martyrdom lies in this word minority. Nazism needed a scapegoat. It found one in the least numerous, the most widely dispersed, the most nearly helpless group. The attack upon the Jew was the first employment of the Nazi strategy — which is always the bully's strategy — of bringing overwhelming power against the weakest of its chosen enemies.

Nazism, as we know, never planned to stop at that point. The persecution of the Jew was the beginning of an insane attempt to reduce all mankind to servitude and to exterminate all who resisted. The Jew was the first number on a list which has since included people of other faiths and of many races —Czechs, Poles, Norwegians, Netherlanders, Belgians, French—and which, should Hitler win, would take in our

The lead editorial from page 24 of THE NEW YORK TIMES, *December 2, 1942, commenting on the Wise disclosure of November 24 and providing the statistics of 2,000,000 Jews killed and 5,000,000 more in danger of extermination.*

Rabbi Stephen S. Wise. (ZIONIST ARCHIVES AND LIBRARY)

The cover page of CONGRESS WEEKLY, *December 4, 1942. This issue was largely devoted to the Wise revelations of November 24, 1942. The Hebrew words read "Rivers of water flow from my eyes over the destruction of my people."*

"All the News That's Fit to Print."

The New York Times.

LATE CITY EDITION

VOL. XCII. No. 31,009.

NEW YORK, FRIDAY, DECEMBER 18, 1942.

THREE CENTS PER NEW YORK CITY

BRITISH CUT ROMMEL'S DESERT ARMY IN TWO AND MAUL HIS ENCIRCLED ARMORED FORCES; FLYING FORTRESSES BLAST BIZERTE AND TUNIS

U. S. PLANES STRIKE

Eight-Hour Tunis Raid Marks Six-Day Air Offensive by Allies

FIVE AXIS CRAFT DOWNED

No Losses for Allied Fliers— Rain and Mud Slow Down Operations on Land

By FRANK L. KLUCKHOHN
Special Broadcast to THE NEW YORK TIMES

ALLIED HEADQUARTERS IN NORTH AFRICA, Dec. 17—The Anglo-American air force inflicted heavy blows today on Tunis and Bizerte, while the Germans raided Tebessa. American fliers shot down three and damaged five Axis planes without losses to themselves.

The United Nations Air Forces attacked points important to German land army concentrations. A significant observation was that there were fewer of the crack German pilots brought from France in the air and that for almost the first time in this vital battle to control the skies and provide an air umbrella over forces in Tunisia the Allies were somewhat ahead.

According to Allied headquarters today, vital air battles were an Allied success, with the naval base and docks at German-held Bizerte and city docks and shipping at Tunis pounded by Boeing Flying Fortresses, large fires burning, at least one vessel probably destroyed and five Axis planes destroyed and three others damaged. More important from the immediate viewpoint, perhaps, were the attacks on enemy land battle installations.

Mateur Rail Yards Hit

Boston bombers escorted by Lightnings made an inferno of the railway yards at the important front-line junction of Mateur. Other Bostons hit the despersal area at Massicault, about ten miles south of Tunis.

Lightnings on a coastal sweep were attacked by a number of Messerschmitts but shot down the Junkers 88 the Messerschmitts were escorting.

British Hurricane bombers blew up ammunition dumps in the same area, starting blazing fires. The

WARSHIPS OF THE FRENCH FLEET BURNING AT TOULON

British official aerial photograph showing vessels afire after they were scuttled to prevent their falling into the hands of the Nazis. At extreme right is the damaged battleship Strasbourg, which was described by the British as partially submerged.

New York Times Radiophoto, passed yesterday by British censor

FORTRESSES ERASE 12 ZERO ATTACKERS

Big Bombers Fell All of Group of Japanese Planes in the Solomons—Warship Hit

By CHARLES HURD
Special to THE NEW YORK TIMES

WASHINGTON, Dec. 17 — A group of Army Flying Fortresses operating in the Solomon Islands on Wednesday destroyed an entire force of twelve Japanese Zero fighter planes that attacked the Americans in the vicinity of New Georgia Island, the Navy reported in a communiqué issued here today. One of the Flying Fortresses was lost but its crew was rescued.

This is one of the most notable air victories yet achieved by our bombers in combat with enemy fighter planes, although Army Air Force records have shown consistently for a long period an advantage of about six to one enjoyed by American heavy bombers in contests with both the Japanese Zeros and up-to-date fighting planes, such as the Messerschmitt 109-G and Focke-Wulf 190.

It was considered probab'

City Is in Confusion in Test Of Double Air Raid Signals

New York City's first test of the double alarm air raid signal system took place last [night] with results that were not entirely satisfactory. It was [twenty] minutes from the first audible alarm until the all-clear [sounded]. In the Times Square area and elsewhere there was a considerable amount of confusion as lights went on, pedestrians started to move and traffic began to roll at the second audible signal.

This signal was evidently mistaken for the all-clear by many of the thousands of amusement seekers on the streets at the time. It appeared that some at least of the more than 50,000 air raid wardens who had responded to the preliminary yellow signal were also confused, for some of them gave conflicting instructions to the bewildered men and women who were trying to obey instructions.

The yellow signal, mobilizing the city's protective services and relayed to such important centers of activity as railroads, utilities, war factories, hospitals and theatres, went out at 8:56 P. M. The first audible signal was sounded on the sirens at 9:20, when the blue signal, which has hit'

11 ALLIES CONDEMN NAZI WAR ON JEWS

United Nations Issue Joint Declaration of Protest on 'Cold-Blooded Extermination'

Special to THE NEW YORK TIMES

WASHINGTON, Dec. 17 — A joint declaration by members of the United Nations was issued today condemning Germany's "bestial policy of cold-blooded extermination" of Jews and declaring that "such events can only strengthen the resolve of all freedom-loving peoples to overthrow the barbarous Hitlerite tyranny."

The nations reaffirmed "their 'nemn republi

DESERT TRAP SHUT

Eighth Army Units Drive South From Coast to Divide Axis Force

OTHERS PUSH FROM EAST

Allied Aircraft Hammer at Enemy Troops That Had Escaped to the West

By GRANT PARR
Special Cable to THE NEW YORK TIMES

CAIRO, Egypt, Dec. 17—A considerable portion of the German Africa Corps has been cut off and apparently trapped by a British force of mixed arms that swung up from the southeast yesterday, broke through to the sea at Wadi Matratin, some sixty-five miles west of El Aghelia, and then took up positions southward.

Unless General Field Marshal Erwin Rommel succeeds in uniting his forces, part of one armored division and a motorized infantry division appear to be in the hands of the Allies.

Despite heavy fighting, the bisecting force is holding firm along the dry watercourse that extends [down] from the coastal road, [the] same time is blocking [coastal] and shore area.

[Whatever] efforts to break through only resulted in heavy Nazi casualties yesterday, and later reports indicated that the fighting was still going in favor of the British.

British Column Pushes Ahead

Chances that the Africa Corps would seriously delay the British Eighth Army's work and drive appeared for the moment remote.

[The Berlin radio, heard by The United Press, said that Marshal Rommel was "now elsewhere on another job," but did not indicate where he had gone.]

The bisecting of the Axis forces was carried out by a strong column equipped for traveling across the desert. It pushed quickly through the mined and defended areas around El Aghelia and moved west across the desert several miles south of the coastal road.

The Germans who were fighting as a rear guard along the road itself did not dare to move too rapid'

THE

Reconstructionist

Vol. VIII.   December 11, 1942   Tebet 3, 5703   No. 16

EDITORIALS

יִזְכֹּר

On Wednesday, December 2nd, American Jewry mourned the loss of fellow Jews,

  60,000 Austrian Jews
160,000 German Jews
  65,000 Bohemian and Moravian Jews
600,000 Polish Jews
120,000 Netherlands Jews
  96,000 Yugoslavian Jews
  35,000 French Jews
630,000 Rumanian Jews
   8,500 Bulgarian Jews
  70,000 Slovakian Jews
  25,000 Latvian Jews

slain or enslaved by the savage Nazis. We bow our heads in grief. Let Israel now say:

How long, O Lord; wilt Thou forget me for ever?
How long wilt Thou hide Thy face from me?
How long shall I take counsel in my soul,
Having sorrow in my heart by day?
How long shall mine enemy be exalted over me?
Behold Thou, and answer me, O Lord my God;
Lighten mine eyes, lest I sleep the sleep of death;
Lest mine enemy say: 'I have prevailed aaginst him';
Lest mine adversaries rejoice when I am moved.

AMERICA AND THE ARABS

TWO disturbing items which appeared recently in the newspapers, both dealing with America and the Arab world, should awaken us to the seriousness of the task facing us of winning American official and public opinion for Zionist demands in Palestine.

At a dinner of the Foreign Policy Association, Professor John S. Badeau, dean of the American College in Cairo, when asked a question about the demands for a Jewish army, heatedly replied that the creation of such an army would be dynamite as far as the Arabs are concerned, for they see in it a means of establishing a Jewish state in Palestine. This is the

The front page of THE RECONSTRUCTIONIST, *December 11, 1942.*

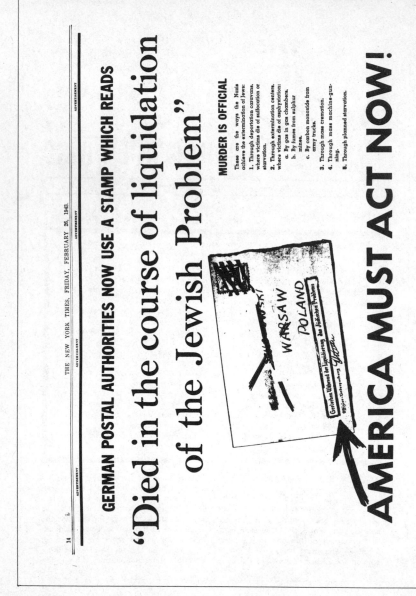

Advertisement in The New York Times, *February 26, 1943, page 14, urging attendance at the March 1 rally. Note the graphic presentation of the tragedy of European Jews.*

Hitler thought up TOTAL WAR. He has now thought up TOTAL MURDER.

The tortured and enslaved populations of the occupied countries will tell you what Total War is. Ask the Czechs, the Poles, the Greeks, the Dutch, the French, the Belgians, the Yugoslavs, or the Norwegians. They know what happens when the Nazi invader sets foot on peaceful soil.

Total Murder is reserved for the Jews of Nazi-held Europe. Will it end with them?

Total Murder has nothing to do with war—even Nazi war. It is not killing in order to terrorize the civilian population of an occupied country. It is a vast organized crime, whose sole purpose is to gratify the blood thirst of Hitler.

TOTAL MURDER is a Nazi invention.

There have been pogroms and massacres before in history. They have been perpetrated by bands of inflamed hooligans, outlaws, hirelings. Savage atrocities have been committed repeatedly in times of war.

But never before has the cold, systematic extermination of defenseless human beings—several million men, women and children—been set up as a government policy to be carried out by government agents under government orders.

Have you ever heard of a *Vernichtungskolonne?* It is a new Nazi word. It means Extermination Squad. It has only one function—to corral innocent and helpless men, women and children, who happen to be Jews, and to murder them.

Have you ever heard of a *Vernichtungstelle?* It is another special Nazi word. It means Extermination Center. It is a place for the systematic, efficient murder of human beings —so many thousands a day. It is the place to which men, women and little children who have been rounded up in the ghettoes of Poland, or kidnapped from all the lands of Nazi Europe, are brought for mass execution in gas chambers or by electrocution or by burning alive. It is the place where those who have escaped the planned starvation and disease of the ghettoes; mass deportation in sealed trains, are finally murdered.

TWO MILLION JEWS HAVE ALREADY BEEN EXTERMINATED!

These are not atrocity stories. They are bitter facts attested by authoritative sources of information.

The Nazis boast of their determination to kill every remaining Jew in Europe. Brazenly they admit the most terrible indictment ever drawn up against any group that pretends to belong to the human race.

The Nazis have begun to doubt the success of their TOTAL WAR, and, as the hour of defeat approaches, want to relish the satisfaction of TOTAL MURDER—the murder of a whole people.

Large numbers of the three million remaining Jews can still be saved. Roumania, Bulgaria, Hungary may let Jews leave their territories before the final plunge into the hands of the Nazis. If havens would be provided for them.

The conscience of the world cries out:

GIVE THEM SANCTUARY!

The voice of Christendom has spoken in England, in France, in Norway, and Sweden. Their proposals are practical measures to meet the immediate situation. The Archbishops of Canterbury, York and Wales have called upon humanity to act without delay. They have issued this declaration:

The Bishops of England and Wales declare that the sufferings of these millions of Jews and their condemnation, calling immediate rescue, to cruel and certain death constitute an appeal to humanity which it is impossible to resist.

They believe it is the duty of civilized nations, whether neutral or Allied, to exert themselves to the utmost possible extent to provide Sanctuary for these victims.

They therefore urge the government of the United Kingdom to give a lead to the world by declaring its readiness, in consultation with the governments of united and neutral nations, in finding immediate refuge territories within the British Empire as well as elsewhere for all persons threatened with massacre and who can escape, whether they be Jews, or for those who have already escaped to neighboring neutral countries and can make room for other fugitives to take their places.

It is not enough to indict and name the murderer. It is time for America and the United Nations to act!

Every hour sees the murder of more thousands. Many of those who will be saved will be fierce and eager fighters in the armies of the democracies. All who will be allowed to perish will be an Eternal Badge of Shame on the soul of mankind.

THE TESTIMONY

From United Nations Information Service:

The means employed in deporting from the Occupied... in the street, seized, all imagination. In particular, children, old people and those too weak to work are available—irrefutable news—that places of execution have been organized at Chelm and Belzek, where those who survive shootings are murdered *en masse* by means of electrocution and lethal gas. The Germans do not attempt to conceal that they intend to murder all the Jews, not only those of Polish nationality but those of other European nationalities also.

From Manifesto of women of Poland, received by Polish Prime Minister General Sikorski:

During these weeks we are witnessing mass executions. People are being murdered by entire families or groups—men, women and children. Hundreds of towns and villages are thus disappear...

...ized. This is labelled the Liquidation of the Jewish element. Each day two thousand Jews are taken from Warsaw and thousands from other cities and packed and loaded half alive, corpses are machine-gunned and buried half alive... Each day whole families are converted by gas or lime vapours in closed railway trucks. Others are machine-gunned and buried half alive, corpses are converted into fertilizer. Each day, whole families with small children are available...

In the streets of the ghetto, the soldiery shoot them like game. In Lublin children were thrown out of windows, in small towns whole groups of Jews are driven to death on foot or in carts by the Cathedral invoking 'Deitel for help. All of them perished. The number sent to the extermination of Jews has by now been almost reached. The raving monster is seeking new victims. The hunt is now already started in the central part of southern Poland, among the Jewish population escaped so far from the wholesale slaughter. There is now talk of an order for killing all the lunatics of old age homes. Tomorrow we will tremble for the lives of our fathers and mothers, and today we tremble for those of our children. In Demblin whole train-loads of people are being rounded up and driven in unknown directions.

Come to: **MADISON SQUARE GARDEN**

ON MONDAY EVENING, MARCH 1ST

To Appeal to America to act now!

AUSPICES OF:
AMERICAN FEDERATION OF LABOR
AMERICAN JEWISH CONGRESS
CHURCH PEACE UNION
CONGRESS OF INDUSTRIAL ORGANIZATIONS
FREE WORLD ASSOCIATION

Admission Cards
May Be Obtained
at Room 809
330 W. 42 St.

Partial view of the 50,000 people who stood outside of the old Madison Square Garden during the rally of March 1, 1943. (ALEXANDER ARCHER)

Drawings by D. R. Fitzpatrick and Edmund Duffy for "Divide and Conquer" and "The Unconquered People" pamphlets by Office of War Information

LIQUIDATION

THESE people are men like our husbands, women like us, children like our children.

They are Jews, our people.

They are not victims of the war. They are victims of an implacable hatred.

Every stroke of the clock ticks off another defenseless life, tens, hundreds, thousands of lives, only because they bear the name of Jew.

Not long ago you heard the radio announce a ban on pleasure driving in seventeen Eastern states. Suppose you had heard instead a decree that two million people from these states were to be taken to a special center to be exterminated. Too horrible to imagine?

Yet that incredible thing has happened to two million human beings like ourselves, and is happening to many more, only a day's air flight from our shores.

A letter was addressed to a Jew in Poland. It was returned unopened to its sender in Sweden, and stamped across the envelope were these words: "Died in the course of the liquidation of the Jewish problem." That routine Nazi message tells the whole dreadful story of the Jewish massacres.

What about the living? What about those who manage to escape from the slaughterhouse of Europe? What about those who will survive at the end of the war? Where will they go?

Their road to hope is Palestine. Palestine, built by Jewish devotion and toil, is ready and eager to receive them. There they will find home and freedom and opportunity. There they will know again the meaning of human dignity and worth.

What can *you* do to assure that future? Your job, immediate and imperative, is to *enroll more members* in Hadassah and Junior Hadassah. In that way you will extend Hadassah's health and rehabilitation work in Palestine for the masses of Jews who will settle there. In that way you will help build Palestine as a Jewish Commonwealth, so that our people shall no longer be homeless but have the standing of nationhood in a free world.

You must do that urgent job *now!*

Page 4 from the HADASSAH NEWSLETTER *of March 1943.*

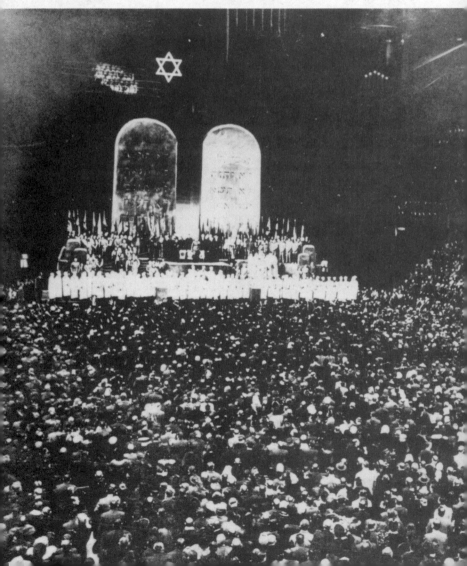

The scene at Madison Square Garden on March 9, 1943, during Ben Hecht's
WE WILL NEVER DIE PAGEANT, *presented by the Bergson Group.*
(INSTITUTE FOR MEDITERRANEAN AFFAIRS)

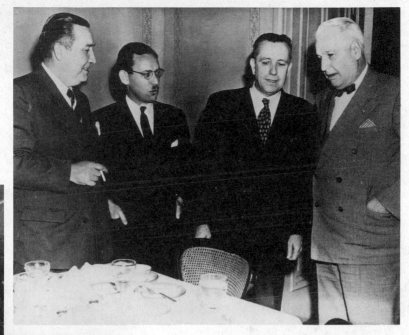

*Planning the Gillette-Rogers Resolutions in the fall
of 1943. Left to right: Senator Warren Magnusson
(Dem., Wash.); Peter Bergson; Oscar Chapman,
Assistant Secretary of the Interior; Senator Guy M.
Gillette (Dem., Iowa).* (INSTITUTE FOR
MEDITERRANEAN AFFAIRS)

Vice President Henry A. Wallace, on the steps of the United States Capitol, reading the petition from the Orthodox rabbis whom President Roosevelt refused to meet, October 6, 1943. To the left of Wallace in the photo is Rabbi Reuven Levovitz; on his immediate right, partially hidden, is Rabbi Bernard Rosenthal, Dean of the Orthodox Rabbinate of Philadelphia; on his far right is Rabbi Eliezer Silver, President of the Union of Orthodox Rabbis. (INSTITUTE FOR MEDITERRANEAN AFFAIRS)

Left: Rabbi Abraham Kalmanovich, Dean of the Mirrer Yeshiva, and a leader in the Vaad Ha-Hatzala. Right: An unknown participant in the pilgrimage to Washington. (Institute for Mediterranean Affairs)

My Uncle Abraham Reports...

By Ben Hecht

I have an Uncle who is a Ghost.

But, he is no ordinary Ghost like so many dead uncles.

He was elected last April by the Two Million Jews who have been murdered by the Germans to be their World Delegate.

Wherever there are Conferences on how to make the World a Better Place, maybe, my Uncle Abraham appears and sits on the window sill and takes notes.

That's how he happened to be in Moscow a few weeks ago.

My Uncle Abraham sat on the window sill of the Kremlin and listened with great excitement, to one of the Finest Conferences he has ever attended since he has been a World Delegate.

He heard every word that Eden, Molotov and Hull spoke.

Last night my Uncle Abraham was back in a Certain Place where the Two Million murdered Jews meet. It is the Jewish Underground. Only Ghosts belong to it.

When the Two Million Souls had assembled, my Uncle Abraham arose and made his report to them as World Delegate.

"Dishonored dead," said my Uncle Abraham. "Fellow Corpses, and Ghosts from All Over. Of the Moscow Conference I have this to report. The Conference made a promise that the world was going to punish the Germans for murdering all the different peoples of Europe—Czechs, Greeks, Serbs, Russians, French hostages, Polish officers, Cretan peasants. Only we were not mentioned. In this Conference, which named everyone, only the Jew had no name. He had no face. He was like a hole in Europe on which nobody looked."

A Ghost from the Lime Kilns of Warsaw spoke.

"Why is this?" asked this Ghost, "why is it that we who are dead are without a Name in the Conferences of Fine People?"

"This I do not know," said my Uncle Abraham, "I can only report what exists. Jews do not exist, even when they are dead. In the Kremlin in Moscow, in the White House in Washington, in the Downing Street Building in London where I have sat on the window sills, I have never heard our name. The people who live in those buildings—Stalin, Roosevelt and Churchill—do not speak of us. Why, I don't know. We were not allowed by the Germans to

stay alive. We are not allowed by the Four Freedoms to be dead."

A Woman Ghost from the Dynamite Dumps of Odessa spoke.

"If they didn't mention the two million murdered Jews in the Conference, isn't that bad for four million who are still alive? The Germans will think that when they kill Jews, Stalin, Roosevelt and Churchill pretend nothing is happening."

And from the Two Million Ghosts came a great cry.

"Why is this silence? Why don't they speak of Us?"

My Uncle Abraham raised his hand.

"Little Children," my Uncle Abraham spoke: "Be patient. We will be dead a long time. Yesterday when we were killed we were changed from Nobodies to Nobodies. Today, on our Jewish tomb, there is not the Star of David, there is an Asterisk. But, who knows, maybe Tomorrow—!"

This ended the Meeting of the Jewish Underground.

My Uncle Abraham has gone to the White House in Washington. He is sitting on the windowsill two feet away from Mr. Roosevelt. But he has left his notebook behind.

* * * *

HELP Prevent 4,000,000 People from Becoming Ghosts

There are four million Jews still alive in Europe.

They can be saved. Experts agree on that.

Sweden and Denmark have just proved it by saving 6,000 Jews in a few days.

This Committee considers it a sacred duty to do all humanly possible to save them.

Our offices and representatives in Washington and in London, in Palestine and in Turkey, are steadily working in this direction, trying to get large-scale government action. This action will have to express itself in the creation of an Intergovernmental Agency to save the Jewish people of Europe and in declaring the doors of Palestine and other countries under United Nations control open for escaping Jews. For, it is now strictly a race for time against death.

Every day that passes dooms thousands who can be saved.

This Committee is asking the American people for a half million dollars with which it hopes—and believes—results can be secured effecting the rescue of the four million martyred Jews in Europe.

We need your financial help immediately. By your support will be determined the speed, scope and affectiveness of our work to save the Jewish people of Europe.

Emergency Committee to Save the Jewish People of Europe

One East Forty-fourth Street, New York 17, N. Y. MUrray Hill 2-7237

Page 11 of THE NEW YORK TIMES, *November 5, 1943, with Ben Hecht's sardonic story on the omission of the Jews from the Allied condemnation of Germany for its atrocities.*

munities to the demands of the hour."* Citing the fact that only *The Nation* and the *New Republic* had outlined plans for rescue and for the amelioration of the position of European Jewry, the students stated:

> It seems almost incredible, but the Anglo-Jewish press has done little beyond documenting the tales of horror. Most of us, it appears, have already given up European Jewry in our hearts; others have acquiesced in their helplessness. . . .

This indictment of American Jewish leaders, which was directed primarily at religious leaders of all denominations, was an echo of a more general *J'accuse,* published by Hayim Greenberg in February 1943, under the title "Bankrupt."[80] Opening his indictment (his term) of American Jewry with the sardonic suggestion that world Jewry "should proclaim a day of fasting and prayer for American Jews," Greenberg bemoaned

> the vacuity, the hardness and the dullness that have come over them . . . a kind of epidemic inability to suffer or to feel compassion—that has seized upon the vast majority of American Jews and their institutions. . . . If moral bankruptcy deserves pity, and if this pity is seven-fold for one who is not even aware how shocking his bankruptcy is, then no Jewish community in the world today (not even the Jews who are now in the claws of the Nazi devourer) deserves more compassion from Heaven than does American Jewry.

---

*Noah Golinkin, Jerome Lipnick, and N. Bertram Sachs, "Retribution Is Not Enough," *Reconstructionist*, March 5, 1943, p. 19. It is difficult to know precisely whether rabbis were alerting their congregants or not. If, however, one may judge from the sermon summaries in *The New York Times* for the Sabbaths following November 25, December 2 (the day of prayer), December 8 (the delegation to Roosevelt), and December 17 (the U.N. declaration), there was nothing on the Holocaust for November 28 or December 5; Herbert S. Goldstein and Israel Goldstein spoke about the mass murders on December 12; William F. Rosenblum spoke about them on Sunday, December 13, at a special service of prayer and intercession for the victims of Nazi murders; and only Louis I. Newman spoke about the United Nations declaration on December 19. Through titles announced and sermons reviewed, one sees but four sermons, out of a total of about fifty, which clearly centered on the dreadful news. Allowing a liberal margin for error, it would still appear that the JTS students were fairly accurate in their assessment of the role of the rabbis.

The author proceeded to condemn the American Jewish Committee and the Jewish Labor Committee for their noncooperation in community efforts with respect to the massacres. He castigated Zionist groups and the different religious denominational organizations for their petty rivalries in the face of a historic disaster. Commenting on the United Nations' determination to exact retribution from the enemy, he criticized Jews for failing to understand that it was far more crucial "that millions of Jews should be saved *before the victory*, than that a few thousand Nazis should be punished or executed *after the victory*." Greenberg accused some of the Zionists of giving up on the European Jews and instead exploiting the issue to strengthen the case for a Jewish National Home in Palestine. ("A home for whom? For the millions of dead in their temporary cemeteries in Europe?") Even the American Jewish Congress, which the author considered to be the only Jewish organization which remained alert, drew his ire.

> It would be criminal negligence, to conceal from the public the fact that at a time when the Angel of Death uses airplanes, the A.J. Congress employs an oxcart-express . . . [and] does not display that will and that tempo which it should manifest at such a time.

Standing at the opposite end of the spectrum from the intellectually detached editor of the *Menorah Journal,* this anguished Jew could not comprehend how "shamefully strong" our nerves were in this greatest catastrophe:

> We have become so dulled that we have even lost the capacity for madness and—may God not punish me for my words—the fact that in recent months Jews have not produced a substantial number of mentally deranged persons is hardly a symptom of health. . . . A state of hysteria is today . . . more normal for Jews than dull, even temper and an attitude of "business as usual."[81]

Why were American Jews not more aroused by the terrible news from Europe? One possibility is that the facts were so unprecedented that they were simply not believed. A Gallup poll, taken in January 1943 shortly after the United Nations declaration, showed that more than half of the general population in America did not believe the reports. Even in December 1944, three quarters of Americans believed that Hitler had murdered fewer than 100,000 Jews.[82] The figures of 2 million murdered and 4 million in danger of extermination, which appeared regularly in the general and Jewish press, beggared the imagination. Perhaps, therefore, Jews could *know* the facts and at the same time *not know* them.

Walter Laqueur addresses the problem of the meaning of "to know" and "to believe" the facts of the Holocaust in his book, *The Terrible Secret.* He tells of a meeting during the war between Judge Felix Frankfurter and Jan Karski, a recently arrived Polish emissary, who told the judge about the mass slaughter in Europe.

> Frankfurter told Karski that he did not believe him. When Karski protested, Frankfurter explained that he did not imply that Karski had in any way not told the truth; he simply meant that he could not believe him—there was a difference.[83]

Even with knowledge buttressed by acceptance and belief, however, it appeared to many that the only recourse was to try to win the war quickly. "Rescue through victory" may have been a State Department slogan designed to blunt direct requests for rescue activity, but many Jews also, as has been seen from the press, considered it to be the only practical program available.[84]

In addition, there was a further factor that may have contributed to the policy of American Jews in this period. With the change in the tide of the war in both North Africa and in the Soviet Union during the late fall of 1942, there was a growing belief that the end of the war was not far off. This may have dulled the sense of urgency for immediate action, even as it gave impetus to a new and somewhat distracting concern over ensuring Jewish rights in the postwar period.

The illusion that an Allied victory in the war might be imminent was entertained by some of the best informed American Jewish leaders. In November of 1942, Stephen S. Wise wrote to his wife: "It may even be that my dream of 1942 seeing the end of the war will come to pass."[85] With hindsight these hopes may appear to have been wishful thinking, but they were taken seriously by many Jews of that day. In more than one case, as we have seen, the expectations about the war's early conclusion deflected concern away from immediate problems and toward postwar programs.

On the first anniversary of Pearl Harbor, one day before the American Jewish delegation met with Roosevelt to present to him a memorandum on the massacres, Edgar J. Nathan Jr., Borough President of Manhattan, addressed 3,000 prominent Jews at a "prayer for victory" in Temple Emanu-El. His message was that victory will be meaningless unless the rights and freedoms of all minorities are guaranteed in postwar Europe.[86] Rabbi Israel Goldstein, speaking in his own synagogue on Saturday, December 19, two days after the issuance of the United Nations declaration, cautioned that now is the time to plan for peace; it would be too late if we wait.[87] Rabbi Goldstein's judgment may have been correct, but nevertheless his preoccupation with the postwar issues may have deflected concern away from the rescue program.[88]

The Central Conference of American Rabbis institutionalized this preoccupation by creating an American Institute on Judaism and a Just and Enduring Peace and holding a four-day conference on the subject in Cincinnati in late December.[89] A United Palestine Appeal conference in Buffalo was similarly engaged in postwar planning for the resettlement of 2 million Jews in Allied countries and in Palestine.[90] The Jewish Agency for Palestine anticipating "a complete Axis defeat [in 1943] . . . allocated 10% of its 1943 budget . . . to facilitate the smooth transition of Jewish life in Palestine from a wartime to a peacetime condition."[91] And the American Jewish Committee, at its thirty-sixth annual meeting, on January 31, 1943, adopted a statement regarding problems facing the Jewish community, none of which addressed the current tragedy in Europe and most of which were concerned with such postwar matters as rehabilitation for innocent victims of the war, resettlement of refugees who would not be able to return to their homes, and equality of rights for Jews so that they might be "free to abide in peace and honor."[92] Thus, at a time when the best Jewish brains might have been employed in mapping out a strategy for saving hundreds of thousands of Jews immediately, rabbis, scholars, and communal leaders were absorbed in charting a course for a world that was more than two years—and 4 million deaths—away. They did not know that then, of course.

The extent to which American Jewry was distracted by post-war planning in this period is most evident in a preliminary meeting called to form an American Jewish Assembly, which ultimately became the American Jewish Conference.[93] idea was promoted by Henry Monsky, president of B'nai B'rith, in a letter to thirty-two national Jewish organizations, inviting them to a preliminary meeting in Pittsburgh, January 23–24, 1943. Monsky identified the purpose of the meeting as follows:

> to consider what steps should be taken to bring about some agreement on the part of the American Jewish community with respect to the post-war status of Jews and the upbuilding of a Jewish Palestine.[94]

This meeting was an outgrowth of the concern of American Zionists to gain communal acceptance for the establishment of a Jewish commonwealth in Palestine. Such acceptance, it was argued, was the best response to the massacres in Europe (which demonstrated the need for a Jewish refuge) and the best answer to the White Paper (which barred the door to the only place that would otherwise have been open to Jews). The Zionists were happy that the American Jewish Assembly was being convened under the neutral auspices of B'nai B'rith.[95]

The letter inviting thirty-four organizations to the Pittsburgh meeting made no mention of rescuing European Jews or alleviating their plight. These matters were not on the agenda of the preliminary meeting, nor were they touched upon in any of the first twenty-three speeches delivered at the meeting. It remained for Isaac Lewin, representing Agudat Israel of America but speaking also in behalf of Polish Jewry, to urge that "within two weeks another conference [be called] for the purpose of finding steps to save Jews not only in Poland but in the whole of Europe."[96]

> In order to ensure the post-war status of Jewry . . . one must first ensure that there will be Jews left in Europe after the war. . . . [Our efforts should be directed] not alone

to save the object, but also the subject: the people who will
benefit from all these rights after the war and who will be
able to help build the Land of Israel.[97]

The proposals upon which the meeting agreed mentioned
the extermination plans but contained no reference to rescue
or to providing immediate aid to European Jewry.[98] The purposes of the forthcoming assembly were stated as follows:

to consider and recommend action on problems relating
to the rights and status of Jews in the post-war world.

to consider and recommend action upon all matters looking to the implementation of the rights of the Jewish people with respect to Palestine.

to elect a delegation to carry out the program of the
American Jewish Assembly in cooperation with duly ac-
credited representatives of Jews throughout the world.[99]

The omission from the agenda of any current concern for
helping the remaining Jews of Europe was noted by Rabbi James
G. Heller of Cincinnati who, apparently at the eleventh hour,
was allowed to present the only resolution of any kind to be offered at the meeting. The resolution expressed solidarity with
the suffering Jews of Europe, protested their annihilation, and
offered the hope that the United Nations would "save those who
can yet be saved, help refugees find asylum and send food to
the starving." This resolution was "adopted unanimously under
a rule of suspension of rules."[100] But the agenda of the assembly looked to the future, not to the present. A solution to the
Jewish question would be found after the war. Unfortunately,
as Pierre van Passen had warned, at the then current rate of
killing there would be no Jewish question left to solve.[101]

PRAYER AS A RESPONSE

Although American Jews did not respond in unprecedented
fashion to the unprecedented crisis, some significant responses
were forthcoming. A day of prayer and fasting was observed on
Wednesday, December 2. It was well advertised and promoted

by the Yiddish press. The organizations that appealed for universal participation covered almost the complete spectrum of the community: the American Jewish Committee, American Jewish Congress, B'nai B'rith, Synagogue Council of America, the Zionist organizations, the Union of Orthodox Rabbis, and Agudat Israel. The Jewish Labor Committee joined in a fifteen-minute work stoppage with a provision that the time lost be made up so as not to retard the war effort. The extent of participation is not clear. *Congress Weekly* reported on compliance throughout the country, conveying the impression that the observance was both wide and deep. *The Day*, on the other hand, bemoaned the sparse participation in a march on the Lower East Side. The Jewish Theological Seminary students complained that the day of prayer was unsuccessful and a writer in *Hadoar* admitted sadly that out of 5 million Jews in America no more than 30,000 to 50,000 were involved in this observance. Most Jews became aware of the observance only after it was over.[102]

There were some further suggestions about expanding the religious expression of prayer and mourning. The Federation of Polish Jews proclaimed a week of mourning from December 17 through December 24 and asked rabbis to speak about the massacres on the Sabbath that fell on December 19.[103] Commenting favorably on the value of such an observance, the *Morning Journal* urged that the mourning be extended further and that all fund-raising banquets be banned.[104] The JTS students suggested several observances which are of interest: a *shiva* (mourning) day in all synagogues to supplement the "unsuccessful" December 2 effort and a week of special services and programs in all synagogues, centers, and Y's under the heading of "Aid European Jewry Now Week." During that week all regular activities would cease.[105] There is no evidence that any of these ideas were ever implemented.

SUGGESTIONS FOR IMMEDIATE ACTION

Several proposals for action were made during the period between November 25 and March 1. None of them came to fruition.

Although the official delegation to Roosevelt on December

8 avoided the suggestion of rescue,[106] the Jewish Labor Committee convention, at its opening session, did urge that "practical measures . . . be taken immediately to save the tortured Jews of Europe, who otherwise may not live to see the day of victory."[107] This was the first such request made by American Jews, though the idea was already commonplace in England.[108] The rescue proposal was raised next by Henry Monsky on December 23, 1942, speaking in behalf of B'nai B'rith. Having expressed gratitude for the United Nations declaration, he added:

> We trust that the declaration on the part of the Allied Governments will be followed by concrete measures (1) to rescue those who still survive and can escape to territories under the jurisdiction of the United Nations,[109] (2) to intervene with neutral countries for their admission, and (3) to make arrangements now for a tribunal to punish the perpetrators of the atrocities.[110]

Asylum for those who might escape the Nazis was not offered in the United States, although more than 10,000 Jewish refugees did enter the country between July 1, 1941, and June 30, 1942.[111] Most American Jews proposed asylum in neutral countries rather than in the United States for reasons we have discussed previously.[112]

A further proposal was made to send food to Jews under Nazi control as was being done for the Greeks in similar circumstances. The first to suggest this idea was Rabbi Aaron Kotler, who claimed he was prevented from sending food to Poland by other Jewish organizations. The idea was reactivated by Philip S. Bernstein in an article in *The Nation* in which he set forth a number of proposals. It was endorsed by the *Jewish Spectator* and by Rabbi Wise, who added the assurance that we do not wish "to break the blockade or impair the defense of the United Nations." Hayim Greenberg in the *Jewish Frontier* was less timid than Wise.

> We must muster the necessary courage and come out with an open request for an official relaxation of the blockade in favor of European Jewry. It is entitled to that "privilege" because no other ethnic group in Europe is threatened with complete annihilation."[113]

None of these proposals was accepted by the United States because of fear that the Germans would get the food, reluctance to weaken Great Britain's blockade, and a policy that the Nazis were responsible for taking care of their captive populations. A food-parcel program was finally financed by the War Refugee Board in August 1944, by which time it was unfortunately too late.[114]

The Committee for a Jewish Army of Stateless and Palestinian Jews published a huge advertisement in *The New York Times,* signed by a host of military officials, political, religious, and communal leaders, educators, writers, journalists, and artists, calling for the creation of a Jewish legion of 200,000 to serve under the Supreme Allied Command in the Middle East and ultimately in Europe. The idea won considerable Jewish support in Palestine, but it was viewed in the United States largely as a publicity gimmick for Peter Bergson and his Revisionist Zionist organization, which would later reappear under different auspices for other purposes.[115]

One of those purposes was a campaign to rescue 70,000 Romanian Jews who were housed in camps in Transnistria, a Ukraine district north of Odessa. Shortly after the first public news of the possibility of rescuing them was carried in the *Times* (February 16, 1943, p. 11) the Committee for a Jewish Army published a full-page advertisement in the *Times,* authored by Ben Hecht, proclaiming:

> FOR SALE TO HUMANITY 70,000 JEWS. GUARANTEED HUMAN BEINGS AT $50 A PIECE. ATTENTION AMERICA! THE GREAT RUMANIAN [sic] BARGAIN IS FOR THIS MONTH ONLY.

The advertisement requested that donations be sent to the Committee for a Jewish Army, in order to facilitate this rescue immediately.

The story of this abortive rescue effort is a tragic one. It reveals the divisiveness that existed in the Jewish community, the tendency to exploit issues for political aggrandizement, and—saddest of all—the reluctance of the Allies to aid the rescue of Jews from Europe, even when such rescue was feasible.[116]

Cables from Riegner in Geneva confirmed the feasibility of the rescue as early as March and April of 1943.[117] In the meantime, Stephen S. Wise had already cautioned American Jews not to send funds to the committee. "The authorized Jewish organizations," he said, "are pursuing this matter energetically, and in case this possibility should be shown in fact to exist, everything will be done to make possible the exit of these Jews from Rumania [sic] and to organize their migration."[118]

The *New Palestine,* supporting Wise's position, wondered where the money the Committee for a Jewish Army would receive would go. "Perhaps [it will] be used to finance further full-page ads exhorting contributions of more money," it said. "There are no limits to irresponsibility."[119]

The most exasperating part of the whole episode, however, was not the divisiveness between the Zionist establishment and the Revisionists, but rather the obstructionist policy of Breckinridge Long and the State Department and the cynical opposition of the British Foreign Office. State delayed approval of the necessary transfer of funds to finance the rescue, and the FO opposed the operation out of concern for "the difficulty of disposing of any considerable number of Jews should they be released from enemy territory."[120] This chilling diplomatic double-talk, Henry Morgenthau, Jr., concluded, added up to a "sentence of death."[121] Coming as it did in December 1943, eight months after the feasibility of rescue was established, the British opposition and the State Department's continued obstructionism demonstrated how hopeless the Jewish cause was. Had Jews in America done their best, this episode suggests that not much in the way of rescue would have been accomplished.

PUBLIC PROTESTS

Part of doing their best would have been to hold public rallies and demonstrations designed to arouse the Jews themselves and to stimulate public opinion to support efforts in behalf of European Jewry. Until the March 1 rally, only a few such demonstrations were held. The first was a small rally on December 22 at the Hotel Diplomat in New York, sponsored by the American Federation for Jews in Poland.[122] A second, larger protest meeting was scheduled for Carnegie Hall on December 28. Sponsored by the Jewish People's Committee, it was well publicized by *The Day, Morning Journal,* and *Freiheit.* The *Forward* ignored it, presumably because the committee was a Communist-front organization.[123] The rally featured as principal speakers Rabbi Joseph H. Lookstein, president of the Rabbinical Council of America (the English-speaking Orthodox Rabbinical body), Representative Emanuel Celler (Democrat, of New York), and Michael Quill of the Transit Workers Union, a prominent labor leader.[124]*

Two of the more impressive demonstrations were by Jewish schoolchildren. One was held in the City Council chambers in Chicago on January 7, 1943. The children asked Mayor Kelly to "transmit their demand to President Roosevelt that the United Nations take steps to save Jewish children in other countries from Hitler's systematic extermination."[125] It was one of the few formal Jewish demands for rescue. The other children's demonstrations brought together 3,000 New York Jewish children on February 22, for prayer for the safe deliverance of the Jewish children in Europe. The *Reconstructionist* was pleased by this Brotherhood Week rally, because it signified an end to shielding children from the bitter truth. The demonstration, it editorialized, "may or may not do the European children good; it will certainly enhance the character of our own youngsters."[126]

MADISON SQUARE GARDEN, MARCH 1, 1943

The Jewish community of New York finally responded, in proportion to the extent of the tragedy, in a mass rally of unprecedented size, held in Madison Square Garden on March 1. The stimulus for this rally is generally considered to be a cable from Riegner, which arrived on January 21, 1943, reporting that "Germans were killing Jews in Poland at the rate of 6,000 a day, that Jews in Germany were being deprived of food . . . [and] that Jews in Rumania [sic] were starving to death." Plans were

---

*I was eleven years old at the time, and I recall my father describing how moved he was by the meeting. I also remember the involvement in a prayer of the children of Ramaz—the demonstration school that my father founded and that I attended, which bears the acronym name of my maternal great-grandfather, Rabbi Moses Z. Margolies. In an earlier period, Rabbi Margolies himself delivered a moving speech before a Madison Square Garden anti-Nazi rally.

immediately made, Henry Morgenthau, Jr., recalled in 1947, "for mass protests beginning with a meeting at Madison Square Garden."[127]

This contradicts a *JTA* report on January 21, 1943, that on January 20 the American Jewish Congress announced a mass meeting scheduled for February 2. The meeting obviously could not have been inspired by a cable that was received the next day. This February 2 meeting was to be cosponsored by the AFL and CIO and the Church Peace Union, the same organizations under whose auspices the March 1 rally was ultimately held. However, this February 2 meeting never took place. Y. Fishman, writing in the *Morning Journal,* confirmed the connection between the two meetings when he complained that the March 1 rally had been delayed for a month.[128] One must assume that the American Jewish Congress had acted out of disappointment at the lack of response in the American Jewish community, and that its plans for a February 2 mass meeting were canceled when the March 1 rally was announced.

Additional organizations joined the four primary groups in sponsoring the March 1 rally. They covered the complete spectrum of the community: social, religious, community relations, and Zionism.[129] The B'nai B'rith and the Jewish Labor Committee did not sponsor the rally but joined in cooperation. The American Jewish Committee was noticeably missing from the list of cooperating groups.[130]

Publicity for the rally was extensive. Readers of the *Times,* who had not been provided with reports of the mass murders since December 18, 1942, saw an impressive full-page advertisement on February 26, 1943, which told the essentials of the genocide story and which featured an envelope addressed to a Warsaw Jew, with the return rubber-stamped legend: "Died in the course of the liquidation of the Jewish problem."[131] *The Day* and the *Morning Journal* promoted the rally for several days in front-page stories and editorials. Both papers printed for several days the English text of a telegram to Roosevelt which all readers were asked to send:

> Jewish community of our city overwhelmed with grief over continued extermination of Jews in Axis countries. Two million are already dead, while same fate awaits those who

remain. Associate ourselves fully with the Madison Square Garden demonstrations March 1st, under the auspices of American Jewish Congress, American Federation of Labor, CIO, Church Peace Union, Free World Association and other leading organizations. Beg you as spokesman of humanity to act at once without delay, to secure exit of Jews from Nazi Europe and creation of havens for them under United Nations' guarantee in Allied and neutral countries as well as Palestine. Confident initiation of such action will result in saving thousands of people and serve not only as warning to Axis nations but a tremendous impetus to the morale of all those who are striving to bring about victory to the democracies.[132]

The *Forward* ignored the rally until March 1, when it featured it on page 1. The Jewish labor movement was more concerned with the protest organized four days earlier by the Workman's Circle and the Jewish Labor Committee. Nevertheless, the paper did report and editorialize on the proceedings of the rally for the following three days.

The rally was attended by more than 75,000 people, only 20,000 of whom could gain entrance to the Garden. More than 50,000 people jammed the surrounding streets to hear the speeches over loudspeakers.[133] Speakers included Wise, Weizmann, Senator Wagner, William Green (president, AFL), Bishop George Tucker (presiding bishop of the Protestant Episcopal Church), George N. Shuster (president of Hunter College), Atkinson, LaGuardia, Justice William O. Douglas, Sir William Beveridge, Governor Dewey, and English author Sir Norman Angell. The last named touched on a sensitive subject when he spoke of refugees: "We cannot say: 'Let them go, but they must not come to us.' We cannot begin to move in the matter so long as we close all doors against all but a small trickle of immigration."[134] Among thirteen speakers only Angell, Atkinson, and Green (very cautiously) proposed the humanitarian gesture on the part of the United States to admit refugees. This may be an indication of how difficult it was even in 1943, with the then state of knowledge of the Holocaust, to combat the antialien sentiment in the United States.

Nevertheless, the eleven-point program of action adopted by the assemblage, for presentation to Roosevelt and through him to the United Nations, did include the matter of easing restrictions for refugee admission into the United States. It was number three on the list. The proposals were as follows: (1) The United States should negotiate through neutral countries the release of Jews from German control; (2) the United States should establish sanctuaries for those who are released; (3) the United States should revise immigration procedures; (4) Great Britain should accept refugees; (5) the United Nations should urge Latin America to ease restrictions on refugees; (6) England should open Palestine; (7) the United Nations should provide financial guarantees to neutral states that have provided and will provide sanctuary; (8) the United States should provide for the feeding of the victims, who are starving under Nazi control; (9) the United States should provide financial guarantees for rescue programs; (10) the United States should provide an intergovernmental agency to implement the program; and (11) the United States should take immediate steps to implement the intention to bring the criminals to justice.[135]

The rally stimulated strong press reactions from sources that had been relatively reticent, at least for the preceding ten weeks. Noteworthy was a March 3 editorial in the previously detached *New York Times* which closed with the words: "It is for the United States to set a good example, revising in the interests of humanity the chilly formalism of its immigration regulations." Anne O'Hare McCormick, interpreting the meaning of the mass murders and, accounting for the world's callousness on the basis of being "drugged by horror," warned that

> if the Christian community does not support to the utmost the belated proposal worked out to rescue the Jews remaining in Europe from the fate prepared for them, we have accepted the Hitlerian thesis and forever compromised the principles for which we are pouring out blood, wealth and toil.[136]

Many important consequences resulted from this rally. Not the least of them was the strong press coverage, which established that there was not the slightest doubt that the campaign to wipe out the Jews of Europe had reached its awful climax.[137]

The rally also stimulated political action. The House of Representatives heard two pleas for rescue of the victims but passed (March 18) only a resolution of condemnation for the Nazis and promises of retribution. In the Senate the subject of rescue was not even mentioned, although the Senate did unanimously condemn the Nazis. The Council of Churches in Cincinnati issued a plea to Roosevelt that contained most of the eleven-point program of the rally—with the notable exception of the revision of United States immigration policy.[138]

The most significant and immediate consequence of the rally may have been that it accelerated plans for a conference on refugees that had originally been intended for Ottawa but was switched after the rally to Bermuda.[139] The catalytic effect of the "Stop Hitler Now" rally was evident from the fact that State suddenly, two days after the rally, released a note from Cordell Hull to Lord Halifax, the British ambassador, agreeing to a conference on refugees. Halifax had proposed such a conference in an aide-mémoire on January 20, 1943, but there had been no reply from Hull until February 25. Now the reply was abruptly released, before the British had had a chance to digest its contents. This quickened pace moved Freda Kirchway to credit the rally with having stimulated the creation of the conference.[140] It is to be noted, however, that the site was moved to Bermuda, where prorefugee pressure groups could not attend.

And finally the rally stimulated formation, in April, of the Joint Emergency Committee for Jewish Affairs. Its constituent organizations were the American Jewish Congress, B'nai B'rith, Jewish Labor Committee, American Emergency Committee for Zionist Affairs, Agudat Israel of America, Union of Orthodox Rabbis, and the Synagogue Council of America. The committee's first act was to transmit to Sumner Welles, on April 14, a memorandum of suggestions for the Bermuda Conference. It was virtually an exact replica of the proposals adopted at the Madison Square Garden rally.[141]

At about the same time as the March 1 rally was being planned, the Committee for a Jewish Army was opening what its chronicler, Isaac Zaar, called a second moral front with the staging of Ben Hecht's pageant *We Will Never Die* in two packed performances in Madison Square Garden on March 9, 1943.[142] The pageant was performed in Washington before many dignitaries on April 12.[143] The committee, which had attracted considerable political support, was able to persuade Governor Dewey to declare March 9 a day of mourning in New York. It was clear that this nonestablishment group was largely ignored by the Jewish leadership, although it inspired much enthusiasm on the part of many nonactivist, unaffiliated Jews because of its passionate pleading of the cause of European Jewry.[144]

WHAT THE WISE REVELATIONS REVEALED

When Stephen S. Wise revealed the plan of the Nazis to murder European Jewry, he set in motion a series of actions and disclosures that established the Final Solution as fact. One might have logically assumed that the Allies, the United States Government, and certainly American Jews would have used this information as the foundation for expressions of deep concern and the formulation of a program of rescue to the extent possible. The concern was forthcoming at the beginning. It waned after December 17 and it was reawakened by the March 1 rally. A program of rescue, however, did not develop early in this period and was not even proposed by the Jewish community until more than three months had passed.

The slow development of a consensus for rescue among American Jews is not difficult to explain on practical grounds, although it may pose some difficult moral questions. The State Department was unwilling to act in behalf of rescue, and anti-Semitism in America still constituted an inhibiting influence on Jewish assertiveness. An opinion-research poll, conducted in December 1942, asked its respondents if they thought "Jews have too much power in America." Fifty-one percent answered affirmatively.[145] When asked if they thought anti-Jewish feeling was increasing or decreasing in this country, 47 percent answered "increasing," and only 12 percent said "decreasing."[146] In such a climate it was difficult to summon the courage to challenge the antialiens in government, to ask for a break in the blockade in order to send food to the starving, and to attenuate the established policy of "rescue through victory."

In addition, as previously noted, many Jews mistakenly anticipated an early end to the hostilities. This dulled their sense of urgency, and it distracted them with postwar considerations when their ingenuity might have been applied to alleviating the most terrible suffering in Jewish history. Gerhard Riegner, recalling those days of unresponsiveness to his alarming cables, explained that most Jews, in addition to their fear of anti-Semitism, simply didn't believe the extent of the carnage.[147] A remark by Matthew Wohl, vice president of the AFL speaking on November 29, 1942, supports this judgment. Perhaps, he said, "it is impossible for ordinary men to conceive of flesh and blood capable of such cruel and monstrous behavior."[148]

March 1, however, and the preparations for the Bermuda Conference, marked a change in the Jewish communal response to the tragedy of European Jewry. Thereafter a new activism and boldness arose, a new determination to help the victims *now*, rather than wait until after the war when there might be no victims left. Several tests of this new spirit were about to be experienced in the months ahead. But first, a challenge was posed by a new spirit in Europe among the victims. On April 19, the day the Bermuda Conference was launched, one of the most heroic episodes in Jewish history began to unfold. The embattled remnants of the Warsaw ghetto rose up against the mighty German military machine, determined to die at the greatest possible cost to the enemy. How did the Jews of America react to this remarkable uprising?

Chapter five

THE WARSAW GHETTO UPRISING

On April 19, 1943, the eve of Passover, a campaign of resistance against the Nazis began in the ghetto of Warsaw. The struggle that ensued during the following weeks revealed for the first time the determination of some Jewish victims of persecution to die, if necessary, as fighters for freedom and Jewish dignity, while inflicting heavy losses on the enemy.[1] The Warsaw ghetto uprising, which was the first national, military struggle of the Jews since the Bar Kokhba rebellion in the second century, has come to symbolize modern Jewish heroism. It constitutes an important inspirational force in the Israeli army's defense of its country. As Gerald Reitlinger put it, "The ghetto rebellion has become a Jewish epic. . . . ."[2] In this chapter we shall try to analyze what American Jews knew about this uprising and how they reacted to it.

THE EVENT

About 500,000 Jews were crowded into the Warsaw ghetto on Tisha b'Av eve, July 22, 1942, when the Nazis began a mass deportation of the inhabitants. Within two months the operation was completed. On Yom Kippur, September 21, 1942, there were 37,000 Jews left in the ghetto—officially. Unofficially, about

20,000 more were still there, having remained hidden during the deportations.[3]

The Jewish Combat Organization (ZOB) determined to resist any future deportations. Its first test came on January 18, 1943, when the ghetto was surrounded and a "second liquidation" began. Caught by surprise, five ZOB battle groups, nevertheless, fought back for three days and inflicted losses on the Germans while suffering more extensive losses themselves. The Germans withdrew and tried to induce the ghetto inhabitants to leave Warsaw for factory work near Lublin. This ruse was countered by the ZOB with posters that urged the Jews not to comply.[4]

The Jewish National Committee (ZKN, the political arm of the ZOB), following the abortive *Aktion* of January 18, sent a radio message to Jewish leadership in New York on January 21:

> We notify you of the greatest crime of all times, about the murder of millions of Jews in Poland. Poised at the brink of the annihilation of the still surviving Jews, we ask you:
> 1. Revenge against the Germans.
> 2. Force the Hitlerites to halt the murders.
> 3. Fight for our lives and our honor.
> 4. Contact the neutral countries.
> 5. Rescue 10,000 children through exchange.
> 6. 500,000 dollars for purposes of aid.
> Brothers—the remaining Jews in Poland live with the awareness that in the most terrible days of our history you did not come to our aid. Respond, at least in the last days of our life.[5]

At 6:00 A.M. on Passover eve, April 19, 1943, the "last days" began for Warsaw Jewry as 2,000 heavily armed SS troops entered the central ghetto, with tanks, rapid-fire guns, and three trailers loaded with ammunition. The ZOB was ready to confront them in battle, even though its leaders sensed that the outcome was foreordained. They hoped that the revolt would spread outside the ghetto walls and ultimately involve the general population of Warsaw. Perhaps the Germans foresaw this possibility, for they threw maximum force at the ZOB to smash the insurrection.[6]

There was a double irony in the date of April 19. On the

one hand, it was the eve of a Jewish festival that celebrates the freedom for which these fearless fighters were about to die; on the other, it coincided with the opening of the Bermuda Conference, at which the United States and Great Britain were engaged in a public relations charade about the problem of rescuing Nazi victims. The ghetto fighters were simplifying this problem by their death.[7]

The major resistance lasted five days and involved about 1,000 Jewish fighters and 5,000 German troops, backed by tanks, howitzers, massive antiaircraft artillery, and flamethrowers. The ghetto became an inferno. Following the five days, guerrilla warfare continued on a large scale until the destruction of the central bunker at Mila 18 on May 8 and the death that day of the leaders of the ZOB, including Mordecai Anielewicz. The battle ended after twenty-eight days, on May 16, with the blowing up of the Tolomackie Street Synagogue and the oratory of the Jewish cemetery, both of which were outside the ghetto. The ghetto itself "became one huge cemetery."[8]

While observers generally agree that the Warsaw ghetto uprising was a precedent-shattering event in Jewish history, with crucial symbolic meaning for Israel and world Jewry today, there is some dispute as to how significant the battle was from the military point of view. There are essentially two positions on the matter. One maintains that the Germans had to commit 5,000 soldiers, many of them crack troops, in order to crush a stubborn and powerful foe. Their casualties on the first day alone were 200 dead and wounded. Ultimately the casualty figures reached 1,000.[9] The other position maintains that the total casualties for the Germans were sixteen dead and eighty-five wounded and that, as a purely military struggle, it was of minor significance compared to other insurrections that were going on at the time.[10]

The dispute over casualties and military significance is immaterial. The Warsaw ghetto uprising is important for the fact that a group of Jews—at a time when organized, armed revolt was but a dream, and in the absence of significant partisan aid—rose up against the most terrible machinery of death and made Jewish resistance and revenge a reality.[11]

A POSTSCRIPT TO THE UPRISING

On May 12, as the Warsaw ghetto fighting reached a conclusion, the Bund representative on the Polish National Council in London, Shmuel Zygelboym, committed suicide as an act of protest.[12] He left behind a letter addressed to General Wladyslaw Sikorski, prime minister of the Polish Government-in-Exile, which read in part:

> I cannot remain silent. I cannot live while the rest of the Jewish people in Poland, whom I represent, continue to be liquidated.
>
> My companions in the Warsaw Ghetto fell in a last heroic battle with their weapons in their hands. I did not have the honor to die with them but I belong with them and to their common grave.
>
> Let my death be an energetic cry of protest against the indifference of the world which witnesses the extermination of the Jewish people without taking any steps to prevent it. . . . . Having failed to achieve success in my life, I hope that my death may jolt the indifference of those who, perhaps even in this extreme moment, could save the Jews who are still alive in Poland. . . .[13]

The desperate act of this distressed man was not without significance. As will be observed, the American Jewish community was moved by Zygelboym's self-inflicted martyrdom. *The New York Times'* judgment that "possibly Samuel Zygelboym will have accomplished as much in dying as he did in living" was not without truth. For the first time in the Holocaust, a Jewish leader had responded to the brutal facts of a supremely cruel world by an act of supreme self-sacrifice.

THE JEWISH PRESS REPORTS THE UPRISING

The response of American Jews to the epic of the Warsaw ghetto depended upon what information was available and how accurately that information conveyed the significance of the event.

The reportage in the press must be viewed first against the

background of confusing information about Warsaw Jewry that was published during the months before the uprising. On February 5, the *JTA* reported from Jerusalem that Warsaw was now *Judenrein*. On February 14, however, the same organ described terrible conditions of life in the Warsaw ghetto, thus contradicting its earlier report. An editorial in *Congress Weekly* in mid-February, entitled "Warsaw Without Jews," implied that the ghetto was already empty, an implication rendered explicit a week later: "The Nazis have made good their threat. The city which for centuries was a cultural and religious center for millions of Jews of Eastern Europe, is a city without Jews now."[14] The magazine, however one month later, reported editorially that "there are still 200,000 Jews within the confines of the Warsaw ghetto." The liquidation of the ghetto was apparently far from complete. It was in that editorial that brief mention was made about Jewish resistance, probably a reference to the January 18–21 skirmishes. Finally, the *JTA* reported on April 14 that only 40,000 Jews remained in the ghetto, where only a miracle could save them from death.[15]

With these confusing and contradictory reports in their minds, American Jews saw their first factual report on the uprising on April 22. The following brief item appeared on page 1 of *The New York Times*, three days after the uprising began:

SECRET POLICE RADIO ASKS AID, CUT OFF

Stockholm, Sweden, April 21. The secret Polish radio appealed for help tonight . . . and then simply went dead. The broadcast as heard here said: "The last 35,000 Jews in the ghetto at Warsaw have been condemned to execution. Warsaw again is echoing to musketry volleys.

"The people are murdered. Women and children defend themselves with their naked arms.

"Save us. . . ."

No one who read the *Times* that morning could have missed the item, which was positioned at the top of a middle column on page 1. Nevertheless, the brevity of the report detracted from its importance, and there was barely a hint of the revolt which was actually well in progress by April 22. The hint was clarified by the *Times* in a far less visible report from London, which appeared the next day on page 9:

WARSAW'S GHETTO FIGHTS DEPORTATION

Tanks Reported Used in Battle to Oust 35,000 Jews

London, April 22. Armored cars and tanks have moved into Warsaw where the ghetto populace is resisting deportation of the city's remaining 35,000 Jews. The battle was still raging when the Polish exile government in London received its latest news last night.

Those resisting are the most active elements left after the mass murders and deportations of last fall. The Polish underground has supplied arms and sent trained commanders for a last stand which is said to be costing the Germans many lives.[16]

This brief item did give the bare facts of the uprising, but it failed to signify its importance. The shortness of the report and the absence of detail—probably not available—left the reader unimpressed by the event. On May 7, two weeks later, there was another brief report on page 7 of the *Times* about how "Jews have fought the Nazis since April 20." (On April 25 a long report reviewed addresses given at the third Seder, sponsored by the Jewish Labor Committee for Palestine before 6,000 people in the Astor and Commodore Hotels; no mention of the Warsaw ghetto appeared in reports of the speeches.) On May 15 a report from London, quoting Rabbi Irving Miller, stated that the Warsaw ghetto Jews had been liquidated.[17] The full meaning of the Warsaw drama was not revealed in the *Times* until May 22 and June 4 when longer reports were published about the nature of the battles, the extent of the German losses, and the suicide of Zygelboym.[18] From the *Times'* reportage it would have been unreasonable to expect a significant response to the uprising until at least one week after it had ended. Contrary to its performance in the previous three periods, the "newspaper of record" was not a very useful source of information for this event, perhaps because the facts were unavailable.

The *Times* was not alone in the paucity of its reportage. The daily Jewish press was hardly more generous in providing information. The *JTA* reported the same radio broadcast as in the *Times,* from the same Stockholm source, but on April 23, one day later than the *Times'* story. And it placed the item on page 2 of its four-page bulletin. The *Forward* gave the same item two bold headlines and a long column-one front-page story on April 22. The *Morning Journal* reported it also on April 22 but gave it less prominence and space than did the *Forward,* though it still placed the story on page 1. *The Day,* which in the previous three periods was the most responsive Jewish newspaper to Holocaust stories, did not publish the Stockholm account until April 24. Although it placed the story on page 1, *The Day* did not give it the kind of prominence one might have expected.

The *JTA* coverage can be summarized as follows: It had stories on April 23 (page 2), April 30 (page 2),[19] May 2 (page 2), May 6 (eight lines on page 1), and on May 10, when the story was featured on page 1 with many details of the fighting and the heroism. Even at this late date, however, when the battle was virtually over, the only source for the story was from the city Kuibyshev in the Soviet Union, where the Jewish Anti-Fascist Committee provided the first "eyewitness account." Such eyewitness stories from this particular source were often unreliable. On May 12, the *JTA* provided some additional information, although still on page 2. The significance of the uprising began to become apparent only with front-page *JTA* reports on May 16 and May 23. On June 1, *JTA* reported that Wise and Goldmann had released appeals from Warsaw, which they had just received, although they had been sent from the ghetto as much as a month earlier.[20] Finally, the *JTA* published a page 1 report of the extraordinary results of the fighting: 2,300 Nazis were killed or wounded, 5,000 Jews were either shot or perished in the flames, and 14,000 Jews were deported to an unknown destination. The size of the uprising and its heroic nature had become apparent only after the struggle was over.

The *Forward* provided the most complete coverage of the uprising with the page 1 story on April 22, another headlined story on page 1 on April 24, and an editorial on the same date calling on the United States and Great Britain at the Bermuda Conference to heed the call of the Warsaw ghetto and save the Jews of Europe. Some insight into the hopelessness with which the *Forward* viewed the ghetto revolt can be gained from the fact that the editorial called for saving the Jews of Europe and not the Jews of Warsaw. After April 26 there passed a week without any mention of the event, and then widely scattered stories appeared until May 9, from which date either the uprising or Zygelboym's death was treated as front-page news or in an editorial or feature article almost daily. It is clear, however, that the facts of the uprising were still elusive. On May 15, a front-page story spoke of only a ten-day battle with the Germans. Nevertheless, the *Forward* alerted its readers as best it could about the facts and nature of the struggle. Perhaps the greater interest manifested by this paper was due to the predominance of the Bund in the Warsaw struggle. In this respect it is noteworthy that the only organization in America that scheduled a mass meeting as a memorial to the ghetto fighters was the Jewish Labor Committee. Needless to say, the *Forward* vigorously promoted that meeting (at Carnegie Hall), beginning with an editorial on June 3, although the meeting was not to be held until June 19. The Jewish Labor Committee provided the only American Jewish response during the uprising when it sent a radio message of support and solidarity to the Warsaw ghetto on May 10, which was probably received only by General Stroop, who was in charge of the liquidation of the ghetto.[21]

The *Morning Journal* gave as much coverage as its news sources supplied. The paper published the first editorial on this event in the Jewish press on April 23, revealing remarkable sensitivity about the significance of the struggle. It advised the Jewish world to "take seriously the radio call from the Warsaw ghetto." The conscience of all Jews must be aroused. The United Nations and the Bermuda Conference must be similarly affected by the call for help. The next mention of the event, however, was not until May 2, when it was featured again on page 1 and described as a four-day battle. The gap in coverage, as with the *Forward* and *JTA*, must be attributed to the lack of news. On May 7 the paper headlined a seventeen-day fight and then, from May 9, as with the *Forward*, there were regular stories and several editorials. The *Morning Journal*'s William Zuckerman gave his readers one of the earliest analyses of the symbolic significance of this event. "Jews died fighting," he wrote on May 13, "rather than like sheep led to the slaughter." Describing this uprising as "the culmination of a spirit of resistance that had been developing for several years," Zuckerman expressed the hope that it would embolden American Jews to work harder to save the few survivors left in Poland. By May 24, the paper had given full details and analysis of the event, including the names of prominent Warsaw Jews who died in the uprising.

What with the scarcity of information, neither the *Forward* nor the *Morning Journal* was able to describe the uprising properly until after the battle was over. For *The Day*, however, this delay was deliberate and intentional. Samuel Margoshes, whose "News and Views" columns and editorials were usually the most responsive to Jewish suffering and the most inspiring in terms of urging community response, was silent on this subject from April 24, when he mentioned it briefly, until May 12. On the latter date he explained his own dilemma:

> I did not write about the heroic resistance of the Jews in the Warsaw ghetto immediately after the strange news broke, for the simple reason that I distrusted the information. Frankly, it seemed unbelievable to me. For how is it possible, I queried, for unarmed people to stand up, even for ever so short a time, against the greatest military machine the world has ever seen. I know, moreover, how in these days, rumors are flying all over Europe, what with censorship making impossible the checking of information, and propaganda machines deliberately set up for the dissemination of false reports. I confess now that I took the reports . . . [as] Nazi propaganda designed to afford a pretext for Nazi atrocities.
>
> However, I see now that I was mistaken. There was an upflare of Jewish resistance in the Warsaw ghetto, and it was one of the miracles of our age. . . .[22]

Beginning with May 12, *The Day*'s editorial policy shifted, and it began to cover the uprising as the precedent-making event that it was. The confession of incredulity on the part of Margoshes, however, may help to explain why the world—general and Jewish—was so slow in its response to this heroic struggle. The implausibility of a Jewish revolt against the Nazis, combined with a shortage of reliable news until after the battle had ended, may have created conditions in which a vigorous Jewish response could not have developed and should not have been expected.

The English periodicals, which were usually responsive to Holocaust issues, supply further evidence that the facts were unknown or not believed until late in May. The *Reconstructionist's* first strong editorial on the uprising did not come until late June. *Congress Weekly* barely mentioned it as a news item on May 7 and in the next issue described it incorrectly as a four-day battle between the Germans and a few Jewish "saboteurs," whom they had come to arrest, a battle fought predominantly by young Jewish boys who struggled until they were overcome.[23] Not until May 21 did the magazine editorialize about the uprising, sadly admitting that whatever aid might be sent would arrive too late to be of any help.[24]

The *Contemporary Jewish Record* gave further evidence of the paucity and lateness of the news. Its June issue had only a short item on the SWIT broadcast and nothing more on the subject, while its August issue had a full accounting of the uprising.[25] *The Ghetto Speaks,* a series of news releases issued by the American Representative of the General Jewish Workers' Committee of Poland, revealed a surprising lack of insight into the meaning of this uprising as late as June 1, 1943. The June press release did not explain the relationship between Zygelboym's suicide and the ghetto struggle despite the inclusion in the release of many important details about the revolt.[26]

THE DELAYED RESPONSE

Once the news became available, the Jewish press reacted with a sense of awe and admiration. The three Yiddish dailies saluted the heroes and urged greater efforts to win the war and more energetic activity to save European Jews.[27] *Congress Weekly* praised the *Manchester Guardian* for its judgment that "the battle of the Warsaw ghetto was a decisive event in this global war. Others are much slower in realizing it. No Jew should be counted among the latter."[28] The comparison between the ghetto fighters and the Maccabees was drawn by such different observers as Stephen S. Wise and Henry Hurwitz.[29] The *Jewish Spectator* cautioned that while we should pay tribute to the heroic fighters of Warsaw, "we do not forget . . . the courage of hundreds of thousands who died meekly and without as much as raising a hand, not because they were cowards but because a tradition of millennia has weaned them from the literal application of demanding a life for a life."[30] Strong editorial reactions appeared in the June issues of the *Jewish Frontier* and *Liberal Judaism*. *Hadoar* printed a large memorial to the intellectual leaders of Warsaw whom it mentioned by name.[31]

In addition to press reactions, there were a few communal responses. The only important meeting on the subject was convened by the Jewish Labor Committee before 3,000 participants in Carnegie Hall on June 19. Speakers included the Polish ambassador to the United States, Jan Ciechanowski, Adolph Held, chairman of the JLC, James B. Carey, secretary-treasurer of the CIO, and Dr. Wise.[32] Non-Jewish responses included a call by the London *Evening Standard* for April 19 to be observed every year as "Jewish Day" in commemoration of the Jewish fight for freedom.[33]

In general, however, all responses were confined to rhetoric. The Archbishop of Canterbury probably expressed the thinking of many Jews when he wrote to Schwartzbart: "It is fearful to be so powerless while these appalling things are going on, but I see no means of action open to us."[34]*

Shmuel Zygelboym's suicide stimulated a number of thoughtful reactions in the press. The *Jewish Frontier* explained editorially the anguish of this man. He had received a message from the Warsaw fighters urging him to ask the Jewish leaders for aid but warning him as follows:

> Jewish leaders abroad won't be interested. At eleven in the morning you will begin telling them about the anguish of the Jews in Poland, but at 1 P.M. they will ask you to halt the narrative so they can have lunch. That is a difference

---

*The biggest response was evident a year later when the first anniversary of the uprising occurred. Manifestos were issued, a march was held, rabbis were mobilized, and commemorations were held throughout the United States. See *NYT*, April 16, 1944, p. 32; April 17, pp. 4 and 10; April 19, p. 5, and April 20, p. 10; editorial on April 21, p. 18; April 23, p. 35, and April 25, p. 1. See also *JTA*, April 13, p. 4. See also *NP*, April 21, 1943, p. 353, and Shlomo Mendelsohn, "The Battle of the Warsaw Ghetto," *Menorah Journal* 32 (Spring 1944). *Hadoar* devoted its entire issue of April 21, 1944, to the Warsaw ghetto uprising. The *Hadassah Newsletter*, March–April, 1944, capped an otherwise beautiful commemorative essay about the forty-two-day battle with an announcement of a forty-two-day membership drive "in tribute to the heroic fighters of Warsaw." Members were urged to use forty-two days to enroll as many new members as they could.

which cannot be bridged. They will go on lunching at their favorite restaurant. So they cannot understand what is happening in Poland.[35]

They urged Zybelboym to plead for help in the American Embassy in London and in the British Foreign Office and to be ready to go on a hunger strike until death if his pleas were rejected.

(There is some evidence that Zygelboym did intend to do just that: lie down in front of 10 Downing Street and refuse to take food until the British Government took action to save the surviving Jews in Poland. But Isaac Deutscher, a Trotskyist friend, dissuaded him from this "unrealistic and romantic idea.")[36]

In any event, persuaded that help would not be forthcoming and depressed over his inability to alleviate his brothers' suffering, Zygelboym took poison as an act of protest against the world's callousness. His farewell letters made no accusations of indifference against the Jews in free lands, observed the *Reconstructionist*. "But he might with propriety have leveled his accusation against them also."[37]

Was his act warranted? Should he have kept on fighting? asked the *Jewish Frontier* rhetorically. His death, like that of a kamikaze pilot's intentional crash onto the deck of a battleship, was a "suicide dive upon the hardened conscience of the world. Perhaps the steel will be shattered; perhaps the imagination will be stirred."[38]

A CALL THAT WENT UNANSWERED

On the fifth day of the uprising in the Warsaw ghetto an appeal was issued by the ZOB explaining why they fought:

> In the name of the millions of murdered Jews; in the name of all those who were burned, tortured and slaughtered; in the name of those who are still fighting heroically though condemned to certain death in an unequal struggle, we call to the world to listen to us today.
>
> The Allies must avenge our death and our suffering. Our Allies must finally realize that a tremendous historic responsibility will fall upon those who remained passive in the face of the unbelievable Nazi drive against a whole

people whose tragic epilogue we witness today. The desperate heroism of the people of the Ghetto must stir the world to an action equal to the greatness of the moment.[39]

This call was not answered by the world or by American Jews. No help was smuggled in, no government bestirred itself on behalf of Warsaw's beleaguered ghetto population. In June, when the battle had long been lost, the *Jewish Frontier* editorialized:

> The Jews in the Warsaw Ghetto received no answer to their call; no one was tactless enough to besiege the embassies of the Allied nations, as the perishing in their simplicity had begged, nor did anyone starve himself to death as a futile gesture. . . .
> The Warsaw ghetto has been "liquidated." Leaders of Polish Jewry are dead by their own hand. And the world which looks on passively is, in its way, dead too.

But the lack of response cannot be wholly explained by indifference. The news of the uprising came slowly, sporadically, and not always from reliable sources. As stated above, the initial reports of the revolt against the Nazis were often rejected as either propaganda or fantasy. By the time the facts became known and the heroic struggle was understood as a modern epic of Jewish courage and fortitude, the time for useful assistance had passed. "We shall not forgive the world or ourselves," said the Yiddish poet, H. Leivick,

> that the calls of Jewish fighters in the ghettos did not reach us in time, that we sat quietly here while our brothers were leaping into the flames, facing the enemy with feeble weapons but strong hearts. . . .[40]

The poet could not forgive, but he provided testimony that explains the inaction.

It took time for the full meaning of this struggle to become clear to the world.[41] Until that time came, the accusation of indifference may be unfair. If there was a betrayal of the Warsaw ghetto fighters, as Elie Wiesel alleges, it did not take place during the uprising but rather after it. When the world realized what had happened, what the fighters had achieved and what they had credulously hoped for, and still nothing was done to save European Jewry, the betrayal had begun. Wrote Wiesel in 1972:

> And suddenly it beomes clear for whom we first should have pity . . . not for the victims (it is too late for pity) but for humanity. For with open eyes it betrayed Feigele [the name of a Jewish child], and itself as well.[42]

The answer to the call of the ghetto fighters could only come through a program of rescue for the remaining Jews of Europe. Such a program was being discussed as the last embers of the Warsaw ghetto died down. How American Jews would react to that program might mean the difference between life and death for hundreds of thousands of Jews. It might also constitute a measure, in retrospect, of American Jewry's answer to the last call from Warsaw.

Chapter six

THE CAMPAIGN FOR A RESCUE AGENCY

Washington, Jan. 22—President Roosevelt set up by Executive Order today a War Refugee Board "to take action for the immediate rescue from the Nazis of as many as possible of the persecuted minorities of Europe, racial, religious or political, all civilian victims of enemy savagery. . . ."

The President's order said that the functions of the new board "shall include, without limitation, the development of plans and programs and the inauguration of effective measures for a) the rescue, transportation, maintenance and relief of the victims of enemy oppression and b) the establishment of havens of temporary refuge for such victims."

The New York Times,
January 23, 1944, p. 11

The establishment of the War Refugee Board (WRB) in January 1944 marked a significant turn in American policy toward rescue and relief for the Jews of Europe. This change in policy can be seen as a belated response to the shocking facts concerning the murder of European Jewry—facts that had become available more than a year earlier in late 1942. The change can also be understood as an answer to escalating Jewish demands for rescue. These were given initial communal expression in the resolutions of the March 1, 1943, rally in Madison Square Garden and the proposals submitted to the Bermuda Refugee Conference in April 1943.[1]

It may be argued that the immediate cause for the WRB's establishment was not pressure from outside the administration but rather from within—namely a disturbing memorandum presented by Secretary of the Treasury Henry Morgenthau, Jr. as a "Personal Report to the President."[2] Originally entitled "Report . . . on the Acquiescence of this Government in the Murder of the Jews," this memorandum was a detailed documentation of the State Department's sabotage of the rescue effort. It indicted the department in general and Breckinridge Long in particular for their record of procrastination, concealment, and misrepresentation. Roosevelt discussed the contents of the report with Morgenthau on Sunday, January 16, 1944. The Secretary also presented him with another memorandum on the creation of a governmental rescue agency. Five days later, the War Refugee Board was established.[3]

Nevertheless, the President's prompt response to the Morgenthau report must also be considered in relationship to the broadening political support, nationwide, for rescue—support that Roosevelt, the preeminent politician, could not ignore in an election year. It is reasonable to assume that this improved political climate was related to the more vigorous espousal of rescue by segments of the Jewish community in the months following the Bermuda Conference.[4]

In this chapter we will analyze some of the public Jewish response to the issue of rescue during the last half of 1943. We will then explore the role played by the Jewish community in the campaign to create the War Refugee Board.

THE NEED FOR A RESCUE AGENCY

The summary paragraph of the memorandum submitted on April 14, 1943, to the Bermuda Refugee Conference by the Joint

Emergency Committee for European Jewish Affairs stated: "The United Nations are urged to establish an inter-governmental agency, to which full authority and power should be given to implement the program of rescue here outlined."[5]

The entire memorandum had addressed itself to rescue and relief. But it was the new agency specifically which—it was hoped—would reach the victims themselves behind the enemy lines. If a program of rescue was not possible, then the agency was to provide relief in the form of food, clothing, and medicine. An Intergovernmental Committee on Political Refugees (IGC) had been formed at the Evian Conference in July 1938, but it had involved itself only in resettlement of refugees after they had escaped. The need now was for an agency to help the victims while they were still under Nazi control.

Jewish organizations and individuals were keenly aware of that need. The Nazi machinery of death was operating with speed and efficiency, and the death toll was now up to 3 million. On August 27, 1943, *The New York Times* summarized the grim details in the following table:

By Extermination

Countries	Total Number of Dead	Organized Murder	Deportation	Starvation Epidemics	Killed in Actual Warfare
Germany	110,000	15,000	75,000	20,000	—
Poland	1,600,000	1,000,000	—	500,000	100,000
U.S.S.R.					
Occupied	650,000	375,000	—	150,000	125,000
Lithuania	105,000	100,000	—	5,000	—
Latvia	65,000	62,000	—	3,000	—
Austria	19,500	1,500	10,500	7,500	—
Romania	227,500	125,000	92,500	10,000	—
Yugoslavia	35,000	15,000	12,000	5,000	3,000
Greece	18,500	2,000	8,500	6,000	2,000
Belgium	30,000	—	25,000	5,000	—
Holland	45,000	—	40,000	5,000	—
France	56,000	2,000	34,000	15,000	5,000
Czechoslovakia	64,500	2,000	47,500	15,000	—
(a) Protectorate	(27,000)	(2,000)	(15,000)	(10,000)	—
(b) Slovakia	(37,500)	—	(32,500)	(5,000)	—
Danzig	250	—	250	—	—
Estonia	3,000	3,000	—	—	—
Norway	800	—	600	200	—
Total	3,030,050	1,702,500	345,850	746,700	235,000

This table appeared four months after the adjournment of the Bermuda Conference. The report of that conference had not yet been issued. The Joint Emergency Committee on European Jewish Affairs was maintaining a policy of silence pending the issuance of the report, a silence that was not received kindly by some Jews.[6]

In the absence of continuing communal pressure from the established community, a nonestablishment organization founded by Peter Bergson, which had staged its first rallies in March and April of 1943, held an Emergency Conference to Save the Jews of Europe. This conference, which was convened at the Commodore Hotel in New York City on July 25, launched a campaign to create a separate rescue agency.[7] Bergson's group, in one form or another, had gained the active or nominal support of an impressive array of public figures, including thirty-three Senators, 109 Congressmen, fourteen governors, fourteen ambassadors, sixty mayors, 400 rabbis—and twice that number of Christian clergy—500 university presidents and professors, a score of military leaders, several Cabinet members and hundreds of stage and screen personalities.[8]

The Bergson group was a continuous source of annoyance and embarrassment to the Jewish establishment organizations. In 1942, David Ben-Gurion had labeled it a front for the Irgun terrorists in Palestine. The *Jewish Frontier* described it disparagingly as "a semiprivate body of men . . . a group of promoters, press agents, and commentators. . . ."[9] Nevertheless the Emergency Conference received supportive messages from President Roosevelt, Secretary of State Hull, Secretary of the Treasury Morgenthau, Eleanor Roosevelt, Chief Rabbi Herzog of Palestine, and Chief Rabbi Hertz of England, among others. Hull's message contained the same caveat that was often used as a deterrent to rescue efforts:

> You will readily realize that no measure is practicable unless it is consistent with the destruction of Nazi tyranny; and that the final defeat of Hitler and the rooting out of the Nazi system is the only complete answer. This Government, in cooperation with the British Government, has agreed upon those measures which have been found to be practicable under war conditions and steps are now being taken to put them into effect.[10]

Professor Max Lerner, chairman of the International Relations Panel of the conference, was not intimidated by Hull's reminder about the primacy of the victory effort. After having read the President's and the Secretary's messages to the assemblage he stated the main concern of the Conference as follows:

> We wish to state our earnest conviction that the Inter-Governmental Agency (IGC), as well as the other steps taken to date have been catastrophically [this word omitted from *JTA*'s report] inadequate to cope with the magnitude of the problem and that no appreciable saving of lives has resulted from them. . . . Only a governmental agency specifically charged with the task of saving the Jewish people of Europe and given sufficient authority to act can successfully accomplish the task [a precise description of WRB almost six months before its establishment].
>
> We of the Conference do not believe that our work has been completed. It has just begun. The Conference has, therefore, decided to become the Emergency Committee to Save the Jewish People of Europe. We shall continue our efforts within the framework of a victory with unconditional surrender, until the job is done.[11]

The conference, which enlisted the participation and leadership of Senator Edwin C. Johnson of Colorado, Representative Will Rogers, Jr., of California, and former President Herbert Hoover, who addressed the closing session, marked the beginning of a spirited campaign to create the governmental agency of which Professor Lerner had spoken.

On Wednesday, October 6, the Emergency Committee was instrumental in bringing 500 rabbis to Washington for a prayer meeting at the Lincoln Memorial. *The New York Times* described the rabbis' plea to Vice President Wallace and his response. The story also reported that Bergson, accompanied by a number of leading rabbis, presented a petition to the President's secretary, Marvin H. MacIntyre. The rabbis mentioned were Rabbi Bernard L. Levinthal, "Dean of the American Rabbinate," Rabbi Israel Rosenberg, co-president of the Union of Orthodox Rabbis, Rabbi Wolf Gold, vice president of the Union of Orthodox Rabbis, and Rabbi Solomon M. Friedman (the Boyaner Rebbe), president of the Union of Grand Rabbis of the United States and Canada. "The mission," the *Times* said, "was under the auspices of the Emergency Committee which is launching a legislative campaign for the establishment of a special inter-governmental agency."[12]

The petition that the rabbis delivered was the same as the one on which the Emergency Committee had pledged to obtain 10 million signatures.[13] The petition said in part:

> The extermination of an entire people arouses the decent instincts of mankind to demand that immediate and effective measures be taken to stop such barbarous action.
>
> Therefore, we, the undersigned Americans, call upon the Executive branches of our Government to create a special Inter-governmental Agency to save the Jewish people of Europe with powers and means to act at once, and on a large scale.
>
> We also respectfully petition our Government to convey to the British Government, which was entrusted with the Mandate over Palestine, the conviction of Americans that it is against all justice that the Jews alone, of all peoples, are not allowed free entry to Palestine, and their desire that the doors of Palestine be open to all European Jews escaping the death trap of Europe.[14]

The Emergency Committee had hoped that this impressive gathering of rabbis would be received by the President himself. The President, however, decided against it, a decision that was supported—if not inspired—by Jewish presidential adviser Judge Samuel Rosenman. It is only by chance that the role played by this influential Jew came to light through the diary of a member of the White House staff who happened to be present at the time:

> October 6, Wednesday, 1943 . . . A delegation of several hundred Jewish rabbis sought to present [Roosevelt] a petition to deliver the Jews from persecution in Europe, and to open Palestine and all the United Nations to them. The President told us in his bedroom this morning he would not see their delegation; told McIntyre to receive it. McIntyre said he would see four only—out of five hundred. Judge Rosenman, who with Pa Watson also was in the bedroom, said the group behind this petition was not rep-

resentative of the most thoughtful elements in Jewry. Judge
Rosenman said he tried—admittedly without success—to
keep the horde from storming Washington. Said the leading Jews of his acquaintance opposed this march on the
Capitol.[15]

Far from being a "horde," this impressively large group of
rabbis demonstrated exceptional concern and commitment in
coming to Washington, D.C., two days before the holiest night
of the year, for Yom Kippur began that year on Friday night,
October 8. Many had come from hundreds of miles away and
had hundreds of miles to journey back. Travel was not easy or
pleasant in wartime, and of course that was long before the day
of fast airplane flights between American cities. Most of these
rabbis must have arrived home by train on Friday, just in time
to lead their congregations in prayer. Those who know what *Kol
Nidre* night is for a congregational rabbi will appreciate how extraordinary was the group that Judge Rosenman sought to de-
precate in the eyes of the President.

About a month prior to this rabbinic demonstration sponsored by the Emergency Committee, the established Jewish
community convened the first session of the American Jewish
Conference in New York's Waldorf Astoria Hotel. The conference, which brought together 501 delegates representing sixty-
five national Jewish organizations, had three primary concerns:
to secure the rights and status of Jews in the postwar world; to
consider the establishment of a Jewish commonwealth in Palestine; and to create an ongoing democratic organization representing American Jewry. According to the *Jewish Frontier,* one
additional item had to be added: "the rescue of European
Jewry."[16]

Historians are in general agreement that the main purpose
of the conference was to deal with the first three concerns cited
above rather than with the issue of rescuing European Jews.[17]
A reading of some of the Jewish press reactions to the planning
of the conference, however, makes it plain that the European
Jewish tragedy loomed large in the minds of the planners. This
marked a significant departure from the planning and execution of the Pittsburgh Assembly in January 1943, where the
tragedy was treated as a mere afterthought. In August, Stephen

S. Wise anticipated that the concerns would be different. "The Conference's earliest task," he wrote, "will be to survey the status of the Jewish people in the world today. Verily, it will be the most mournful review of a people's life, if only a tithe of the tragic tale be truly told." [18]

An editorial in *Congress Weekly* was even more specific on the role of the Jewish catastrophe at the Conference: "While the primary task of the American Jewish Conference is to deal with the postwar Jewish situation, it is safe to presume that the pressing question of immediate rescue action will be a principal item on the agenda." [19] The editorial predicted that the delegates would have "to contradict the wishes of the highest authority of the land" in pursuit of a rescue policy. What would be called for was nothing less than a spirit of *Kiddush ha-Shem* (a readiness for ultimate sacrifice in sanctification of God's name) paralleling the heroic sacrifices made by the Warsaw ghetto fighters. This oblique reference to the inactivity of Roosevelt in bringing succor to European Jews was one of the few criticisms of the President printed in a Jewish journal during the Holocaust years.

On August 29, 1943, two days after the publication in *The New York Times* of the table (see page 162) describing the extermination of more than 3 million Jews, the American Jewish Conference held its opening session. That session demonstrated that the plight of European Jewry was to have central significance at the conference. The session began with the singing of "The Star Spangled Banner," followed by a memorial service "in tribute to the martyred Jews who met their fate under Axis rule." [20] Psalms and prayers were recited by national rabbinic leaders. Rabbi Naftaly Riff, vice president of the Union of Orthodox Rabbis, recited *Kaddish* (the prayer for the dead) and Cantor Ben Zion Kapov-Kagen chanted the *El Moleh Rachamim* (the memorial prayer). Only after this service was concluded did Henry Monsky deliver his keynote address. That address set forth the six goals of the conference, the first of which was "to immediately inaugurate practical and effective measures of relief and rescue for the Jews in occupied Europe." [21] Monsky's address was followed by that of Wise who "suggested that the gathering appoint a delegation to seek an immediate audience with President Roosevelt to lay before him the demand of the organized Jewish community of this country for action without further delay to rescue the remnants of European Jewry."[22]

The issue of rescue was also on the formal agenda of the conference. One of the six committees charged with formulating resolutions for adoption by the plenum was named the Committee for the Rescue of European Jewry. One of the symposia presented at a plenary session was "Rescue of European Jewry." In that symposium, Rabbi Israel Goldstein, vice president of the Zionist Organization of America, criticized the American government for not undertaking a large-scale rescue program, which had been submitted to it on many occasions.[23]

A Resolution on Rescue of European Jewry was passed by the conference. Among other measures, it urged the following:

> A solemn warning addressed by the leaders of the democracies to the Axis governments and their satellites . . . that the instigators of crimes against the Jews, as well as the accomplices and agents of the criminals, will be brought to justice. . . .
>
> A special intergovernmental agency should be created which, working in consultation with Jewish organizations, should be provided with the resources and armed with the authority to seize every opportunity to send supplies through appropriate channels, provide the means for Jewish self-defense and coordinate and expand the work of rescue through the underground.
>
> The Conference recognizes that all the victims of Nazi oppression, irrespective of race or faith, are entitled to aid and succor from the United Nations. But the situation of the Jews in Europe is unique in its tragedy. They have not only been more deeply wounded than any other people, but alone among all the subject communities they have been doomed to total destruction by an act of state. For every one of them—men, women and children—the alternative to rescue is deportation and death.
>
> In the name of the Jews of America, the Conference respectfully addresses a most earnest appeal to the President of the United States not to suffer democracy to go down in defeat on the first front opened by Hitler in his war on civilization. The Conference affirms its faith that democracy has it in its power to deny victory on this front

to Hitler and to take the fate of the Jewish people in Europe out of his hands.

It is not yet too late. But time presses.[24]

This resolution, the committee structure of the conference, its opening program, and the plenary sessions devoted to rescue, all suggest that the established Jewish organizations in America were at last awakening to the need for forceful action in behalf of their European brethren. While the main concerns of this conference remained Palestine, postwar plans, and a democratic organization for American Jewry, these concerns no longer eclipsed the mass murder of European Jewry.[25] While the Zionists insisted that rescue be linked to the fight for a Jewish commonwealth in Palestine,[26] there was at least a clear consensus that rescue of some kind was also a matter that had to be fought for. The only disappointing element in that consensus was that, unlike the exuberant quality of the agreement on Palestine, the unanimous vote on the rescue resolution was registered without passion or enthusiasm. Perhaps, as one editorial writer put it, because American Jews were pessimistic about the chances for its ever being implemented.[27]

"OMISSION IN MOSCOW"[28]

The new sensitivity of American Jews to the issue of rescue was manifested twice during the last two months of 1943. The first manifestation was a reaction to the Moscow Declaration, a joint communiqué issued simultaneously in Washington, London, and Moscow on November 1, 1943, warning the Nazis that they would be prosecuted after the war for all atrocities and crimes committed against civilians. The communiqué, which was signed by President Roosevelt, Premier Stalin, and Prime Minister Churchill, was issued at the conclusion of a conference of the three powers in Moscow. It noted that the retreating "Hitlerites and Huns are redoubling their ruthless cruelties" as evidenced by what the conquering armies were finding in liberated territories. The communiqué went on to warn as follows:

At the time of granting of any armistice . . . those German officers and men and members of the Nazi party who

have been responsible for or have taken a consenting part
in the above atrocities, massacres and executions will be sent
back to the countries in which their abominable deeds were
done in order that they may be judged and punished. . . .

Thus, Germans who take part in wholesale shooting of
Polish officers or in the execution of French, Dutch, Bel-
gian or Norwegian hostages or of Cretan peasants, or who
have shared in slaughters inflicted on the people of Poland or in territories of the Soviet Union . . . will know
that they will be brought back to the scene of their crimes
and judged on the spot by the peoples whom they have
outraged. . . .

The above declaration is without prejudice to the case
of German criminals, whose offenses have no particular
geographical localization and who will be punished by the
joint decision of the governments of the Allies.[29]

There was an immediate outcry from the Jewish community.
They did applaud this direct warning to the Germans in an effort to inhibit participants from their genocidal efforts, but at
the same time they denounced the glaring omission of any specific mention of Jews, who were the primary subjects for annihilation. In this declaration, they had been consigned to the vague
category of victims of "offenses [that] have no particular geographical localization."[30]

The Day, Morning Journal, and Forward, all carried articles and
editorials critical of the omission.[31] For the most part, however,
their criticism was subdued. The Anglo-Jewish periodicals were
more assertive about the subject. The New Palestine cried out
against the negation of "the most significant element in the
monstrous situation: namely, that our people have been massacred as such [their emphasis], as Jews, not as citizens of the
invaded countries. . . ."[32] The Jewish Outlook and the Reconstructionist both deplored the silence of United Nations leaders,
including Roosevelt, concerning the specifically Jewish aspect of
the tragedy.[33] The Jewish Spectator noted poignantly the classi-
fication of millions of murdered European Jews as the "anonymous sufferers of this era," murdered as Jews but remembered
only as Germans, Austrians, and Poles, thereby, in effect, denying them even a spiritual kever yisroel (a Jewish burial).[34]

Congress Weekly pointed out that the omission in Moscow was not only an affront to the dead but also a threat to the living.

> What can be the effect of such a declaration? Let us remember that the Germans are more than half convinced that it is relatively safe to murder Jews. Anti-Semitism is a policy for which they believe they find sympathy abroad. . . . [They] are likely to read the present declaration as indicating that the account of their crimes against Jews will not be as strictly kept as those against other groups. . . .

The writer added a final rebuke:

> To almost every plea for rescuing the Jews of Europe—by feeding them, by evacuating them, by obtaining recognition for their status as war prisoners—it may have been possible to oppose arguments of practical difficulties. *But a warning by the United Nations that the Jews cannot be killed with impunity lies wholly within the discretion of the Allies* [their emphasis].[35]

The anonymity of Jewish suffering had a historical precedent. On January 13, 1942, the St. James Conference in London of eight governments-in-exile plus the Free French National Committee had issued a scathing denunciation of Nazi atrocities— without one word about crimes against Jews. When the World Jewish Congress formally protested this omission on February 18, the answer it received from General Sikorski, Prime Minister of the Polish Government-in-Exile—three months later—was that a specific reference to atrocities against Jews "might be equivalent to an implicit recognition of the racial theories which we all reject."[36] There seems to be some evidence that Roosevelt also intentionally avoided singling out the Jewish suffering in Europe and that he preferred to bury it under the collective suffering of all European nationals.[37] At a press conference on November 5, 1943, when he was asked whether rescue for Jews had been discussed in Moscow, he replied vaguely, "The heart is in the right place. It is only a question of ways and means."[38] Margoshes commented later in *The Day* that if you looked for the heart, you might not find it.[39]

In an obvious attempt to reply to the criticism about this

Moscow omission, Secretary Hull, addressing a joint session of both Houses of Congress on November 18, reported crimes by Nazi leaders "against the harassed and persecuted inhabitants of occupied territories—against people of all races and religions, among whom Hitler has reserved for the Jews his most brutal wrath. Sure punishment will be administered for all these crimes."[40]

The "correction" seemed to satisfy most of the Jewish community, although a week later the president of Junior Hadassah, addressing the opening session of the group's twentieth annual convention, still assailed the omission of the Jews from the Moscow Declaration as "incomprehensible."[41] Nevertheless, *The Day* was pleased with Hull's clarification,[42] and *Opinion* wrote that while the omission was regrettable, "Secretary Hull's statement does much to undo what might have been the deeply evil result of the failure to make mention of Jews as foremost in suffering under Axis wrongs."[43]

The group that responded most publicly and passionately to the omission was the Emergency Committee to Save the Jewish People of Europe. The committee cabled Roosevelt that the failure to mention the Jews will suggest to the "diabolical Nazi criminal mind" the indifference of the United Nations to "Hitler's proclaimed intention to proceed with the extermination of the entire Jewish people of Europe. There is, therefore, the grave possibility that the statement might thus prompt, indirectly, the barbarous Nazis to intensify the slaughter of these Jewish people."[44] Ben Hecht wrote a series of sharply worded advertisements that appeared in *The Day* and *The New York Times*. The advertisement ran the length of the page, six columns wide. The following is a nonverbatim summary of the text.

My Uncle Abraham Reports . . .
by Ben Hecht

[A well written story about a] "ghost world delegate of the 2,000,000 slain Jews who goes to conferences and takes notes. He was in Moscow and brought back a report to the other 2,000,000 ghosts and said they promised to punish Germans for murdering Czechs, Greeks, Serbs, Russians, French hostages, Polish officers and Cretan peasants. Only we were not mentioned. In this conference which named everyone, only the Jew had no name. He had no face. . . ."

Jews do not exist even when they are dead. . . . We were not allowed by the Germans to stay alive. We are not allowed by the Four Freedoms to be dead.

A woman ghost from the Dynamite Dumps of Odessa spoke.

"If they didn't mention the two million murdered Jews in the conference, isn't that bad for four million who are still alive? . . ."

[The message:] Help prevent 4,000,000 people from becoming ghosts.[45]

There followed an appeal for funds for the Emergency Committee. This advertisement drew the ire of *Congress Weekly* and *The Day*. While *The Day* approved the cause for which the ads were placed, it did not approve of Hecht or his "so-called Emergency Committee . . . which does its work chiefly by printing paid advertisements."[46]

The committee, nevertheless, maintained its maverick ways and its differing opinions. After Hull issued his clarification, the committee insisted that such an addendum would have meaning to the Nazis only if it were signed by the signatories to the original declaration: Roosevelt, Churchill, and Stalin.[47] In fact, it was not until March 24, 1944, after Hitler's takeover of Hungary, that Roosevelt was prevailed upon to issue a clear statement in his own name warning the Nazis of the consequences of atrocities committed against Jews.[48]

THE GILLETTE-ROGERS RESOLUTION

The new sensitivity of the Jewish community to the rescue issue was manifested again in its promotion of and response to the Gillette-Rogers resolutions introduced in both Houses of Congress on November 9, 1943, the eve of the fifth anniversary of *Kristallnacht*. Sponsored in the Senate by Senator Guy M. Gillette, Iowa Democrat, with nine other cosponsors from both parties, and by Representative Will Rogers, Jr., California Democrat, and Representative Joseph Clark Baldwin, New York Republican, in the House, the resolution said:

Whereas the Congress of the United States, by concurrent resolution adopted on March 10 of this year, expressed its condemnation of Nazi Germany's "mass murder of Jewish men, women, and children," a mass crime which has already exterminated close to two million human beings, about thirty percent of the total Jewish population of Europe, and which is growing in intensity as Germany approaches defeat; and;

Whereas the American tradition of justice and humanity dictates that all possible means be employed to save from this fate the surviving Jews of Europe, some four million souls who have been rendered homeless and destitute by the Nazis; therefore be it resolved, that the Congress of the United States recommends and urges the creation by the President of a commission of diplomatic, economic and military experts to formulate and effectuate a plan of immediate action designed to save the surviving Jewish people of Europe from extinction at the hands of Nazi Germany.[49]

The Gillette-Rogers resolutions were a direct result of the activity of the Emergency Committee to Save the Jewish People of Europe. The *Forward* even headlined the presence of Peter Bergson at the press conference called by Senator Gillette to announce the introduction of his resolution.[50] The Jewish community, however, gave a mixed reception to these resolutions.

The *Morning Journal* on the whole, supported the resolutions, reflecting, perhaps, its warmth toward Bergson and the Emergency Committee.[51] The *Forward* also supported Gillette-Rogers editorially, asserting that since the Nazis had made a special target of the Jews, there was a practical need and a moral imperative to exert special efforts for rescuing Jews. The *Forward,* however, also gave prominence to the opposition in its news coverage and through its columnists.[52] *The Day,* which reported the public support in the New York press (e.g., the *New York Post*)[53] and among public officials like Wendell Willkie, the Republican presidential candidate in 1940, and Dean Alfange, American Labor Party candidate for governor of New York in 1942,[54] nevertheless equivocated in its editorial support for the rescue resolutions. On the one hand, its first reaction was to back them up, since these resolutions could set the stage for saving many Jews;[55] on the other hand, it reported favorably on Stephen S. Wise's opposition to the resolutions, on the grounds that they would prove worthless unless America would open its doors to the refugees and England would unlock the gates to Palestine. In a sense, Margoshes warned, by passing these resolutions, Congress would have a sense of accomplishment and then would feel no further need to act.[56]

The Day's about-face between November 25, when it supported Gillette-Rogers, and December 7, when it joined the opposition, may have resulted from the testimony given by Dr. Wise on December 2 before the House Foreign Affairs Committee.[57] That testimony provided the rationale for the widespread opposition to the resolutions that developed among the Jewish communal leadership.[58] Terming the proposal for a commission to rescue European Jewry "inadequate," Dr. Wise called for an amendment to open the doors of Palestine as the "simplest way of helping the Jews of Europe." Representative Rogers replied that he doubted the wisdom of injecting the ancient and acrimonious issue of Palestine into a specific resolution designed for rescue.[59]

This was the principle on which American Jewish organizations were divided. The American Jewish Conference, which represented a Zionist point of view and which spoke in the fall of 1943 for almost all of American Jewry (except for the American Jewish Committee, which had recently withdrawn from the organization), would not allow the issue of Palestine to be eclipsed even momentarily, not even by the cause of rescue. Dr. Wise, *Congress Weekly* reported, lifted the discussion in the House Foreign Affairs Committee "from the plane of abstract plans to the most immediate practical measures of rescue, and in the first place to the opening of Palestine for such Jews as may be saved from Nazi annihilation."[60] The Emergency Committee, on the other hand, which was a Revisionist Zionist group, felt that the issue of rescue should be considered alone; to complicate it with the Palestinian problem would have involved the United States in a disagreement with an ally in wartime and would have set American policy in opposition to Arab interests at a time when Arab friendship was considered necessary.[61] These were the implications in Rogers' retort to Wise, but they did not convince the Zionists.

The leading Jewish periodicals largely followed the Zionist position. They reacted to the Gillette-Rogers resolutions by ignoring them, at a time when *The New York Times,* the *JTA,* and the Yiddish papers gave them coverage that ranged from moderate (the *Times*) to extensive (the Yiddish press). *Congress Weekly* published an editorial about Gillette-Rogers in the fifth issue following November 9 and then only with reference to Wise's testimony. In the previous four issues, there had been only one small news item referring to these resolutions, although they had been introduced with bipartisan support in both Houses of Congress. The *Jewish Frontier* never mentioned the resolutions, although it attacked the testimony of Undersecretary of State Breckinridge Long, who testified in the House committee hearings. *Opinion* also ignored Gillette-Rogers as did the *Jewish Spectator.* The *New Palestine* contained no reference to the resolutions until the fifth issue following November 9, when it printed a strong article repudiating the Emergency Committee and all of its work.[62]

The split in the Jewish community over Gillette-Rogers, however, did not remain sub-rosa. The Zionist establishment and the Emergency Committee locked horns in a public battle that was liberally reported in the press and periodical literature from November 1943 through January 1944. The most blatant consequence of this internecine struggle was the failure of the Gillette-Rogers resolution to be voted upon in either House of Congress. In the House of Representatives, the Rogers resolution was not even reported out of committee by Chairman Sol Bloom, the New York Democrat, whose allegiance lay clearly with the establishment organizations. Bloom had tried to intimidate Bergson during the hearings by questioning him about his status as an alien. Bloom also attacked the Emergency Committee for a telegram it had sent to 200 people, appealing for funds to "force" passage of the Gillette-Rogers resolutions.[63]

A less measurable, though no less significant, result of this open struggle was its impact upon the American public. A public whose political support was essential if Jews were to be saved was witness to the spectacle of Jewish organizations bickering among themselves over issues that were not at all clear. It must have appeared to outsiders—correctly or not—that American

Jewry was once again allowing itself the luxury of fiddling while European Jewry was burning.[64]

Most of the attacks stemmed from the American Jewish Conference and its constituents, who saw the Emergency Committee preempting the leadership role in rescue and relief and gaining much popular support in the process. The committee, according to the *Reconstructionist,* had filled "a vacuum created by many years of ineffective activity on the part of Zionist bodies and philanthropic organizations."[65] It had properly replaced *shtadlanut* with bold, public initiatives, wrote B. Z. Goldberg in *The Day.* What the American Jewish Congress had once been to the American Jewish Committee, the Emergency Committee was now to the American Jewish Conference.[66] It had awakened the conscience of American Jewry and demonstrated that the highest priority, which ought not to be compromised in any way, was the prompt rescue of as many European Jews as possible.[67]

As the support for the Emergency Committee grew in the press, a full-page advertisement was placed in *The Day* by the committee urging support for Gillette-Rogers and contributions to help the committee in its work. The text contained a letter from Chief Rabbi Herzog of Palestine in support of this effort. Two days later the Interim Committee of the American Jewish Conference issued a sharply worded attack on the committee, in which it made the following charges among others:

1. The committee in all of its guises (American Friends of Jewish Palestine, Committee for an Army of Stateless and Palestinian Jews, and American League for a Free Palestine) constantly presumed to speak for the Jewish people in America without having a mandate or a constituency.

2. The committee did not cooperate with the Joint Emergency Committee for European Jewish Affairs, which represented the broad spectrum of the community. Instead it began to engage in sporadic and sensational competitive activities.

3. The committee raised funds through advertisements for the purpose of saving 70,000 Romanian Jews with no accounting of how much was raised, what was done with the money, and how many Jews were ransomed—if any.

4. The committee has gained the support of well-meaning

people—Jews and non-Jews—who have "mistaken propaganda for performance and advertisement for achievement." These people might otherwise have been "helpful to the truly representative and responsible bodies in organized Jewry."

5. The resolutions sponsored by the committee in Congress have attracted much support among people who mistakenly think that they will be effective instruments of rescue. In fact, the resolutions will achieve little because they are confined solely to an American effort—when an international commission is what is needed—and the issue of opening the doors of Palestine has been specifically avoided.

6. Now the committee has organized the American League for a Free Palestine, which is attacking the World Zionist Organization and seeking to supplant the Jewish Agency.

The statement concluded with this admonition: "Irresponsible action, which destroys coordinated effort and which does not assist the objectives it pretends to serve, must be so characterized."[68]

This statement of charges received wide publicity in the Yiddish press on December 30. The New York Times also carried a big story about it on December 31, together with a rebuttal by Dean Alfange, a vice-chairman of the Emergency Committee. The most interesting treatment of this statement was featured by Margoshes in his front-page column in The Day. On January 3 he printed the text of the American Jewish Conference's blast at the committee while on January 4 he printed the committee's reply. On January 5 he gave his own view, vacillating between criticism and praise for the committee.[69] Rabbi Eliezer Silver, president of the Union of Orthodox Rabbis, was less equivocal. He vehemently protested the charges of the conference, and he called for rabbis to support the rescue work of the committee. Peter Bergson called upon the Union of Orthodox Rabbis to hear a Din Torah (a civil suit) against Dr. Wise as president of the Conference for slandering him and his colleagues, for urging people to stop supporting the committee, and for attempting to kill the Gillette-Rogers resolutions. Wise called Bergson's statements "moral blackmail."[70]

The charges and countercharges resulted in a hideous spectacle in which both sides emerged as losers. The Emergency Committee had struck a responsive chord among the masses of

Jews and among non-Jewish humanitarians. Their methods and motives, however, were suspect, and they accepted no communal restraints. Nevertheless, their sponsorship of the Gillette-Rogers resolutions probably helped the cause of rescue, if only indirectly. Had they been joined by the wider Jewish community, the War Refugee Board would probably have resulted directly from this effort instead of being delayed until Morgenthau's political intervention.

The Zionists were clearly jealous of the work of this independent body, as Rabbi Meir Berlin, president of World Mizrachi (the religious Zionists), was to recall at a later date.[71] Furthermore, they could not reorder their priorities even in the short run. The Jewish commonwealth issue could not be superseded by a program of rescue, even if it meant that immediate rescue would therefore be impossible to achieve.[72]

The Jewish disagreement caused consternation among well-meaning non-Jews, as was noted by Rabbi Isaac Lewin. Gillette and Rogers, Lewin wrote, wanted to arouse the world and enhance the rescue effort for Jews. But Jewish leaders came to them and asked them to withdraw the proposals. "Is not this the most terrible desecration of God's name imaginable?"[73] Senator Gillette recalled the incident a year later. Within twenty-four hours of his introduction of the resolution in the Senate, he began to receive phone calls and personal visits assuring him that those who had asked him to sponsor the resolution "did not represent the Jewish people; that they were upstarts . . . who desired to aggrandize themselves." On the day the resolution was to come up for a vote in the Foreign Relations Committee, one of the cosponsors came over to Gillette and said:

> I wish these damned Jews would make up their minds what they want. I could not get inside the Committee room without being buttonholed out there in the corridor by representatives who said that the Jewish people of America do not want the passage of this resolution.[74]

Perhaps it was all a "dispute for the sake of heaven," as one writer in the *Forward* observed. But in such critical times even a sacred dispute was inappropriate.[75]

THE WAR REFUGEE BOARD IS ESTABLISHED

The division within the Jewish community over the Gillette-Rogers resolutions became somewhat academic in the late afternoon of Saturday, January 22, 1944, when President Roosevelt signed Executive Order No. 9417 bringing into being the War Refugee Board. The board was to be headed by Henry L. Stimson, Secretary of War, Cordell Hull, and Henry Morgenthau, Jr., the latter having served as the catalytic force in its creation. The functions of the board were to organize and implement programs for the rescue, transportation, maintenance, and relief of the victims of enemy oppression and to establish havens of temporary refuge for such victims. These functions were to be performed by special attachés abroad who would hold diplomatic status. (The most famous of these was Ira Hirschman, a New York department store executive, who saved thousands of Jewish lives through his voluntary mission for the board in Ankara, Turkey, and its environs.)[76] The board was instructed to cooperate with private groups and governmental agencies already involved in rescue work. In effect, the WRB was the fulfillment by the executive branch of the American Government of the Gillette-Rogers resolution, which had never come to a vote in the legislative branch.[77]

The creation of the WRB was hailed by the total Jewish community. The Yiddish press was uniformly enthusiastic. The American Jewish Committee, the Jewish Labor Committee, the American Jewish Conference, the Emergency Committee, the World Jewish Congress, the Zionist Administrative Council, and the National Orthodox Conference for Palestine and Rescue were among the organizations that issued statements of praise for the new initiative by the President. HIAS (the Hebrew Immigrant Aid Society) sent $100,000 to the board, which had been given an initial government allocation of $1 million.[78] The Vaad Ha-Hatzala supplied over $1 million, while the Joint Distribution Committee provided in excess of $15 million.

Behind the statements of praise, however, one could detect a struggle in the Jewish community to win credit for the establishment of the WRB. The Emergency Committee did not lose a moment before claiming credit for this victory. Full-page ads appeared in the three major Yiddish dailies, trumpeting its role in this great event.[79] However, when it came to editorial support, only the *Morning Journal*—and the *Answer*—gave credit to the Emergency Committee for creating the model for the WRB.[80] The *Answer*'s February 12 issue was filled with self-congratulatory statements and telegrams from such people as Harold Ickes, Wendell L. Willkie, Ted O. Thackrey (editor of the *New York Post*), and from papers like the *Washington Post* and the *Christian Science Monitor*.

The non-Jewish press saw clearly the connection between Gillette-Rogers and the WRB. The Jewish press, however, representing the established organizations, preferred not to notice the link.[81] The *Conference Record*, published by the American Jewish Conference, cautioned that the WRB was not set up overnight but was rather the outcome of many conferences held by the Rescue Commission of the conference with government officials.[82] *Congress Weekly* identified the roots of the WRB in the March 1, 1943, rally and the recommendations of the Joint Emergency Committee to the Bermuda Conference. This was accurate as far as it went, but it was not the whole story, because it left out the important role played by the Emergency Committee, a role which *Congress Weekly* could not or would not admit. The magazine added a thinly veiled attack on the future role of organizations like the Emergency Committee with respect to the WRB.

> There is room for authoritative and responsible Jewish organizations to play a leading part in the rescue plans, and the War Refugee Board will undoubtedly welcome this cooperation. There is room for the World Jewish Congress . . . the Joint Distribution Committee . . . [and] the rescue commission of the American Jewish Conference. . . . There is a chance for these and other authoritative Jewish bodies to work closely with each other and to collaborate in unison with the WRB.

The editor then added a more pointed attack when he wrote:

> Will the President's action, however, serve to purge our own internal life of the plague of self-styled voluntary saviors whose chief accomplishment is the creation of confusion and bewilderment?[83]

The *New Palestine,* although it praised the establishment of the WRB, was the only organ of the Jewish press to notice that the President's executive order did not specifically mention Jews, although an accompanying statement had singled out the unique refugee status of the Jews of Europe. The editor quoted approvingly Senator Gillette's criticism of this fundamental omission from the formal executive order.[84]

The *National Jewish Monthly* added to its praise of the WRB a discordant note—a reminder that the problem of restrictive rules on immigration to the United States, which was evident in 1939, was still a strong factor five years later. The editor wrote:

> American generosity may have to face the fact that some of the rescued may have to be given at least temporary refuge in the United States. We can't undertake a job of rescue and expect our allies to shelter all the rescued. The responsibility of a rescuer includes giving the rescued a place of refuge in his own house if that is necessary.
>
> No one will ask for a letting down of immigration laws. Our immigration laws can stand firm even while we give shelter to the stricken stranger.[85]

The *National Jewish Monthly* was not alone in its concern for what the restrictionists might say. Representative Celler, upon hearing of the establishment of the WRB, wrote to Roosevelt that "the nation's security must not be imperilled by the admission of spies and espionage agents under the guise of refugees."[86] (This was a commonly cited reason of the State Department for barring refugees after Pearl Harbor. What was strange was its use by Celler—a normally sympathetic Jew—at the moment when rescue became a real possibility.)

DISUNITY AND DELAY

The War Refugee Board was a relatively small operation that came on the scene rather late in the Holocaust period. Its creation marked a significant shift in American policy, from "indifference and inadvertent collusion with the Nazis," to an active rescue program which may have saved as many as 200,000 lives. Had it been created two years earlier, the number of lives saved might have been counted in the millions.[87]

Should the Jewish community have forced the rescue issue at an earlier date? The creation of a WRB was warranted as early as December of 1942, but the issue was not pressed at the time by American Jewry, nor would Roosevelt, preoccupied by America's war effort, have concerned himself with rescuing Jews from the Nazis.[88] Even after the March 1 rally there was little coordinated pressure on the government to create a rescue agency. The Emergency Committee did exert such pressure but its actions, while popular among the masses, were repudiated by most of the Jewish establishment, which fought the committee on ideological grounds for political and financial reasons.

There was even an effort in January 1944 to create an interfaith group in support of European Jews as a counterforce to the committee. It was founded on January 30, 1944, as the National Committee Against Nazi Persecution and Extermination of the Jews of Europe. Its chairman was Justice Frank Murphy of the U.S. Supreme Court, and it included among its leaders Vice President Wallace, Wendell L. Willkie, Governor Leverett Saltonstall of Massachusetts, and other prominent federal and state political figures.[89]

The disunity hindered the effort to move a government that was not at all inclined to change its refugee-rescue policy. Ultimately, it was Morgenthau who effected the change. The Jewish community was only an indirect contributor, by helping to create a political climate that was somewhat receptive to a new direction in America's policy toward refugees. Had the Jewish community been able to overcome its divisiveness, the WRB might have started its life-saving work many months earlier.

It was now the spring of 1944, and the curtain was about to rise on the final act of the Holocaust tragedy. A change in command in Budapest threatened as many as 1 million Jewish lives in Hungary. The next chapter will examine this threat and discuss the response of American Jewry to the plight of the last of the 6 million.

Chapter seven

THE TRAP SHUTS

The occupation of Hungary by Nazi Germany on March 19, 1944, marked the beginning of the last chapter of the Holocaust, the final episode in the Final Solution. The tragedy that unfolded for Hungarian Jewry from that day on was compounded by several factors.

Before the occupation, Hungary had been a relatively safe haven for European Jewry, a veritable oasis on a continent that had become an uninhabitable desert for Jews. The American Jewish community knew it to be the permanent or temporary home of close to 1 million Jews,[1] some of whom had fled there from other lands occupied by the German army. Under the government of Prime Minister Miklos Kallay, who took office in March 1942, Jews were subject to severe employment restrictions, forced labor conscription, and expropriation of property. These economic privations, however, were but petty annoyances by comparison with the deportation and extermination threats to which Jews in other lands were subject. All of this was to change radically when Hitler summoned Regent Nicholas Horthy to his headquarters in Klessheim Castle near Salzburg and informed him that he would no longer tolerate Kallay's "treachery" toward Germany (Kallay was trying to disassociate Hungary from the war) and his failure to eliminate Hungary's Jews. Hitler told the regent that Germany had to occupy Hungary. When Horthy arrived back in Hungary on March 19, he found the occupation completed. A new prime minister, General Dome Szotjay, formerly Hungarian minister in Berlin, was appointed to head the government, but the real rule in Hungary had passed to the SS.[2] The *Jewish Frontier* was to describe it as follows:

> Look at your map. You have been studying geography since 1939. Horror-stricken, you watched the march of the Nazi hordes across Europe. . . .
>
> You have seen the tentacles of the Nazi monster reach out into France, Belgium, Holland, Denmark, Norway, Italy. You have heard the sealed trains rumble back across Central Europe. . . . You have averted your face from the slaughter-house of Poland. The murder of three million human beings was something that you would not bring yourself to watch. . . .
>
> There was one spot on the map, however, where you sought some scant comfort. That was in the Balkans. You said to yourself, "Here is the remnant." 800,000 Jews in Hungary; 250,000 in Rumania [sic]. These could be saved from the extermination-squads. . . .
>
> Look at your map again. The circle has closed. The last remaining Jewish communities in Europe, outside of Russia, are caught in the vise. Since the German occupation of the Balkans, the death-trap has snapped shut. Already reports reach us that the Nazi over-lords have ordained a quick "solution to the Jewish problem" one of their first tasks in the Balkans.[3]

There was a second compounding factor to the tragedy of Hungarian Jewry: Germany was clearly going to lose the war against the Allies, but there were strong grounds to fear that she was determined to win the war against the Jews. Such a fear had been given official expression by the Moscow Declaration on November 1, 1943. Citing new evidence of atrocities, massacres, and extermination, the joint declaration of Roosevelt, Stalin, and Churchill had observed:

> The brutalities of Nazi domination are no new thing and all peoples or territories in their grip have suffered from the worst form of government by terror. What is new is

that many of these territories are now being redeemed by the advancing armies of the liberating powers and that in their desperation, the recoiling Hitlerites and Huns are redoubling their ruthless cruelties. This is now evidenced with particular clearness by the monstrous crimes in the territory of the Soviet Union which is being liberated from Hitlerites. . . .[4]

This fear was publicized again on March 20, 1944, by Nahum Goldmann, chairman of the Administrative Committee of the World Jewish Congress, at a press conference in New York, following his return from London. Citing reports from occupied Europe on the possibility of rescue, Goldmann warned:

To speed up rescue is doubly necessary now before the invasion of Europe. There is justified fear that the period before the final collapse of the Nazis may become the worst chapter in this tragedy. The retreating Nazis will try to exterminate the Jews before they withdraw."[5]

Goldmann's apprehension had already been corroborated by a report five days earlier from the Jewish underground in Poland: "The Nazi barbarians, faced with certain defeat, are killing off the pitiful remnants of the Jewish population in Poland."[6] His anxiety was to be substantiated, for the Nazis moved decisively to pave the way for the annihilation of Hungarian Jewry.

A third factor compounding the tragedy of Hungarian Jews was the timing of the German occupation. It began just twelve days before the British White Paper, terminating Jewish immigration into Palestine, was to go into effect, March 31, 1944, and on the very day that Congress decided not to pass a resolution against this British move, March 19. American Jews had mounted a powerful campaign in Congress to obtain passage of resolutions in both Houses calling upon the United States to "use its good offices and take appropriate measures to the end that the doors of Palestine shall be opened for free entry of Jews into that country. . . ."[7] The resolutions, which attracted broad political and editorial support, were ultimately shelved because of testimony offered by General George C. Marshall, chief of staff of the Army, and Henry L. Stimson, Secretary of War.[8] This was not the time to create a breach in the alliance with Great Britain. The Congressional decision not to protest the closing of the only doors which might have been open as a refuge for Hungarian Jewry took on an added irony in that it became public on March 19, 1944, the day the trap was sprung in Hungary.

The White Paper connection provided a further ironic element. The campaign waged by American Jewry against British policy—an exhausting one and ultimately futile[9]—reached its climax with a mass rally of 20,000 at Madison Square Garden. This rally required extensive mobilization of communal energies, which could not readily be mobilized for a new crisis. By an unfortunate twist of fate, the White Paper rally took place on March 21, 1944—the same day that *The New York Times'* front page carried the story of Germany's occupation of Hungary. The tragedy was thus complete, compounded by a haven that no longer existed, a potential refuge whose doors were about to close, an American Jewish community that was poorly organized and worn out from a fruitless struggle, and a ruthless Nazi regime that was determined to win one final victory against the helpless Hungarian Jews.

WHAT DID AMERICAN JEWS KNOW?

The threat to the lives of Hungarian Jews was clear to American Jewry from the beginning of the German occupation. On March 22, 1944, the news was carried on the first page of the *JTA* and on page 1 of the three major Yiddish dailies.[10] "ONE MILLION HUNGARIAN JEWS FRIGHTENED FOR THEIR LIVES AFTER NAZIS TAKE OVER HUNGARY" was the headline in the *Morning Journal*. Immediately the paper warned that

> in the past, United States Jews have been negligent in saving Jews, especially from Hungary, in which rescue opportunities existed but were not exploited. But even now it is not completely too late. Many lives can yet be saved.[11]

In the days that followed, the Jewish press reported on a series of Nazi actions and ordinances that made the Hungarian scene a replica of *Kristallnacht* and its aftermath in Germany, with the addition of Nuremberg-type laws and the beginning of mass deportations. Below is a sampling of what the American Jewish reading public found in the papers.

On March 23 the papers headlined reports of the looting of Jewish shops, the arrest by the Gestapo of many Jews, and a promise by a German Foreign Office spokesman to eliminate Jews from "various phases of life" in Hungary.[12] Margoshes reacted to the news with a sense of resignation, concluding that only total victory by the Allies will save Hungary's Jews. An editorial in the same issue of The Day reflected the same hopelessness, adding that these Jews could have been saved, but those who should have helped did not.

On March 24 the Times carried a plea from Dr. Israel Goldstein for rescue efforts: "The Nazi occupation of Hungary portends catastrophe for hundreds of thousands of Jews in Europe. . . . There is not an hour to lose in carrying out a large-scale rescue action in whatever places and by whatever means still remain available."[13] Despite the urgency of Goldstein's statement, the accounts of Saturday's sermons in the Times, March 26, 1944, p. 5, contained only one report of a sermon devoted to the plight of Hungarian Jewry.

On March 29, JTA and The Day reported that 10,000 Hungarian Jews were arrested and placed in concentration camps. That figure was to rise to 55,000 less than a week later.[14] On April 2, the papers carried reports of the requirement that Hungary's Jews must wear yellow badges and that the Minister of the Interior called for "a merciless war" against the Jews leading to their "liquidation." The first reports of deportations in cattle trains were also carried that day.[15] The word "deportations" had an ominous sound, for just ten days previously the papers had reported that 60,000 Greek Jews who had been deported to unknown destinations were now known to have been gassed in Auschwitz.[16] The danger to Hungarian Jews was clearly not the Nuremberg-type laws but rather the realistic fear that the Nazis would decide to kill all the Jews in frustration over their massive battlefield defeats.[17]

In the ensuing weeks, the papers reported the following events and incidents. The initial reporting date for each follows in parentheses.

The establishment of a Central Jewish Council (*Judenrat*) "to speed up anti-Jewish measures" and to serve, as in other countries, for collection of taxes and choosing deportees (April 14).[18]

Registration and confiscation of all Jewish property (April 16).[19]

The beginning of deportations to death camps in Poland (April 17).[20]

The dissolution of the Zionist Organization of Hungary and various other Jewish groups (April 19).[21]

The transfer of Budapest Jews to "closed districts" with a 7 A.M. to 7 P.M. curfew and the closing of all Jewish firms (April 24).[22]

More than 300,000 Jews in Hungarian concentration camps; sugar and fat ration cards surrendered (April 28).[23]

Prohibitions on Jewish public worship, telephones in Jewish homes, and the owning of radios (May 4).[24]

80,000 Jews have already been deported to death camps in Poland (May 18).[25]

Finally, German newspapers reported on May 26 that "5,000,000 Jews have been eliminated in various countries of Europe." The statement continued, "There are still about 500,000 Jews to be dealt with in Hungary" (May 28).[26]

The Final Solution in Hungary was being carried out in full view of the entire world. The pattern of restriction, registration, concentration, and impending deportation was clear, although definite news of mass deportations was not yet fully available. Between May 15 and June 30, before the world knew the full story, 380,000 Hungarian Jews had already arrived in Auschwitz.[27] There were, as we have seen, preliminary isolated reports and rumors. These continued through June, but they were inconclusive. As late as June 15, the *JTA* carried a confusing story headlined "MASS DEPORTATIONS OF JEWS FROM HUNGARY PREDICTED[!] BY SWISS NEWSPAPER."[28]

On June 20 and again on June 26 the *JTA*, *The Day*, and the

Forward carried lead stories about the mass deportations. These emanated from the Polish Government-in-Exile in London and estimated the number of deportees who had already been murdered at 100,000. These reports were followed on June 30 by a statement from the World Council of Churches in Geneva that 12,000 Hungarian Jews were being deported daily and that the number who had already reached Poland was up to 450,000. The Hungarian Government itself confirmed the terrifying news by announcing in early July a decision "to liquidate all Jews in the country."[29]

The news of the deportations evoked a number of protests from non-Jewish world leaders which may have had an effect upon the Hungarian leadership. An appeal issued by the general secretary of the Federal Council of Churches of Christ in America said in part, "In the face of such conditions I earnestly appeal to American Christians to pray for the Hungarian Jews subjected to such inhuman treatment. Even if we see no practical way of going to their assistance, we must at least cry out in protest and identify ourselves in sympathy with the victims. . . ."[30] On June 26, Secretary Hull issued a condemnation of Hungary's complicity with Nazi brutality, echoing a similar statement by the House Foreign Affairs Committee five days earlier. King Gustaf V of Sweden personally intervened with Admiral Horthy to save Hungarian Jews from further persecution. Pope Pius XII also made representations to the Hungarian regent. In apparent response to all of these protests, Horthy announced a halt to the deportations on July 18.[31]

HOW DID AMERICAN JEWS RESPOND TO THE CRISIS OF HUNGARIAN JEWRY?

From the above press accounts, it is clear that the final chapter in the Final Solution was written in public, before the eyes of the whole world. The actual news of the deportations came out slowly, but the threat to Jewish lives was painfully clear almost from the moment of occupation on March 19. What was the public response of American Jews to this rapidly unfolding tragedy? One might measure that response first by considering how American Jews reacted to a number of events and issues that dominated this period.

THE ROOSEVELT WARNING

On March 24, 1944, President Roosevelt issued a public appeal to Germans and other Europeans not to cooperate in the Nazi crimes against humanity and to help the potential victims of those crimes escape death. He warned that anyone who knowingly took part in the deportation of Jews or others to death camps would be punished after the war. Calling attention in particular to the plight of Hungarian Jewry, the President said, "That these innocent people, who have already survived a decade of Hitler's fury, should perish on the very eve of triumph over the barbarism which their persecution symbolizes, would be a major tragedy."[32]

The reaction to this historic statement—it was the first time that Roosevelt had referred officially to the specific Jewish tragedy*[33]—was not uniformly enthusiastic. The American Jewish Conference, the World Jewish Congress, and the Emergency Committee all issued strong statements of support.[34] The American Jewish Committee, which had publicly called for such an official statement one day before it was issued,[35] was effusive in its expressions of gratitude to the President, conveyed in a letter from its own president, Judge Joseph M. Proskauer.[36] But in the press, only *Opinion* and Glatstein in *The Day* expressed unequivocal editorial praise for the President's initiative. Stephen S. Wise's magazine waxed eloquent in its encomiums for the American leader and concluded:

> The Nation is grateful to the President for his expression
> of moral and spiritual leadership and, irrespective of politics and the pettiness of partisanship, all American Jews
> bless the name of him who, the moment peril approached

---

*S. Friedman, *No Haven for the Oppressed*, p. 227, indicates that the original draft submitted to Roosevelt began with the words "One of the blackest crimes in history, the systematic murder of the Jews of Europe, continues unabated." In the actual statement delivered by Roosevelt, the Jews were mentioned only after all other suffering nationalities had been listed.

the surviving Jews of Hitler's Europe, spoke out on their behalf not only with the strength of his own great person but with the moral force of a great nation in his support.[37]

Not everyone was as heartened by Roosevelt's warning as *Opinion*. What was the purpose of urging Hungarians to help Jews to escape if the doors of the United States and Palestine were to remain closed to them? Why should neutrals like Turkey be expected to open their doors while the Allied nations were unwilling to open theirs? The President's statement was praiseworthy but what was really needed was to "translate fine principles into performances."[38] Menachem Ribalow, in *Hadoar*, expressed the hope that Roosevelt's statement would lead to the kind of enlightened action that the desperate conditions now required.

> One possibility is that he who asks for justice and mercy from others, will be the first to act justly and mercifully in his own home: i.e. that America herself will relax her immigration quota and open her gates to refugees.[39] And if she will do it, there is hope that Canada will follow her example. And so will other countries.
>
> A second possibility is that the gates of Palestine will be opened. . . . America can play a major role in this too.
>
> And if both of these possibilities come about, . . . it will be a great achievement. And, to the message of Roosevelt, from which the rays of morality shine, there will be added an additional power, the power of redemption.[40]

Trude Weiss Rosmarin, in the *Jewish Spectator,* was less sanguine about the redemptive power of the President's statement. Reflecting what may have been the unspoken thoughts of many Jews, she editorialized about the statement under the heading "Too Late."

> We are bowed down with grief at the tragedy that has overtaken eight hundred thousand Jews in Hungary. No doubt, the expressions of sympathy of our President, speaking in the name of the United Nations, are a welcome and soothing balm. Nevertheless, our hurt is not assuaged for we know with utter and unshakable certainty

that at least half of these doomed eight hundred thousand could have been saved had they been given the opportunity of a haven of refuge in the Jewish homeland. . . .[41]

The President's warning, many Jews apparently felt, would have had practical significance had it been combined with the abrogation of the White Paper and the opening of Palestine to those who might still be saved. Otherwise, while it was a gratifying statement, it offered little hope of achieving gratifying results.[42]

THE FREE PORTS PROPOSAL

The WRB and its director, John Pehle, were also concerned that a closed-door policy against Jews would severely limit the usefulness of the President's warning. A way had to be found to open the doors of the United States and the neutrals. An idea suggested by Samuel Grafton in his April 5 column in the *New York Post* provided the solution. Why not create a system of "Free Ports" for people? A Free Port was a place where merchandise could be stored for a while until a decision as to its ultimate destination was made. Such a temporary haven for refugees could also be established without deciding on their ultimate resettlement. The idea itself was not new; it had been proposed by Jews as far back as 1938. The packaging, however, was new, and it appealed to Pehle. He held a news conference on the subject that attracted front-page coverage by *The New York Times*.[43]

The response of the Jewish community was almost universally supportive. *The Day*, the *Forward*, and *Congress Weekly* gave Free Ports their strong endorsement, as did the Philadelphia and Boston weeklies.[44] The Jewish Labor Committee urged Roosevelt to enact the Free Port program immediately, and it solicited the support of the CIO for this idea.[45] The *Jewish Frontier* saw it as the instrument for the rescue of "hundreds of thousands" of Balkan Jews. The American Jewish Conference hailed it as something that "may yet help to stave off the death sentence . . . for the last surviving Jews of Europe."[46] Its communal rival, the Emergency Committee, was so pleased with the idea that it devoted most of its editorial in the *Answer*[47] to claiming credit for proposing it. The *Jewish Spectator* and the *New*

Palestine, alone among the Jewish newspapers and periodicals, cautioned that while Free Ports might be a good idea they would not solve even the short-run problems of homeless Jews. That solution could only be in Palestine.[48] It might be argued that the Zionists were apprehensive about Free Ports because they represented a settlement plan outside Palestine, something which they felt was impractical and which would also divert energies from the main struggle to revoke the White Paper.[49] The Zionist-dominated American Jewish Conference, however, took a strong position in favor of Free Ports, which suggests that those who were suspicious of the Free Port idea may have been motivated by other considerations than Zionism.

Events quickly confirmed the suspicions of the skeptics. Roosevelt announced his intention to establish Free Ports on June 2 and one week later he declared that Fort Ontario, near Oswego, New York, would be converted into an "emergency refugee shelter" to accommodate 1,000 refugees. The Presidential order required that the 1,000 chosen (they turned out to be 984) should "include a reasonable proportion of various categories of persecuted peoples. . . ."[50] A reaction came immediately from Rep. Samuel Dickstein, New York Democrat, chairman of the House Immigration Committee, who asked Congress to act to admit an unlimited number of refugees to Free Ports. *The New York Times* editorialized on June 11 its hope that more than a mere thousand could be accommodated, for that figure represented but a minute fraction of the masses of homeless people. Six other Congressmen introduced bills to provide for additional facilities, but hearings never took place. Congress had to finish its pressing business in time to adjourn for the national political conventions.[51]

The editor of *Hadoar,* who had earlier joined the chorus of enthusiasm in the expectation that the Free Ports idea would restore some sense of moral balance to America, now expressed profound disappointment with such a pitifully small gesture: "Is this the act of salvation for which we waited with such longing? . . . Whence will help come? Who will save those who can still be saved? A dreadful question—for the world, for America, for ourselves."[52]

A disappointed *Jewish Spectator* commented, in a resigned editorial entitled "Who Will Be the Lucky Thousand?" that Fort

Ontario was neither a solution to the pressing refugee problem nor even a generous gesture.[53] Marie Syrkin, contemplating Roosevelt's sensitivity to bigots and restrictionists who might express their opposition at the polls[54] to a more magnanimous gesture, urged the President not to succumb to fear of such a reaction, but rather to face the issue of homeless refugees honestly and generously:

> If the United States can permit itself to declare to the world that its maximum contribution to the refugee problem is the admission of 1,000 people, what answer can be expected from smaller and poorer nations, who have coped with sporadic streams of refugees for years?[55]

BOMBING AS A DETERRENT

One of the issues that confronted Jewish leaders was the proposal to bomb Budapest, the railroad lines leading to the death camps, and even the camps themselves, as a means of impeding the process of mass murders.[56]

The bombing of Budapest began on April 3, 1944.[57] In response, the Hungarian regime threatened to move Jews into the target areas—a threat which drew a severe Allied warning on May 15: This threat will not stop us from bombing, but if Hungary carries it out, that will constitute murder, and whoever is involved in this will be punished after the war.[58] The bombing was not presented as an act of retribution, however. A *JTA* dispatch on December 7, 1942, had reported that many Germans believed that the bombing of their cities was "God's punishment for the brutal handling of Jews." The same message might have been brought home to the Hungarians by broadcasts and the dropping of leaflets after the bombings, to discourage Hungarian cooperation with the SS.[59]

Only two Jewish periodicals called for such bombing. The *Jewish Forum,* in an open letter to the President, asked that Budapest be wiped "off the face of the earth." *Congress Weekly* called for "telling Budapest, not with words but with deeds, that humanity will not stand for the murder of the last million." Help, rather than revenge, was the goal. If there was no way to help on the ground, then why not help from the air? Or was this a foolish encroachment on the military priorities of the Allied High Command?[60]

From the vantage point of today, one cannot help but wonder why American Jews did not launch a campaign to induce Washington to threaten the Hungarians with massive bombings if deportations continued and, on the other hand, to offer immunity from bombing if no Jews were deported. Perhaps the best answer was suggested by Raul Hilberg: "The Jews could not think of 'interfering' with the war effort, and the Allies on their part could not conceive of such a promise. They could not think of Jews in planning their missions."[61]

Hilberg's analysis may help to explain also the lack of a concerted campaign to bomb the rail lines leading from Hungary to Auschwitz and Treblinka and the camps themselves. The Nazis themselves worried about the crippling effect of a raid on the rail lines. In a *JTA* report out of Zurich, the pro-Nazi Hungarian government was reported as speeding up deportations from Budapest before the principal rail lines were severed by Allied bombing.[62] Cutting the lines was not a difficult task. Survivors of Auschwitz, for example, who were deported from the Carpathian Mountains in May of 1944, report that had the Allies bombed one railroad junction in Csop, located today on the Russo-Czech-Hungarian border, no train could have traveled from the Carpathians to Poland. The bombing would have taken minutes but the crippling effect would have lasted for weeks or months. No such raid ever took place.[63]

As early as June 12, 1944, a cable from Isaac Sternbuch of Montreux arrived in New York, informing certain Jewish circles that deportations had reached 10,000 to 15,000 persons daily. He requested intervention with "Roosevelt, Churchill and possibly Moscow" to arrange for the bombing of the railroad junctions in Kaschau and Presov, through which the trains passed on their way from Hungary to Auschwitz. The request was honored, but the answer was that "the conduct of the war did not require such measures."[64]

The bombing of the death camps themselves was another possibility. It was suggested publicly by liberal groups in London and reported in the American Jewish press.[65] It was proposed editorially in the *Jewish Frontier,* as was the bombing of the railroad lines.[66] Apparently the idea was current in June of 1944 because Y. Fishman in the *Morning Journal* opposed it on the grounds that many Jews would be killed in raids on the camps. A. Leon Kubowitzki, head of the World Jewish Congress Rescue Division, had similar misgivings about the proposal and so expressed himself in a letter to John Pehle.[67] He asked instead for paratroopers and underground raids on the camps, which would achieve the desired results but with less loss of Jewish lives. Chaim Weizmann, on the other hand, submitted two requests to Anthony Eden urging the bombing of the camps. All of these requests came to naught. Either the Jews did not press their case strongly enough, or the Allies were too resistant—both probably. The Allied position was particularly inflexible. On August 14, 1944, John J. McCloy, assistant secretary of war, wrote to Kubowitzki regarding a proposal for bombing the camps and the rail lines:

> After a study it became apparent that such an operation could be executed only by the diversion of considerable air support essential to the success of our forces now engaged in decisive operations elsewhere and would in any case be of such doubtful efficacy that it would not warrant the use of our resources. There has been considerable opinion to the effect that such an effort, even if practicable, might provoke even more vindictive action by the Germans.[68]

How much more vindictive the Germans could be than to murder millions of Jews in these camps is difficult to imagine. Nevertheless, Auschwitz and its rail connections were never bombed, and American Jews accepted the decision in silence, a silence which may have unintentionally aided the Nazis to carry out their murderous program in secrecy.

THE RESPONSE OF THE JEWISH PRESS TO THE HUNGARIAN CRISIS

The threat to 1 million Hungarian Jews was clearly understood. One might have expected the Jewish press to respond with outrage and pain as it did following *Kristallnacht*. Such was not the case, however. The fire was missing and in its place came resignation and bitterness.

The *Morning Journal* was the most consistent in its expression of fear for the fate of Hungarian Jewry and in its demand for action. Y. Fishman, in his regular feature, *Fun Tag zu Tag* ("From Day to Day"), was critical of the Madison Square Garden rally on March 21, for not having altered its program in the face of the front-page report of *The New York Times* on that same day, telling of the Nazi takeover in Hungary. The speakers' messages had been prepared in advance, of course; nevertheless, "the meeting should have been transformed into a rally protesting the plight of Hungarian Jewry."[69] Week after week the paper warned of the disaster that lay ahead and urged American Jewish activity in behalf of their brothers and sisters in Hungary:

> In the past, when such news came here, there was a flurry of meetings and protests. . . . But now people are passive; there are dinners and banquets and many expressions of thanks to the WRB and to individuals who save Jews. . . .[70]

The paper suspected that while thanks might be in order, a "recognition cult" was being created for the WRB that could obscure the liquidation of Hungarian Jewry. As late as the end of June the paper was still bemoaning the plethora of nice words—the Hull statement was then the most recent example—and the paucity of effective acts. "American Jewish organizations have absolutely not done enough to save the Jews of Europe."[71] On June 25, in a page 1 column, Fishman exclaimed: "The news from Hungary is terrible; one can literally go out of his mind listening to it. Once again we must protest."

The Day and the *Forward* were similarly critical of the pace of rescue, but their comments lacked the same sense of urgency manifested by the *Morning Journal*. Margoshes, in particular, was more subdued in his reaction than in any other period of the Holocaust included in this study.[72]

The weekly and monthly Jewish periodicals, on the whole, covered the news from Hungary with regularity and concern, but with differing reactions. There were two notable exceptions. The *Reconstructionist* discussed Hungarian Jewry only once [73] in seven issues between March 31 and June 23. This is somewhat surprising, because in previous periods the *Reconstructionist* had been quite sensitive to Jewish suffering. The *National Jewish Monthly* devoted insignificant space to the plight of "900,000 Jews in Hungary" [74] in its April and June issues but featured this subject in the news section of the May issue. No editorial space was assigned to the Hungarian situation in any of the issues, though each issue usually carried nine editorials.

Opinion magazine editorialized on the Hungarian situation in April, May, June, and July. Its reaction was optimistic at first; it later became one of passive resignation. In his Passover message, Wise warned of the threat to Hungarian Jewry but expressed the hope that the threat would not materialize. He anticipated a United Nations warning to Hungary that would forestall Hungary's sinking "to the base depths of the Axis powers." In May, an editorial suggested that not much more could be done for Hungarian Jewry than to hope, to broadcast warnings and requests for mercy, and to pray for a speedy Russian victory in Hungary. This was one of the first examples of a press response born out of a sense of futility, helplessness, and despair. As Wise put it, "The issue is in the hands of God." [75]

The feeling that there was not much American Jews could do in this new crisis stimulated a mood in the press that alternated between anger and despair, mostly the latter. Trude Weiss Rosmarin was angry at the callousness of the world, which had reached its climax with the White Paper closing date, twelve days after Hitler's takeover in Hungary. "The time has come for us to speak out openly and unafraid," she wrote. "Four million of us are slain and your beautiful phrases will not bring them back to life! If you would honor our dead—save the living that can be rescued!" Even the exclamation points bristle with anger in this blazing editorial. [76] Yet, two months later, even Rosmarin's mood had changed from anger to despair:

> The voice of our brother's blood cries out to us from many lands in these crucial days. There is little we can do to halt the slaughter to which every hour and every minute so many of our people succumb. What we are able to accomplish, however, is to act so that these dead and their ideals shall not be forgotten. [77]

Different organs stuck the same notes in various ways. The *Jewish Frontier* bitterly accused the Allies of allowing the doors of Palestine to be shut when they knew what was coming. Now all that was left to the Jews was to help to destroy the Nazis as rapidly as possible. The *New Palestine* bemoaned the past (the Warsaw ghetto anniversary was in April 1944) and the present and declared: "We stand helpless, and seemingly hopeless to aid them or to rescue them. . . ." The WRB has proved to be too little and too late. The world does not care; but

> If the blame is to be leveled against anyone, it should be done so against all of us, against American Jewry as a whole, for lacking foresight and initiative in pressing the issue vociferously enough to bring forth action earlier.[78]

The same sense of despair informed the extensive comment of the *Jewish Outlook,* which had not been so responsive in earlier periods. The magazine observed that only the end of the war would bring any relief in a world which had closed its doors more tightly than ever. Perhaps with this last condition in mind, its editor went on to suggest:

> It seems that the murderers, far from fearing retribution at the hands of assured Allied victors, are convinced that destruction of their Jewish neighbors will find favor in the eyes of the liberators. They believe that the outside world hates Jews far more than it detests the most barbaric inhumanity.[79]

This was an anger of which the Jewish press had not been previously capable. Frustration and resignation allowed the *Jewish Outlook* to mention the previously unmentionable.

This, then, was the mood of most of the press. There was little to be done for Hungarian Jewry, and what little was done turned out to be pitifully inadequate—for example, the fiasco of Fort Ontario. Rather than wallow in unproductive despair, *Congress Weekly* suggested that Jewish energy be "directed toward procuring guarantees for the future in the fields of relief and reconstruction, and the restoration of rights and status."[80] As for Hungarian Jews, they were abandoned—though not forgotten.

THE PUBLIC RESPONSE

In view of the depressed mood of American Jewry as reflected in the press, it was to be expected that the public communal response to the Hungarian crisis would be weak. And so it was. This is not to ignore the often vital role played privately by organizations like the JDC, the National Refugee Service,[81] the American Jewish Committee,[82] and the American Jewish Conference. The last named felt obliged to go public on July 11 with a list of its private representations in behalf of Hungarian Jewry.[83] Two months earlier, however, *The Day*'s feature writer had bemoaned the fact that the conference had been uninvolved, confining its activities to the issuance of memos on the crisis. A review of the *Conference Record* of June 1944, would seem to support this feature writer's perception.[84] Another private organization, the Va'ad Ha-Hatzala, which was deeply involved in vital rescue work in Europe, went public during this period with appeals for funds. Its campaign was officially supported by the *Morning Journal* and the Union of Orthodox Rabbis led by Rabbi Eliezer Silver.[85]

Most Jewish organizations, however, were not engaged in public activities in reaction to the plight of Hungarian Jews. On April 19, for example, one month after the Nazi takeover, *The New York Times* covered several public events commemorating the first anniversary of the uprising in the Warsaw ghetto. Nowhere in its coverage can one see a reference to the fact that a new catastrophe, far greater in numbers than the destruction of the ghetto, was at hand. The burning of Warsaw in 1943 was mourned; the conflagration that was about to engulf Hungarian Jewry, however, was barely mentioned.[86]

During the months of June and July, conventions were held by the Central Conference of American Rabbis (Reform), the Rabbinical Assembly (Conservative), the Rabbinical Council of America (modern Orthodox), and Agudat Israel (European Orthodox). Only the last named discussed the issue of rescue.[87] Perhaps one of the reasons for the omission was that the present was already lost and Jewish energies might be better directed toward the future, a future which appeared to be close at hand after the Allied invasion of Normandy on June 6.[88]

The most active public response was provided by the Emergency Committee to Save the Jewish People of Europe. In addition to publishing advertisements in the Yiddish press, to sound the alarm, and to solicit funds,[89] the committee sponsored three rallies. The first was held on April 2, 1944, in the Hotel Astor, for about 1,000 American Jews of Hungarian descent. The rally called for warning the Hungarian government, radio appeals to Hungarian citizens, opening neutral countries to refugees, and opening Palestine to those who might escape.[90] The second was held in a packed Carnegie Hall on April 30 and called primarily for the abrogation of the White Paper in light of the new emergency.[91] The final rally was held in Town Hall on July 19.[92]

While this third rally by the nonestablishment Emergency Committee was being promoted, the Rescue Commission of the American Jewish Conference met and decided to invite representatives of other Jewish organizations to a meeting to discuss a major demonstration "to call public attention to the situation in Hungary."[93] The decision to hold such a rally was reported in *The Day* and the *Morning Journal* on July 20, 1944, four months after the German occupation of Hungary and several weeks after the news was confirmed that half of Hungary's Jews had already reached the extermination camps. The lateness of the hour was noted with a tinge of bitterness by the *Morning Journal* which, throughout this period, was the most responsive of the newspapers.[94]

The rally, which took place in Madison Square Park on July 31, 1944, was organized hastily and without adequate promotion. Only during the last four days before the event did advertisements appear in the Yiddish press. Nevertheless, the estimates of the crowd varied between 50,000 and 100,000.[95] Speakers at the rally included Wise, Monsky, and Held. An eight-point declaration was adopted for presentation to Roosevelt. After demanding warnings, open borders in neutral countries, Allied nations, and the United States, the rally finally brought up the issue of the murder camps. It carefully avoided a specific call for bombing, but it did urge other action: "All measures should be taken by the military authorities, with the help of the underground forces, to destroy the implements, facilities, and places where the Nazis have carried out their mass executions."[96]

"PROTESTS DO HELP" was the headline in the next issue of

the *National Jewish Monthly* as it reviewed the rally (its attendance figure was 40,000).[97] One cannot help wondering why, if
protests did help, the *National Jewish Monthly* and others did not
call for them during the first four months of this crisis. It is
possible, that there was a simple answer for the delay. American Jews may simply have been too unorganized and discouraged, exhausted from the horrible news and despondent over
their inability to have an effect upon the tragic fortunes of their
European brethren. There was a hint of all this in a depressing
editorial in *Congress Weekly* on the July 31 demonstration.

> They walked down New York's Broadway in groups of
> three, four and five—men and women, stooped, some still
> erect; most of them gray-haired or graying. . . .
>   Their sons did not come. Many of them are away on the
> battlefields fighting and dying. . . . The men and women
> in the professional and business offices did not come. But
> they—these men and women from the shops, from the lit-
> tle stores, this graying generation which planted the seed
> of a powerful Jewry in America—they came. . . .
>   A decade or two will pass, and there will be fewer and
> fewer of these to whom the woe of their brethren across
> the sea is their own woe. . . .
>   May Providence grant that the meeting of July 31, 1944,
> be the last of its kind to which they are called. . . . Would
> that these men and women in the afternoon and evening
> of their life be granted the privilege of seeing a world in
> which no appeals will have to be made for the rescue of
> human beings. . . .[98]

FOUR MONTHS AND 400,000 LIVES

The occupation of Hungary by the Nazis, presented a challenge to the American Jewish community which that community did not meet. Four months passed before a public response
of any significance was mounted. By that time it was known that
400,000 Jews had been deported to Auschwitz. In some ways it
was the perfect time for a rescue campaign. The WRB provided the mechanism. The facts and the threat were clear to Allied governments. Jews knew already what was at stake. Five
sixths of the Holocaust was already past history.

Why was the public response so weak? There may be several explanations. The White Paper went into effect despite an energetic Jewish effort to stop it, and the closing of the doors of Palestine was directly related to the rescue problem—there was no place to which escapees, if any, could go. The rally against the White Paper had consumed much communal energy. On the day of the rally, the news about Hungary broke in the press. There was no possibility of mobilizing the community immediately for another protest demonstration, particularly in view of the fact that the White Paper rally failed to achieve its goal. Communities are composed of people. They cannot rise daily to peaks of emotional excitement. In addition, there is reason to believe that despair and hopelessness had already enveloped American Jewry. The news from Europe was growing more horrible by the day. Hungarian Jewry was trapped. And there was little that could be done about it except to scream. Perhaps there should have been more screaming. Perhaps, like the Federal Council of Churches, the Synagogue Council of America should at least have called for days of prayer. Depressed people, however, rarely act forcefully in their own best interest. One can see in the press many indications of that communal depression. Perhaps more than anything else it helps to explain the lack of a response to the plight of Hungarian Jewry.

The rally on July 31, *Congress Weekly* pointed out, was held on the day following Tisha b'Av (the ninth day of *Av*), a national day of mourning for the destruction of the Temple in Jerusalem. The implication of the editorial writer was that American Jews were mourning that day for their European brethren. Looking back, one cannot help wondering whether perhaps on that hot, sultry day, as the Holocaust was reaching its climax and American Jewry was at its most helpless and hopeless, some of the Jews in Madison Square Park may have been mourning for themselves.

Chapter eight

WERE WE OUR BROTHERS' KEEPERS?

> We must stand as a generation, not only condemned
> to witness the destruction of a third of our number
> but guilty of having accepted it without any resis-
> tance worthy of the name.
> Nahum Goldmann, *The Autobiography of Nahum
> Goldmann: Sixty Years of Jewish Life,* p. 148.

Looking back on the public Jewish response in the six periods
covered by this study, one reluctantly comes to the conclusion
that Nahum Goldmann's assessment, twenty-five years after the
events, was probably accurate. In these periods the Nazi effort
appeared to be maximal and unrelenting, the Allies' response
seemed minimal and ineffective, while the American Jews' public resistance was weak and sporadic. A retrospective view of this
study may provide some insight into the reasons for the weak
response.

In the two prewar periods, the critical issue facing the Jewish people was finding a refuge for Jews who wanted, and were
able, to flee from the Nazis. The doors to the receiving nations

were rapidly closing. Entry to America was governed by a quota system that was rigidly enforced. The American Jewish response to this pathetic situation was a muted one, as demonstrated in both the *Kristallnacht* and *St. Louis* episodes. In part, this muted response resulted from the fact that American Jews did not fully appreciate the danger to which their German coreligionists were exposed. They certainly had no idea of the impending Final Solution, upon which even the Nazi regime did not decide until some time in 1941.[1]

But the weakness of this early American Jewish response was more the result of fear than of incomplete knowledge. The American Jew of 1938–1939 was a cowed figure, who was destined to remain in that state for most of the war years. His timorousness, however, was at its height before America's entry into the war. The anti-Semites were at their most brazen. Jews were publicly vilified, accused of warmongering, and castigated as public menaces. Aside from the normal shivers that anti-Semites gave to Jews, American Jews were particularly sensitive in those days to the strident tones of hate because they could see what one unbalanced bigot had accomplished in Germany.[2]

For one who lives in a world where there is a State of Israel, where young Jews wear crocheted skullcaps on college campuses, and where people rally frequently for Soviet Jews, who identify themselves publicly in Moscow and Leningrad as Jews and as lovers of Israel, it is difficult to imagine that there was a time, not long ago, when none of this was possible, let alone normal. In the America of the 1930s Jews put their skullcaps in their pockets upon leaving home, synagogue, or school. Many who carried a Hebrew book in the subway carried it with the front cover facing inward in order to hide its Hebrew character. For most Jews the desire was to blend in with the majority, to be assimilated into the larger culture, to be as American as possible and to conceal or obliterate the obviously Jewish characteristics of language, accent, clothing, behavior, and sometimes even group loyalties. "Be a Jew in your home and a man in public" was an aphorism of nineteenth century European Jewish intellectuals. It was no less a slogan for the apprehensive American Jew of the 1930s and 1940.

An indication of American Jewish insecurity was displayed by *Congress Weekly*, the organ of the most outspokenly Jewish organization of its day. When it adopted a new masthead on February 20, 1939, it made this apologia:

> The American Jewish Congress, true to the Jewish tradition, safeguards the status of Jews in all lands. Loyal to the ideals of America, it unites American Jews on a democratic basis.
>
> There is no inconsistency between loyalty to America and loyalty in Jewry. The Jewish spirit is essentially modern and essentially American.

The tendency, therefore, to maintain a low profile and not to raise "Jewish" issues in the *Kristallnacht* and *St. Louis* periods can be understood. *But to understand is not necessarily to excuse.* When one considers the pain and suffering of German Jews in late 1938 and the terrible agony of 907 trapped refugees on the *St. Louis* in June 1939, the reluctance of American Jews to speak out clearly and demand relief for the victims must be considered a grievous failure, one that ultimately may have cost untold numbers of lives.

The strong restrictionist sentiment in the country provided another reason for maintaining a low Jewish profile on the refugee issue. The public consensus was so overwhelmingly anti-alien that Senator Lewis B. Schwellenbach, Democrat of Washington, confided in 1940 that condemnation of aliens "is perhaps the best vote-getting argument in present-day politics. The politician can beat his breast and proclaim his loyalty to America. He can tell the unemployed man that he is out of work because some alien has a job."[3] The real effort of Jewish groups in those days, therefore, had to be directed not at expanding the quotas but at opposing the restrictionist forces who wanted to stop immigration altogether. The strategy was to mute the refugee issue entirely. Magazines like the *National Jewish Monthly, Opinion,* and *Congress Bulletin,* which regularly denounced Britain for closing the doors of Palestine, were silent on urging America to open her own doors.[4] Even when the Oswego Free Port was announced in June 1944, Jewish periodicals took pains to explain that Free Ports did not represent a change in immigration laws but only provided a temporary refuge for the homeless.[5]

Some observers were less than charitable when they analyzed the frightened reaction of American Jews to the refugee issue during the Holocaust. A contemporary analyst charged in 1943 that many American Jews subordinated the rescue of Hitler's victims to their own concern for safety and security in America.[6] One student of American Zionism, Samuel Halperin, suggests that much of the growth in American Jewry's pro-Palestine feelings during the 1930s was due to a "fear that Jewish refugee immigration into America, especially in the midst of an unresolved economic crisis, would only aggravate American anti-Semitism."[7] It is also possible that the total failure to attack the quota system was not purely the result of Jewish fears. The quotas may almost have been welcomed by Zionists as proof of their contention that only in a Jewish sovereign state might Jews find security.[8] The precise reason for the American Jewish reticence on the refugee issue in 1938–1939 will remain a matter for scholarly inquiry. What is no longer conjectural, however, is the fact that this reticence prevailed at a time when emigration from Germany and the rest of Europe was not only possible, but for the most part encouraged. How many Jews might have been saved from the ashes had American Jewry spoken out strongly in 1938–1939 will never be known.

The situation had changed drastically for the worse by December 1942 when the issue was no longer one of providing havens for immigrants but rather finding ways to rescue the intended victims of the Nazis. By the end of December 1942, any American Jew who had read *The New York Times* or a Jewish newspaper or periodical knew that 2 million Jews had been murdered and about 4 million more were threatened with a similar fate. An immediate, strong public Jewish campaign for dissemination of the facts and a pressing for rescue effort might have been expected. Such a campaign did develop, but it was neither immediate nor strong. It focused around the Madison Square Garden rally of March 1, 1943.

It is possible that the tentative nature of the response was the result of an inability on the part of many to comprehend the "facts" of the Final Solution, despite the numerous news reports. Why should American Jews have believed something that was inherently unbelievable—namely, that Jews were being killed by the millions for the crime of being Jewish? The crime was unprecedented: "They were accused of living, of having been born," wrote Yehuda Bauer.[9] How could anyone comprehend such a possibility?

Those who heard the reports of mass murders from eye-witnesses often did not believe them. A survivor from Auschwitz in its early days, May 1942, complained bitterly about the reaction of those to whom he tried to tell the story:

> The worst thing was that you simply could not get through to those closest to you. That gave you a terrible sense of isolation, as if a steam-roller was about to run you over. You felt like screaming it from the housetops but knew it was just a waste of your breath—no one would believe a word you told them.[10]

The reports were not even believed by the Jews in the Warsaw ghetto when their underground press informed them that deportation meant death.[11] How then could American Jews, so distant from the scene, be expected to accept the "eclipse of sanity"[12] from the world?

Americans in general did not seem to believe the reports, either. In January 1943, the month following the United Nations announcement of the murder of 2 million, a public-opinion poll reported that less than half the American population believed the announcement. Most labeled it a rumor or expressed no opinion. Almost two years later, in December 1944, 75 percent believed that the Nazis had "murdered many people in concentration camps," but when asked to guess how many, most gave figures of under 100,000, perhaps the largest figure they could humanly conceive of. By May of 1945, when all of the camps had been liberated, the median figure was still only 1 million.[13] Americans, it would appear, could not comprehend genocide on so immense a scale. Is it possible, then, that Jews were unable to believe it either?[14]

Aside from the incomprehensible nature of the Final Solution for normal minds, there is a psychological basis for disbelieving the reports about the annihilation of millions of Jews. People often deny those things with which they cannot cope. This is a common tendency among patients with certain illnesses. Many European Jews, starting with German Jews, tried to deny what their eyes beheld. They masked the denial behind misjudgments of the enemy or a false optimism about the future. American Jews may have been similarly affected. Overcome by the pain of their brothers and sisters, frustrated over their lack of power to effect a change in Washington, and frightened by the relentless and efficient process of annihilation, they chose to deny, minimize, or ignore the terrible news that was before their eyes.[15]

If American Jews did not believe the reports, however, American Jewish leaders certainly did. Should not this problem of credibility have elicited from them a strong public relations effort to convey the truth to the largest number? The greater the disbelief, the harder the Jewish establishment should have worked. By means of rallies special observances, days of prayer, banners and posters in Jewish meeting places, restrictions on celebrations, fasting, and other such methods, the leaders of American Jewry should have made it impossible for their followers to ignore the awful truth and to deny the bitter reality. It is difficult to understand why this was not done.

In addition to the problem of disbelief, a realistic distraction mitigated against an adequate Jewish involvement with the Jews of Europe. American Jews had their own personal concerns with regard to the war—husbands, fathers, brothers, and loved ones were in the armed forces, facing danger and possible death. By the end of World War II there were 16 million American men in the armed forces, among them 550,000 American Jews. They were the object of the most immediate concern and worry for their families in the United States, a personal concern and worry that transcended in importance the plight of European Jews.[16]

Still another factor inhibited the Jewish response in this period and throughout the Holocaust: the implicit trust placed by American Jewry in Franklin D. Roosevelt. It is hard to understand the Roosevelt syndrome from this side of the Holocaust, looking back from an age in which all politicians are suspect. American Jews in those days were suspicious of local politicians, but tended to look to the national leadership "as the source of all good."[17] And the best of the good they thought was Roosevelt. His words could "bring solace and hope to millions of Jews who mourn."[18] His declaration against the Nazis would be "an expression of the conscience of the American people."[19] The attitude toward Roosevelt, as revealed in the Jewish press, was reverential and subservient, obsequious in requests and fawn-ing in gratitude for small favors. No matter how little the United States government did for Jews, no matter the President's reti-cence on the Wagner-Rogers Act, no matter the omission of "Jews" from the Moscow Declaration, no matter Secretary Stim-son's testimony against a Congressional resolution deploring the White Paper, no matter that after all the hopes raised by the Free Ports proposal, only one Free Port was established with ac-commodations for a mere 1,000 refugees—there was hardly a word of direct criticism of the President in all the Jewish press read for these six periods. Even the most outspoken writers—Rosmarin, Greenberg, Syrkin, Bergson—refrained from criti-cizing Roosevelt. This uniform pattern suggests the existence of a basic confidence on the part of American Jews in his leader-ship and a fundamental trust that somehow, in some way, Roo-sevelt would do what had to be done.

One of the most bitter critics of American Jewish inaction during the Holocaust, Elie Wiesel, seems to have come sadly to the same conclusion that this press study suggests:

> What happened after Rabbi Wise was released from his pledge [to Welles about keeping the reports of the exter-minations secret until they were confirmed]? Not much. Not much at all. Did he and the other Jewish leaders proclaim hunger strikes to the end? Did they organize daily, weekly marches to the White House? They should have shaken heaven and earth, echoing the agony of their doomed brethren. Taken in by Roosevelt's personality, they, in a way, became accomplices in his inaction. . . .[20]

There are several responses that might be given to the ago-nizing questions posed by Wiesel.[21] But the basic answer was supplied by the questioner himself. An act of civil disobedience would have been directed ultimately against the President. This was unthinkable to Jews at that time. Whatever the President's failings, Jews believed that in a world filled with enemies, Roo-sevelt represented the best that Jews could hope for. He was, after all, winning the war against the arch enemy. There was not even a possibility of exerting pressure on him in 1944, an election year, because, as Marie Syrkin, who lived through the Holocaust, writes:

[There was] a genuine conviction held by most Jews at the time that in a world of enemies, Roosevelt represented the best Jews could hope for. He was the man who had re-called the American ambassador to Germany after *Kris-tallnacht* and had finally managed to get the United States to join the fight against Nazi Germany. The fact that an election was in the offing made American Jews all the more nervous. . . . I recall the near panic that would seize many of us for fear that Roosevelt might fail of election, because the forces against him were viewed as actively dangerous and inimical, whereas we believed that though Roosevelt could perhaps be more daring he was probably judging what the traffic would bear. The last thing the Jews wanted to do was to attack him in an election year and in any way jeopardize his victory.[22]

Roosevelt, then, could not be challenged. He had to be sup-ported. Thus did American Jews become "accomplices to his in-action."

The Warsaw ghetto uprising, discussed in this study, exem-plifies many tragic events of the Holocaust that were unknown to American Jewry and could not be expected to have elicited a contemporary response. Most of these events happened in the period between September 1939 and December 1942. Alarm-ing reports filtered out of Europe during those early years but definitive news upon which might be built strong and enduring responses was not yet available.[23]

The period between July 1943 and January 1944, when a campaign was undertaken to create a rescue agency, revealed some of the ongoing political struggles in the Jewish commu-nity, which seriously inhibited strong action in behalf of Euro-pean Jewry. The divisions between Zionists and anti-Zionists, activists and *shtadlanim,* and establishment and nonestablish-ment organizations, were luxuries that the Jewish community could never afford. During the Holocaust, however, they prob-ably cost many lives.[24] One example: Had Bergson and Wise been able to work together, the War Refugee Board might have been created months earlier, and many lives might have been saved.

In the final period of this analysis, the time of the Hungar-ian deportations, the public Jewish response was pitifully weak. The reasons seemed to center around a feeling of hopelessness, helplessness, and fatigue, emotions that were not unique to this period.[25] In the final analysis, the pace of the Holocaust was not determined in Washington but in Berlin. Moreover, Washington did not evince much interest in saving Jews. How much, therefore, could realistically be done by American Jews? Despair was a realistic state of mind under the circumstances.

WAS ENOUGH DONE?

To ask "was enough done" may be to engage in a futile rhetorical exercise. How can enough be done if 6 million were killed? And if 1 million had been saved, could one say enough was done? When a people is victimized by genocide, no help can be considered enough. America could have done much more. Roosevelt had many options he failed to use, from temporary havens to mortgaging immigration quotas for future years, from warning the murderers more often to bombing the camps and the rail lines leading to them.[26] But Roosevelt was concerned about winning the war. He was not going to be distracted from the war effort without strong Jewish pressure. That pressure never came. Had it come, had Roosevelt acted accordingly, had America's power been exerted in behalf of rescue, there is still no guarantee that many lives would have been saved. Ultimately, the key to saving lives lay with the murderers rather than with even the best intentioned rescuers. This was the unhappy lesson learned by the War Refugee Board.[27] This may also have been the unconscious conclusion of a despairing American Jewry as Hungarian Jews by the tens of thousands rolled, packed in cattle cars, to the gas chambers of Auschwitz.

Perhaps, then, no amount of protesting, rallying, or the exercise of political-pressure tactics would have accomplished much. But in the light of what American Jews knew, might one not have expected that the Holocaust would have been reflected in some way in their daily, weekly, or even yearly lives?

> Day after day, night after night, hundreds and thousands were disappearing into mass graves or burning to cinders. All of this was known to the free world, and yet . . . holidays were celebrated; charity balls and dinners were or-

ganized; people went to the concerts, to the theatre. . . .
Everything went on as if nothing were happening.[28]

This description is not a distorted view of life as it existed in
the American Jewish community during the Holocaust, at least
as far as one can tell from the press. Some observers were of-
fended by the normal, sometimes festive, atmosphere. "Can
United States Jewry say with a clear conscience that we have done
all we could to save Jews in Europe," asked a *Morning Journal*
editorial; "thus far we have contented ourselves with issuing
statements between banquets."[29] A writer for the *Jewish Spectator* bemoaned the "careless gaiety" and "ostentatious luxury" of
Jewish summer crowds at the beach resorts, the "giggling" and
the golfing, the mah-jongg, and the horse races, the casual in-
dulgent life, enjoyed by Jews.[30]

The normal life patterns extended to the literary world also.
The *Menorah Journal* marked its thirtieth anniversary in the
spring issue of 1944, while Hungarian Jewry was being annihilated. Its lead statement, by Henry Hurwitz, expressed thanks
for this milestone, and joy "over the good fortune of our immunity [from war] here." Without a word about the tragedy that
had befallen—and was still befalling—European Jewry, Hurwitz wrote:

American Jewry is now the largest community in the world.
It enjoys complete freedom of expression and conduct. On
its own psychological state, and on the quality of its leadership, depends whether it will rise to spiritual and cultural heights, further enriching American civilization.[31]

Not everyone was so sanguine about the spiritual and cultural heights of American Jewry. One Jewish educator was more
pessimistic about what he saw. Writing in *Hadoar* in January 1943,
one month after the United Nations announced to the world
that 2 million European Jews had been murdered by the Nazis
and that 4 million more were candidates for the same fate, Judah
Piltch looked ahead to a time of spiritual accounting and asked
a troubling question:

And what will happen when my son asks me tomorrow:
"What did you do while your brothers were being exter-

minated and tortured by the Nazi murderers?" What will I say and what will I be able to tell him? Shall I tell him that I lived in a generation of weaklings and cowards who were neither moved nor shocked when they heard of hundreds of thousands of their brothers being led to the slaughter hour by hour, day by day, year by year? Shall I describe this chapter in the annals of American Jewry and admit that our people did not meet the test of history? Shall I tell him that the forces of destruction which enveloped their European brothers did not disturb the slumber of American Jews or arouse them from their inertia? Or shall I defend my generation, saying that we did not have the guts to launch a strong campaign because we knew well that our efforts would be unavailing and that we had no power to affect the situation. I shall, however, certainly not dare to tell my son about the "business as usual" conduct of our lives at a time when the press was informing us about the extermination of complete communities. I would be ashamed to face him with such a description.

And my heart pounds within me because I am sure that I shall have to give an accounting some day. Of course I will tell him of the public fast that the rabbis called for the people in order to mourn their dead. But then I shall have to admit the truth and add that from 5,000,000 Jews less than 30,000 came to the *shuls* and fewer than 50,000 came to the protest meetings called that day by the Jewish organizations.

Apparently our hearts are like stone. We do not tremble at the reports of the European Holocaust. We are still mired in the 49 levels of indifference and passivity, as if nothing has happened in our world.[32]

One looks in vain, during the six periods covered in this study, for a sign that American Jews altered some aspect of their lifestyle to indicate their awareness of the plight of their European brothers. There was no need for civil disobedience; some small gesture would have sufficed to keep the matter at the forefront of their consciousness and to generate feelings of sympathy and solidarity. Why, for example, was there not a regular fast day each month or a special prayer circulated by the Synagogue Council of America to be recited at sabbath services every week? Why could not the Holy Ark in each synagogue have been draped in black, so that an American Jew entering a house of worship would be reminded that European Jews were being slaughtered even as his prayers were being recited. There were other suggestions similar to these made by young rabbinical students at the Jewish Theological Seminary.[33] But none of them was adopted. The result was a painful reenactment of a scene described by the poet Chaim Nachman Bialik in his "City of Slaughter":

> *The sun was shining*
> *The trees were flowering*
> *And the murderer kept on killing*

Among the many tragic lessons of the Holocaust, this may be one of the most instructive. The Final Solution may have been *unstoppable* by American Jewry, but it should have been *unbearable* for them. And it wasn't. This is important, not alone for our understanding of the past, but for our sense of responsibility in the future.

Fear not your enemies,
for they can only kill you.
Fear not your friends, for
they can only betray you.
Fear only the indifferent,
who permit the killers and
betrayers to walk safely
on the earth.

EDWARD YASHINSKY:
Yiddish poet who
survived the Holocaust
only to dic in a Communist
prison in Poland

NOTES
ABBREVIATIONS

The following is a list of abbreviations used in the notes (and occasionally the text) of this study. The names of other publications are written out.

AJHSQ	American Jewish Historical Society Quarterly
AJH	American Jewish History
AJYB	American Jewish Year Book
CB	Congress Bulletin
CJR	Contemporary Jewish Record
CW	Congress Weekly
HIAS	Hebrew Immigrant Aid Society
JDC	American Jewish Joint Distribution Committee
JA	Jewish Advocate
JE	Jewish Exponent
JF	Jewish Frontier
JLC	Jewish Labor Committee
JS	Jewish Spectator
JTA	Jewish Telegraphic Agency Daily News Bulletin
MJ	Morning Journal
NJM	National Jewish Monthly
NP	The New Palestine
NYT	The New York Times

CHAPTER 1: A DIFFICULT QUESTION

1. Saul S. Friedman, *No Haven for the Oppressed* (Detroit: Wayne State University Press, 1973), p. 11, observes that the revisionist school of Holocaust literature began with Rolf Hochhuth's play *The Deputy* in 1964, which accused the Vatican of failing to intervene to save the Jews of Europe.

2. Though a journalist by profession, Morse was sufficiently systematic and thorough in his research to warrant his book's acceptance as history.

3. See Henry L. Feingold in his review essay on Morse, *Six Million*, *AJHSQ*, September 1968, p. 152. "What did these *shtadlanim* do in the face of the emergency? What of Samuel Rosenman . . . or Herbert Lehman, Bernard Baruch, Benjamin Cohen, Felix Frankfurter, Sidney Hillman, David Lilienthal, Isadore Lubin, David Niles and Anna Rosenberg?" See also, Henry L. Feingold, *The Politics of Rescue* (New Brunswick, N.J.: Rutgers University Press, 1970), pp. 10–15, and Friedman, *No Haven*, p. 20.

4. Many Jews, of course, undertook behind-the-scenes efforts during the Holocaust. Some of these have been documented, though much more remains to be done. Among the works that touch on this non-public activity, besides the general works already mentioned, are the following: Yehuda Bauer, *My Brother's Keeper* (Philadelphia: The Jewish Publication Society of America, 1974) and its sequel, *American Jewry and the Holocaust* (Detroit: Wayne State University Press, 1981); Naomi W. Cohen, *Not Free to Desist* (Philadelphia: The Jewish Publication Society of America, 1972); Oscar Handlin, *A Continuing Task* (New York: Random House, 1964); A. Leon Kubowitzki, et al., eds., *Unity in Dispersion* (New York: World Jewish Congress, 1948); Nathan Schachner, *The Price of Liberty* (New York: The American Jewish Committee, 1948); and Milton Goldin, *Why They Give* (New York: Macmillan Publishing Co., 1976). Isaac Lewin, in his "Attempt at Rescuing European Jews with the Help of Polish Diplomatic Missions During World War II," *The Polish Review*, 22:4 (1977), pp. 3–23, discusses some of the private efforts by religious Jewry in America for relief and rescue. He specifically cites the work of the Vaad Ha-Hatzala (Rescue Committee), established in 1941, the Union of Orthodox Rabbis of the United States, and Agudat Israel, the world Orthodox Jewish organization. See also Efraim Zuroff's study on the Vaad Ha-Hatzala and the JDC and Frederick A. Lazin's analysis of the American Jewish Committee's early response to the Holocaust both in *American Jewish History*, 68:3 (March, 1979). See also David S. Wyman, *Abandonment of the Jews* (New York: Pantheon Books, 1984) for a full discussion of the nonpublic activity in behalf of European Jews.

5. There are three major histories of the Holocaust: Gerald Reitlinger, *The Final Solution,* 2nd ed. (New York: Thomas Yoseloff, 1961); Raul H. Hilberg, *The Destruction of the European Jews* (Chicago: Quadrangle Books, 1961); and Lucy S. Dawidowicz, *The War Against the Jews 1933–1945* (New York: Holt, Rinehart and Winston, 1975). Reitlinger's chronology begins on p. 568.

6. The importance of the Jewish press as a representative source of information on what Jews said and felt is demonstrated in David Brody's "American Jewry, the Refugees and Immigration Restriction (1932–1942)," publication of the American Jewish Historical Society, 45:4 (June 1956), p. 220, n.2; Feingold, *Politics,* p. 356, and Bernard Postal, "The English-Jewish Press," *Dimensions in American Judaism,* Fall 1969, p. 30. Postal observes that more than half of the 185 English-language Jewish periodicals in 1969 were sponsored by national Jewish organizations. Only two monthlies were independent. The remaining eighty served local communities or compact geographical areas.

This study has also used an occasional primary source other than the press when the press accounts raised problems. See, for example, chapter 2, note 49. Secondary sources were also used for the same purpose.

7. See Postal, *op. cit.,* p. 31, and Aaron M. Neustadt, "An Orchid for the Jewish Press," *NJM,* November 1946, p. 108.

8. Robert E. Park, *The Immigrant Press and Its Control* (New York and London: Harper and Brothers, 1922), p. 89. Park's statement about the influence of the Jewish press and its validity as a source for understanding the feelings of the Yiddish reading public, was confirmed by Mordecai Soltes, *The Yiddish Press* (New York: Teachers College, Columbia University, 1924), p. 63. Both views were echoed substantially in later studies by B. Z. Goldberg in "The American Yiddish Press at Its Centennial," *Judaism,* Spring 1971, p. 225, and by Morris Laub in "A Lament for the Tog," *Conservative Judaism,* 26:4, pp. 63–66. On the circulation figures, see Nathan Goldberg, "Decline of the Yiddish Press," *Chicago Jewish Forum,* Fall 1944, p. 17, and B. Z. Goldberg, "The American Yiddish Press," pp. 227, 229.

9. On the role of the *Times* as the "paper of record," see the following: Gay Talese, *The Kingdom and the Power* (New York and Cleveland: World Publishing Company, 1969), p. 29; Meyer Berger, *History of the Times* (New York: Simon and Schuster, 1951), p. 563. See also Edwin Emery, *The Press and America* (Englewood Cliffs, N.J.: Prentice-Hall, 1954), p. 654, on Arthur Hays Sulzberger's concern when he took over the paper in 1935 after the death of Adolph S. Ochs to "live up to his responsibilities as the head of the country's 'newspaper of record.' " Talese describes the *New York Herald Tribune* in 1943 as being vastly inferior to the *Times* in terms of reporting the news (p. 198). He as-

serts that *"The Times* was the bible, emerging each morning with a view of life that thousands of readers accepted as reality. They accepted it on the simple theory that what appeared in *The Times* must be true" (p. 7). For the acceptance of the *Times* by New York Jews, see David Wolf Silverman, "The Jewish Press: A Quadrilingual Phenomenon," in Martin E. Marty, et al., *The Religious Press in America* (New York: Holt, Rinehart and Winston, 1963), p. 164.

10. H. S. Linfield, "Jewish Communities of the United States: Number and Distribution of Jews of the United States in Urban Places and in Rural Territory," *AJYB*, 62 (5701, 1940–1941), p. 231. There is some question about the reliability of Linfield's statistics, but there is no scholarly disagreement about the relative size of the four largest Jewish communities in the United States. It is this finding of Linfield which is of consequence for this study. For Linfield's statistics on Philadelphia see p. 236, on Boston, p. 231. See also his table VI, p. 224.

11. Freda Kirchway, "While the Jews Die," *The Nation*, March 13, 1943, p. 366.

12. For the immigration figures cited, see Feingold, *Politics*, pp. 126, 136–37, David S. Wyman, *Paper Walls* (Boston: University of Massachusetts Press, 1968), p. 209, and *JTA*, April 5, 1944, p. 4. Only in 1939 were the relevant quotas filled: Feingold, "Who Shall Bear the Guilt of the Holocaust: The Human Dilemma," *AJH*, 68:3 (March 1979).

13. Feingold, "Roosevelt and the Holocaust: Reflections on New Deal Humanitarianism," *Judaism*, 18 (Summer 1969), pp. 269–70; and Feingold, *Politics*, p. 198.

14. Francis L. Lowenheim, Harold D. Langley, and Manfred Jonas, eds., *Roosevelt and Churchill* (New York: Saturday Review Press/E. P. Dutton and Co., 1975), pp. 73–74. See also Hilberg, *op. cit.*, p. 721.

15. Cohen was interviewed by Saul Friedman on June 5, 1968; Friedman quotes him, *op. cit.*, p. 225.

16. This evaluation is made by Feingold in *Politics*, p. 7, and in "Who Shall Bear," n. 10, pp. 273–74. The population figures are from Linfield, *op. cit.*, pp. 216–17 and 225.

17. Stephen S. Wise, *As I See It* (New York: Jewish Opinion Publishing House, 1944), p. 67.

18. Hilberg, *op. cit.*, p. 671. The public opinion poll is reported in Charles Herbert Stember et al., *Jews in the Mind of America* (New York: Basic Books, 1966), p. 116. The reader should be aware that all data from public opinion polls in the 1930s and 1940s are open to question because of deficiencies in the methods used by the pollsters.

19. See Stember, *op. cit.*, pp. 8 and 121. See also Joshua Trachtenberg, in H. C. Englebrecht and Joshua Trachtenberg et al., *How to*

Combat Anti-Semitism in America (New York: Jewish Opinion Publishing Corp., 1937), p. 33

20. See Wyman, *Paper Walls,* p. 3 ff., Feingold, review of Morse's *Six Million,* p. 153, and *Politics,* p. 128ff, and Samuel Halperin, *The Political World of American Zionism,* (Detroit: Wayne State University Press, 1961), p. 341, n. 42.

21. Feingold, *Politics,* p. 35. See also Wyman, *Abandonment,* p. 337.

22. Feingold, review of Morse's *Six Million,* p. 153. See also Chaim Weizmann, *Trial and Error* (New York: Harper and Brothers, 1949), p. 420. Parenthetically, it might be noted with some surprise that Weizmann's autobiography, published in 1949, contains almost nothing on the Holocaust. It is almost as if the Jewish tragedy in Europe was not a priority item on his personal agenda.

23. See S. Friedman, *op. cit.,* pp. 225–26; Feingold, "Roosevelt and the Holocaust," p. 270; and Lawrence H. Fuchs, *The Political Behavior of American Jews* (Glencoe, Ill.: The Free Press, 1956), pp. 76–78.

24. See Menachem Rosensaft, "The Holocaust: History as Aberration," *Midstream,* May 1977, p. 55.

25. Shlomo Katz, "6,000,000 and 5,000,000: Notes in *Midstream,*" *Midstream,* March 1964, p. 14; Walter Laqueur, *The Terrible Secret* (Boston: Little Brown & Co., 1980), p. 208; Bernice S. Tannenbaum, *NYT,* November 13, 1977, Sec. 4, p. 16.

CHAPTER 2: KRISTALLNACHT

1. Hannah Arendt, *Eichmann in Jerusalem* (New York: The Viking Press, 1963), pp. 207–209, gives a summary of the testimony of Zindel Grynszpan, at the Eichmann Trial. Cf. Bauer, *My Brother's Keeper,* pp. 243–45, A. Kubowitzki, *Unity,* p. 97, and Dawidowicz, *War Against Jews,* p. 100. A graphic description of this background to the pogrom is provided in Rita Thalmann and Emanuel Feinermann, *Crystal Night 9–10 November 1938* (New York: Coward, McCann and Geohegan, 1974), pp.27–42.

2. Arendt, *Eichmann,* p. 209. Grynszpan's motives remain enshrouded in mystery. Arendt argues that he was an emotionally disturbed youngster, who knocked about Brussels and Paris for years without finishing school. Ironically, his victim, Vom Rath, was under investigation by the Gestapo at the time for expressing anti-Nazi views and for harboring sympathy for Jews. Reitlinger, *op. cit.,* p. 11, corroborates this view. The ultimate fate of Grynszpan personally is similarly unclear. Friedman, *op. cit.,* p. 260, n. 55, claims that Grynszpan

was tortured to death by the Nazis on September 1, 1941. Arendt, *loc. cit.*, writes that Grynszpan was never tried by the Nazis and that he survived the war. Reitlinger, *op. cit.*, p. 33, cites a report by Kurt Grossman in *Aufbau* (New York), May 10, 1957, to the effect that Grynszpan was still alive and residing in Paris.

3. See Dawidowicz, *War Against Jews*, pp. 101–102; Reitlinger, *op. cit.*, p. 16, and Hilberg, *op. cit.*, p. 26. *JTA*, November 14, 1938, reported internment figures of between 35,000 and 50,000.

4. *NYT*, November 17, 1938, p. 24. It is hard to recall another subject—except for a war or Watergate—that has been treated so extensively and intensively by the *Times*.

5. "American Press Comments on Nazi Riots," *NYT*, November 12, 1938, p. 4.

6. *NYT*, November 12, 1938, p. 14.

7. *NYT*, November 12, 1938, p. 6. A highly abbreviated list of community leaders who spoke out forcefully in response to *Kristallnacht* would include Herbert Hoover, Mayor LaGuardia (who spoke almost daily), William Green, president of the AFL (who called for a nationwide boycott of German goods), John L. Lewis, chairman of the CIO, Archbishop Michael J. Curley of Baltimore, James L. Conant, president of Harvard, and Norman Thomas, Socialist leader.

8. *NYT*, November 15, 1938, p. 2. See also Morse, *op. cit.*, pp. 231–32.

9. In spite of being a Communist-front organization, the committee was able to capitalize on the general revulsion in the community and attract seventeen governors and a number of senators as sponsors of the rally, *JTA*, November 22, 1938, p. 6. The strong Communist response in this country may have been stimulated by editorials on November 16 and 17 in *Pravda* condemning the pogroms. David M. Szonyi suggests this causal link in his "The Holocaust: Prelude and Postscript," *Jewish Currents*, June 1966, p. 34.

10. This was officially a nonsectarian protest, but it would appear from the leadership that it was organized by Jews. The *NYT*, November 24, 1938, p. 7, reported that one of the prime movers was Charles Ackerman, general manager of the United Independent Retail Grocers and Food Dealers association. The best response to the protest was in the Bronx.

11. *JTA*, December 11, 1939, pp. 1–2.

12. *The Secret Diary of Harold L. Ickes*, Vol. II *The Inside Struggle 1936–1939* (New York: Simon and Schuster, 1954), p. 503.

13. A Gallup Poll, reported in the *Times* December 12, 1938, recorded that 94 percent of its respondents were opposed to the Germans' treatment of the Jews, while 97 percent condemned German treatment of Catholics.

14. Cf. Anne O'Hare McCormick, *NYT,* November 21, 1938, p. 18.

15. Cordell Hull, *The Memoirs of Cordell Hull,* Vol. I (New York: The Macmillan Co., 1948), p. 599.

16. *NYT,* November 30, 1938, p. 1.

17. *CJR,* January 1939, pp. 45–47.

18. Stember, *op. cit.,* p. 140.

19. S. Friedman, *op. cit.,* p. 31, quoting Hadley Cantril, ed., *Public Opinion, 1935–1946* (Princeton: Princeton University Press, 1951), p. 384.

20. S. Friedman, *op. cit.,* p. 86.

21. The number of Jews in Germany in November 1938 was usually estimated in the press at 600,000. Feingold, *Politics,* p. 311, n. 6, suggests that the accepted figure is 500,000 but cites another, possibly more reliable estimate of 343,552 by Bruno Blau, "The Jewish Population of Germany, 1939–1945," *Jewish Social Studies,* 12:2 (April 1950), pp. 161–72. Blau's figure seems to be accepted by Dawidowicz, *op. cit.,* p. 374.

22. Editorial, *NYT,* November 16, 1938, p. 22.

23. *NYT,* December 1938, p. 8.

24. See Andrew Sharf, *The British Press and Jews Under Nazi Rule* (London: Oxford University Press, 1964), pp. 168 and 173.

25. *CJR,* January 1939, p. 49. The quote is from the *Philadelphia Record.*

26. *NYT,* December 1, 1939, p. 12.

27. The *New Republic,* November 30, 1938, p. 87.

28. Editorial, "Condemn and Shame Germany," *The Day,* November 12, 1938, p. 1.

29. The General Jewish Council was the umbrella organization which united, for a brief period, the four major Jewish defense agencies of the day: The American Jewish Committee, The American Jewish Congress, B'nai B'rith, and the Jewish Labor Committee. Its role in effectively silencing Jewish protests over *Kristallnacht* and its aftermath is discussed on page 57.

30. See Margoshes, "New and Views," *The Day,* November 13, 1938, p. 1.

31. *MJ,* November 13, 1938, p. 3, and November 14, p. 1.

32. Editorial, *Forward,* November 18, 1938, p. 8. See also Sholem Asch's article on November 19 in which he predicted that the world would turn against Hitler. "The spectators are beginning to stand up for us. Who Knows? Through our blood Hitler rose and through our blood he will fall." It is noteworthy that the *Forward*'s optimism was not shared by the Jewish Labor Committee whose views it greatly reflected.

33. This function of the Yiddish press was described by the follow-

ing authors: B. Z. Goldberg, "The American Yiddish Press," p. 225; Silverman, "The Jewish Press," p. 139; and Oscar Handlin, *Adventure in Freedom* (New York: McGraw Hill Book Co., 1954). While *The Day* and *MJ* also continued to perform that function during the *Kristallnacht* period, the crisis brought about a reduction for several weeks in the amount of space and the number of editorials and features devoted to general matters. Such a reduction was not apparent in the *Forward*.

34. M. Osherowitz, *Forward*, November 18, 1938, p. 8.

35. *NYT*, December 5, 1938, and MJ, November 23, 1938.

36. In 1938 that judgment seemed to be correct, but historians now question whether Roosevelt ever was "the voice of America's conscience." See Feingold, *Politics*, Friedman, *op. cit.*, and Wyman, *Paper Walls* and *Abandonment*, for their well-documented, critical analysis of Roosevelt's moral posture during the Holocaust.

37. *NP*, front-page article on November 8 and 25, 1938, and a page 4 editorial in the November 25 issue.

38. *Hadassah Newsletter*, December 1938, p. 68.

39. In fact, both the *NYT*, November 28, 1939, p. 4, and the *JTA*, November 27, 1938, p. 4, reported that the tragedy of German Jewry was brought to this Pittsburgh convention through Mayor LaGuardia's strong telegram to the president of Junior Hadassah, condemning German brutality. The telegram had enough of an impact to warrant treatment by these two news sources, but the subject was not deemed important enough to be included in the *Hadassah Newsletter*'s report.

40. *Notes and News*, February 20, 1939, p. 4, n. 54, quoting the address of Joseph Willen at the General Assembly of the Council of Jewish Federations and Welfare Funds in January 1939.

41. *Ibid.*

42. *Jewish Center*, March 1939, p. 1.

43. See Gilbert Murray, "In Defense of Civilization," *Menorah Journal*, 27 (Spring 1939), p. 122ff, and Carnzu Clark, p. 217ff.

44. M. Shoshani, "The Land of Slaughter," *Hadoar*, November 18, 1938, p. 34.

45. *JE*, December 2, 1938, p. 4. This was a courageous position for a Jewish paper to take, as is demonstrated later in this chapter. See also *JE*, November 18, 1938, p. 4. On the whole, the *Jewish Exponent* seems to have been a rather provincial paper, devoting its news columns mostly to Philadelphia Jewish news, anniversaries, and communal events.

46. *JA*, November 18, 1938, p. 4.

47. Nathan Schachner, *op. cit.*, p. 119. Cf. N. Cohen, *op. cit.*, p. 225, and *CJR*, November 1938, p. 20.

48. General Jewish Council, minutes of meeting, November 13, 1938.
49. *Ibid.*
50. The American Jewish leaders who were present at the November 13 meeting of the council, according to the listing in its minutes, were Dr. Stephen S. Wise, Arthur S. Meyer, Sol C. Stroock, Carl Sherman, Edward Greenbaum, Carl Austrian, Richard Rothschild, Henry Monsky, Maurice Bisgyer, Adolph Held, I. A. Goldberg, Isaiah Minkoff, Louis Fabricant, Judge Samuel Rosenman, Sidney Wallach, Sigmund Livingston, Louis Hollander, Joseph Weinberg, I. D. Wolf, Judge A. K. Cohen, Edward Schanfarber, Leonard Finder, Reuben Guskin, George Backer, Lillie Shultz, Louis Segal, and Gedalia Bublick.
51. This statement was carried widely in the Jewish press.
52. Schachner, *op. cit.,* p. 111, and Feingold, *Politics,* pp. 12–13. Harry Alderman, a former editor of the *AJYB,* published by the American Jewish Committee, corroborated in an oral interview (August 3, 1975) the fact that the committee frequently spoke through others and that many statements made by non-Jews at the time were actually the products of the committee's writers and spokesmen.
53. Schachner, *op. cit.,* p. 112.
54. *Ibid.* The view was that of Joseph Proskauer, expressed at an executive committee meeting of the American Jewish Committee, April 9, 1933. The two opposing approaches on the part of American Jews with regard to helping their brethren overseas did not originate with the rise of Hitler. They first appeared in nineteenth-century America in reaction to the Damascus blood libel in 1840 and the Mortara case in 1858. There were those who favored public protests and mass meetings in response to these events while others preferred to exert pressure upon public officials, behind the scenes, in order to enlist their help for beleaguered Jews. See Hyman B. Grinstein, *The Rise of the Jewish Community of New York 1654–1860* (Philadelphia: The Jewish Publication Society of America, 1945), pp. 422–39. Note particularly his description of the *shtadlanut* approach as it was practiced by the leaders of Congregation Shearith Israel in New York, pp. 438–39.
55. Editorial, *CB,* November 25, 1938, p. 2. The reference was to an emergency conference of delegates from all the organizations in the New York area at the Commodore Hotel. The conference resolved that (1) there be no settlement of Jewish refugees in former German colonies; (2) the General Jewish Council be asked to formulate a common policy on refugees; and (3) the economic boycott be intensified.
56. Stephen S. Wise, *Challenging Years: The Autobiography of Stephen S. Wise* (New York: G. P. Putnam Sons, 1949), pp. 264–65. Wise's explanation for his own turn to reticence is open to some question. He

was still reticent during the *St. Louis* episode when there was no public outcry.

57. Justine Wise Polier and James Waterman Wise, eds., *The Personal Letters of Stephen Wise* (Boston: The Beacon Press, 1956), p. 252.

58. See Emanuel Ringelblum, *Notes from the Warsaw Ghetto* (New York: McGraw-Hill Book Co., 1958), p. 291.

59. See Stember, *op. cit.*, p. 121, for the public opinion figures. The "sha-sha" policy is discussed in detail in Engelbrecht, Trachtenberg, et al., *op. cit.*, p. 33.

60. Editorial, "American Jewish Leadership," *Opinion*, May 1939, p. 5.

61. The minutes of the General Jewish Council's metting of December 18, 1938, report on the full compliance with the council's directive except for the Communist groups.

62. *NYT*, November 15, 1938, p. 2. The Communist-led protests reflected the enmity which then existed between the Soviet Union and Nazi Germany.

63. *Freiheit*, November 13, 1938, p. 1, November 14, 1938, p. 1, November 16, 1938, p. 1. This newspaper continuously called on all Jewish organizations to protest and send telegrams to public officials.

64. *Forward*, November 23, 1938, p. 6.

65. *The Day* and *Forward*, November 30, p. 1.

66. See *MJ*, November 15, 1938, p. 6, and *The Day*, November 16, 1938, p. 1.

67. The success of the Communist-led demonstrations, particularly the one at Madison Square Garden on November 21, would support this contention. So does a reading of the "Inquiring Photographer" column in *The Day*, November 20, 1938, p. 16.

68. See Glatstein's article in *The Day*, November 13, 1938, p. 4, and November 20, 1938, p. 4

69. B. Z. Goldberg, "To Scream or to be Silent?" *The Day*, November 25, 1938, p. 4.

70. Editorial, "Paging the General Council for Jewish Rights," *Reconstructionist*, December 2, 1938, pp. 4–5. The writer apparently was overzealous in his readiness to join with the Jewish People's Committee. That suggestion was retracted editorially in the December 16 issue, p. 6, while the fundamental opposition to the council's policy of silence was reaffirmed.

71. See *JTA*, November 30, 1938, p. 1, November 17, 1938, p. 3, and Dawidowicz, *War Against Jews*, p. 105, Feingold, *Politics*, pp. 3–21, Wyman, *Paper Walls*, p. vii and p. 35ff.

72. Stember, *op. cit.*, pp. 145, 148–59; and Louis Adamic, *America and the Refugees*, Public Affairs Pamphlets, No. 29 (New York: Public

Affairs Committee, 1939), pp. 2–3, 20–22. The American Jewish Committee published a pamphlet, *Refugee Facts,* designed to show that the refugee influx was small and non-Jewish and that it would not threaten employment but would, on the contrary, provide consumers who would create new jobs. The committee distributed 250,000 copies under the imprint of the American Friends Service Committee, preferring its own authorship to be anonymous. See Wyman, *Paper Walls,* pp. 9 and 26.

73. The editorial writer in *The Day,* November 21, 1938, p. 6, was surprised at this criticism.

74. Wyman, *Paper Walls,* cites an opinion survey in the *Brooklyn Jewish Examiner* of April 1938 on the question of enlarging the quotas 50 or 60 percent. Four out of six Jewish Congressmen opposed it. Three rabbis expressed fear of widespread public antagonism, which would in the end hurt the cause of the refugees.

75. *NJM,* May 1940, p. 295. This selfish concern was probably accompanied by resentment and prejudice on the part of former East European immigrants against the new refugees from Germany who may have been viewed as "arrogant," "demanding," and "hostile." These are among the epithets recalled by some present-day observers who were asked about this matter.

76. Feingold, *Politics,* pp. 14–15.

77. Adamic, *op. cit.,* p. 30. This concern was expressed by one who was in favor of enlarging the quotas. See also n. 74 for the rabbis' reaction. The same concern is cited by Thalmann and Feinermann, *op. cit.,* p. 142, on the part of the Jews in Sweden who preferred to send money to German Jews to help resettle them outside Europe but were reluctant to bring them to Sweden.

78. Bauer, *My Brother's Keeper,* pp. 184–210. The author shows how Polish anti-Semitism was fostered by a historical, Catholic hatred for the Jew, economic hardship, and fascism imported from Germany. At the Evian Conference in July 1938, Poland demanded resettlement for 50,000 emigrés a year, and she pressed the Jews to ask the conference for this. Romania modeled herself after Poland.

79. *JTA,* November 29, 1938, lead story on p. 1.

80. *NYT,* December 1, 1938, p. 12. Even Louis Adamic whose pamphlet, *America and the Refugees,* was written "to assuage public apprehension regarding the influx of refugees," according to Feingold (*Politics,* p. 363), asserts that this problem of potentially larger refugee migrations from other countries is "one of the chief difficulties which stand in the way of the United States enthusiastically opening its doors. . . ."

81. General Jewish Council, minutes, December 18, 1938.

82. Bauer, *My Brother's Keeper*, p. 232. However, his opposition was voiced in the spring of 1938, before *Kristallnacht.*

83. Morse, *op. cit.*, p. 234, and Selig Adler, "America's Moment of Failure," review of *Six Million, Midstream*, May 1968, p. 67.

84. FDR Library, Official File, 3186, Rosenman to Taylor, November 23, 1938, quoted in Feingold, *Politics*, p. 42.

85. *NYT*, November 26, 1938, p. 3, and *JTA*, November 27, 1938, p. 3

86. *MJ*, November 17, 1938, p. 1.

87. *MJ*, November 23, 1938, p. 3.

88. See the glowing tributes to Roosevelt's statesmanship, the sense of gratitude, and the acceptance of the grand gesture as sufficient, in editorials in *CB, Opinion, NP, JE,* and *JA* in their issues immediately following the President's statement.

89. Editorial, *The Day*, December 14, 1938, p. 6.

90. Editorial, *JF*, December 1938, p. 4.

91. Linfield, *op. cit.*, p. 229.

92. Feingold, *Politics,* p. 127, lists seven such options, all of which were topics of discussion during various periods of the refugee crisis.

93. *NYT*, November 21, 1938, p. 4; *JTA*, December 2, 1938, p. 4; Abba Hillel Silver, "Colonization and Jewish Refugees," *Notes and News*, No. 53 (January 11, 1939), p. 5ff. See also Henry Feingold, "Roosevelt and the Holocaust," p. 274, where he discusses the dilemma of the Zionists, who saw the cost of resettlement elsewhere undercutting support for Palestine and who therefore fought for Palestine to the exclusion of other possible havens.

94. See *JTA*, November 15, 1938, p. 4, November 16, 1938, p. 1, November 17, 1938, p. 6, and November 21, 1938, p. 6. See also *The Day*, November 16, 1938, p. 1, and *MJ*, November 20, 1938, p. 3.

95. *JA*, November 25, 1938, p. 1, and December 2. See also Erdberg in *The Day*, November 29, 1938, p. 1.

96. See Philip Ernest Schoenberg, "The American Reaction to the Kishinev Pogrom of 1903," *AJHSQ*, 68:3 (March, 1974), pp. 262–83 for an interesting contrast between American Jews' religious response to the Kishinev pogrom in 1903 and their response to *Kristallnacht.*

97. For a description of these fund-raising drives see *NYT*, November 30, 1938, p. 10, and *JTA*, December 2, 1938, p. 3, and December 12, 1938, p. 8.

98. *CJR*, January 1939, p. 6, and Bauer, *My Brother's Keeper*, p. 255.

99. Herbert Agar, *The Saving Remnant* (New York: The Viking Press, 1960), p. 93.

100. *Ibid.*, p. 94

101. See *The Day*, December 2, 1938, pp. 1–2, and November 23, 1938, p. 1. See also *MJ*, November 15, 1938, p. 3.

102. *NYT,* November 30, 1938, p. 15, and *JTA,* December 1, 1938, p. 3.

103. *JTA,* December 4, 1938, p. 2, and editorial, *CB,* December 9, 1938, p. 2.

104. See Moshe Gottlieb, "The Anti-Nazi Boycott in the American Jewish Community, 1933–41," Ph.D. dissertation, Brandeis University, 1967, p. 57 and pp. 170–73, and Joseph Tenenbaum, "The Anti-Nazi Boycott Movement in the United States," *Yad Vashem Studies,* 3 (1959), pp. 146–48 and p. 157.

105. *MJ,* November 18, 1938. The report, which was probably in part a reflection of wishful exaggeration, was nevertheless indicative of a heightened interest in boycott activity.

106. See *The Day,* November 18, 1938, p. 3, and S. Margoshes, "News and Views," *The Day,* November 21, 1938, p. 1. See also *NYT,* November 21, 1938, p. 6, and, for the tax proposal, see J. Fishman, *MJ,* November 24, 1938, p. 1. The author of the proposal, Frederick Schuman, Woodrow Wilson professor of government at Williams College, was not worried about German retaliation on American accounts in Germany, because German investments in America exceeded American investments in Germany by $139 million.

107. Feingold, *Politics,* pp. 44–53; Wyman, *Paper Walls,* pp. 53–55. See also Edwin Black, *The Transfer Agreement* (New York: Macmillan, 1984), for a full exploration of this issue.

108. For the Jewish reactions to the Schacht proposal see *CB,* December 23, 1938, pp. 1 and 2, and editorial, *JF,* January 1939, p. 4.

109. The phrase is from *CJR,* January 1939, p. 4.

110. Schoenberg, *op. cit.*

111. Stemberg, *op. cit.,* p. 8.

112. S. Friedman, *op. cit.,* p. 27.

113. Wyman, *Paper Walls,* p. 17; N. Cohen, *op. cit.,* p. 215.

114. Stember, *op. cit.,* pp. 137–38.

115. *JTA,* December 14, 1938, p. 3, reported Welles as follows: "Jews, because of their 'irrational nationalism,' are largely to blame for their persecution."

116. Lowenheim, Langley, and Jonas, eds., *op. cit.,* p. 308.

117. *JTA,* December 20, 1938, pp. 4 and 6, quoted Ickes' speech in Cleveland and Broun's article in the *World Telegram.*

118. Ickes, *op. cit.,* p. 510, entry of Saturday, December 3, 1938.

CHAPTER 3: THE SADDEST SHIP AFLOAT

1. Morse, *op. cit.,* devotes a chapter (pp. 273–88) of his book to the *St. Louis* as an example of the general American response. Gordon

Thomas and Max Morgan Witts, *Voyage of the Damned* (Greenwich, Conn.: Fawcett Publications, 1975), try to reconstruct the entire episode on the basis of research and personal interviews.

2. Wyman, *Paper Walls,* p. 37.

3. Dawidowicz, *War Against Jews,* p. 105. Mark Wischnitzer, *To Dwell in Safety* (Philadelphia: The Jewish Publication Society of America, 1948), p. 199, describes how the Gestapo would provide urban Jews with certificates of proficiency as farmers to enable them to gain entry to countries that would accept only bona fide farmers. See also Feingold, *Politics,* p. 65.

4. Kurt Grossman, in "Refugees, D.P.'s and Migrants," *The Institute Anniversary Volume 1941–1961* (New York: Institute of Jewish Affairs, World Jewish Congress, 1962) estimates that the trade in visas in 1938 and 1939 alone reached $2.5 million.

Although the most widely known of all the tragic voyages was that of the *St. Louis,* many other ships took their hapless cargo on a similar voyage in the late spring of 1939. H. Lang, *Forward,* June 18, 1939, Section II, p. 1, discussed twenty-two such ships filled with homeless Jews. Niger in *The Day,* June 10, 1938, p. 5, warned that the *St. Louis* was not an isolated case. "There have been others like it and there will be future ships on similar journeys," he wrote. The S.S. *Flandre* (French) and the S.S. *Orduna* (British) were refused entry by Cuba, and their complement of Jewish refugees had to be returned to Europe, reported the *NYT,* June 7, 1939, pp. 1, 11. The same was true of the German liner *Orinoco* with two hundred Jews, *JTA,* June 5, 1939, p. 2. That same liner, on a later voyage, received fifty-two Jews who were expelled by Cuba after having found refuge there for six weeks. These Jews too were returned to Germany, *NYT,* June 24, 1939, p. 5.

5. Thomas and Witts, *op. cit.* p. 134. See also Morse, *op. cit.,* pp. 272–74. The figure of 907 is obtained by subtracting, from the passenger total of 936, 6 nonrefugees, 22 refugees who had purchased authorized Cuban visas (price: $500 plus legal fees), and one refugee who died at sea.

6. Jacob Lestschinsky in "Where Do We Stand," *CB,* June 16, 1939, p. 5, indicated sympathy for the position of the Cuban president when he wrote: "Even the Cuban government . . . is deserving of some claim to understanding. The plain fact of the matter is that the government was simply afraid of the demogogic political agitation of the fascists." See also the report in *NYT,* June 1, 1939, p. 16, and a letter to the editor of the *NYT,* June 24, 1939, in which a Cuban correspondent explained that, with 300,000 unemployed on the island, Cuba could hardly afford to accept additional refugees. In fact, under fascist pressure, fifty-two Jewish refugees who were already in Cuba actually were expelled. See *NYT,* June 24, 1939, p. 5, and *MJ,* June 25, p. 1.

7. *NYT,* June 1, 1939, p. 16; June 7, 1939, p. 1; and June 8, 1939, p. 1. See also Morse, *op. cit.,* p. 275.

8. The exchange of telegrams between Bru and Rosenberg is found in *JTA,* June 11, 1939, p. 2, and reflects the tone of other communications between Cuba and the JDC. Rosenberg was obviously concerned about reports that Cuba was planning to expel some Jewish refugees who were already residents.

9. Morse, *op. cit.,* p. 275.

10. Editorial, *NYT,* June 8, 1939, p. 24. The *JTA,* June 12, 1939, p. 4, carried a headline: "NAZIS WARN OF CONCENTRATION CAMPS FOR THOSE WHO RETURN."

11. Morse, *op. cit.,* p. 277; Thomas and Witts, *op. cit.,* p. 239. Thomas and Witts (p. 153) imply that Captain Schroeder lingered off the Florida coast because of his assumption that America would accept at least the 734 if no other solution developed.

12. Quoted in Morse, *op. cit.,* p. 280. On the evening of June 6, when Captain Schroeder finally set his course back toward Europe, proceeding at a slow pace, the passengers did send a telegram to Roosevelt asking for help. There was no reply. *Ibid.,* p. 282.

13. *NYT,* June 9, 1939, p. 21; June 13, 1939, p. 1, and June 14, 1939, p. 11. See also *JTA,* June 12, 1939, p. 4, and Morse, *op. cit.,* p. 283. The final disposition was 214 in Belgium, 287 in England, 181 in Holland, and 224 in France. The 907th passenger turned out to be a traveling salesman from Hungary, who had boarded the *St. Louis* by mistake. In addition, France accepted another ninety-six refugees from the *Flandre,* and England accepted the refugees from the *Orduna.* The JDC posted bonds of $500 for each of the refugees. The sources for the conclusion of the *St. Louis'* voyage include *JTA,* June 20, 1939, p. 3, Bauer, *My Brother's Keeper,* p. 289, Herbert Agar, *op. cit.,* p. 85, and Morse, *op. cit.,* p. 287.

14. Agar, *op. cit.,* p. 85. See also Thomas and Witts, *op. cit.,* pp. 253–54, who write that no American newspaper suggested that the United States should have opened her doors to the *St. Louis* refugees. The *New York Post,* however, did editorialize on June 6, about the failure of the "Western World"—the United States included—to make a place for these refugees. A number of Jewish newspapers asked some questions about that failure. See also Menachem Rosensaft, "An Ill-Fated Voyage," *Midstream,* March 1977, pp. 75–77.

15. Morse, *op. cit.,* p. 280.

16. *NYT,* June 14, 1939, p. 17, and *JTA* for June 14–20, 1939.

17. This is not to be considered as an index of the sermons of *all* rabbis. What it does mean is that those rabbis who advertised their titles did not indicate that the *St. Louis* was their subject and that those sermons which were reviewed, usually through releases sent in by the

rabbis themselves, did not give prominent attention to this subject. There were about ten advertisements and five or six reviews each week. Generally, some of the best-known rabbis in New York were represented in both the advertisements and the reports. They included Stephen S. Wise, David De Sola Pool, Louis I. Newman, William F. Rosenblum, and Herbert S. Goldstein, among others.

18. *NP*, June 16, 1939, p. 4.

19. *The Day*, June 2, 1939, p. 4.

20. *CB*, June 9, 1939, p. 4, and June 16, 1939, p. 4.

21. *Freiheit*, June 3, 1939, p. 4; June 7, 1939, p. 5, and June 10 and 17, 1939, p. 4. See also the *Forward*, June 3, 1939, pp. 4 and 13, and B. James's article, June 16, 1939, p. 4.

22. *Forward*, June 13, 1939, p. 4.

23. *MJ*, June 7, 1939, p. 6. See also June 9, 1939, p. 7, Abe Goldberg's article, "The Tragedy of the Jewish Refugees in the Bosom of the Sea."

24. *Forward*, June 1, 1939, p. 4. *The Day* observation was made on June 5, 1939, p. 4.

25. Editorials, *The Sentinel*, June 16 and 23, 1939, p. 8.

26. June 9, 1939, p. 506 (front page of the paper).

27. *JE*, June 9, 1939, p. 4, and June 23, 1939, p. 4. The same kind of irony was hinted at—or lost—by the editor of *The Sentinel* who wrote (June 9, 1939, p. 8), "The shores of this continent have been approached by slave ships, plague ships, prison ships . . . but surely the *St. Louis* has a special place of its own among the heartbreak ships in American waters."

28. Wyman, *Paper Walls*, p. 14.

29. Stember, *op. cit.*, pp. 79, 129, and 132.

30. *CJR* January 1939, pp. 51–52.

31. Donald S. Strong, *Organized Anti-Semitism in America* (Washington, D.C.: American Council on Public Affairs, 1941), pp. 65 and 68; James Wechsler, "The Coughlin Terror," *The Nation*, July 22, 1939, pp. 92–97; and N. Cohen, *op. cit.*, p. 217. It should be remembered that both New York City and its police department had a large Irish-Catholic population, which made opposition to Coughlin extremely risky.

32. See Stember, *op. cit.*, pp. 112–13 and p. 58. See also the reaction to the Garden meeting in *CJR*, March–April, 1939, pp. 53–58.

33. Strong, *op. cit.*, pp. 138–43 and p. 14.

34. Carl Herman Voss, ed., *Stephen S. Wise: Servant of the People* (Philadelphia: The Jewish Publication Society of America, 1969), p. 233.

35. *MJ*, June 13, 14, 1939, pp. 4, 6. The news of Coughlin and anti-

Semitism superseded the *St. Louis* in the editorial section of the *Forward* on June 14 and *MJ* again on June 20.

36. *Opinion,* July 1939, p. 3.

37. An excellent analysis of the problems faced by American Jews with respect to restrictionism is contained in Brody, *op. cit.,* pp. 219–47.

38. Brody, *op. cit.,* p. 220; *AJYB,* 47 (1945–1946), p. 653. Feingold, *Politics,* p. 3, reports that between 1932 and 1938 the United States sustained a net loss of immigrants.

39. Brody, *op. cit.,* pp. 221–22, quoting the testimony of Max Kohler before the House Committee on Immigration, May 18, 1933.

40. *Ibid.,* p. 222.

41. *AJYB,* 39 (1937–1938), p. 67.

42. Abraham Leon Sachar, *Suffering Is the Badge,* (New York: Alfred A. Knopf, 1939), p. 519.

43. Wyman, *Paper Walls,* p. 5; *AJYB,* 41 (1939–1940), p. 196.

44. Wyman, *Paper Walls,* pp. 10–11.

45. *CB,* June 9, 1939, pp. 1, 8. See also *NYT,* June 8, 1939, p. 9.

46. Editorial, *Colliers,* January 27, 1940, p. 70. The writer tried to refute these fears as groundless.

47. Wyman, *Paper Walls,* p. 13.

48. Dorothy Thompson, quoted in Wyman, *Paper Walls,* p. 72, cautioned that raising the issue of expanding refugee quotas would be "political dynamite."

49. S. Friedman, *op. cit.,* p. 33, and Wyman, *Paper Walls,* pp. 69–71. Wyman quotes here a revealing memorandum sent by a representative of the highly supportive American Friends Service Committee on November 25, 1938, two weeks after *Kristallnacht,* stating that "to our knowledge no one is trying to change the quota. It is considered highly dangerous to attempt such a step and might jeopardize even the present quota."

50. Feingold, *Politics,* p. 42. See also Reuben Ainsztein, "Facing the Truth," *Jewish Quarterly,* 16 (Spring 1968), p. 39.

51. H. Lang, *Forward,* June 6, 1939, p. 3. See also Ben Zion in the *Forward,* November 24, 1938, p. 3. For press accounts of the Celler and Dickstein bills see *NYT,* March 25, 1938, p. 1, and November 20, 1938, p. 3. See Brody, *op. cit.,* pp. 227–28 for background analysis.

52. *AJYB,* 41 (1939–1940), p. 195. See also Feingold, *Politics,* pp. 149–51, S. Friedman, *op. cit.,* pp. 91–104, and Wyman, *Paper Walls,* pp. 75–98.

53. Wyman, *Paper Walls,* p. 91, and Feingold, *Politics,* p. 151.

54. Wyman, *Paper Walls,* p. 95, and Stember, *op. cit.,* p. 149.

55. Wyman, *Paper Walls,* pp. 70–71. Houghteling's wife had been

part of a nasty opposition to the Wagner–Rogers Bill. She was quoted as saying at a cocktail party that the trouble with the bill was "that 20,000 children would all too soon grow up into 20,000 ugly adults." Feingold, *Politics*, p. 150.

56. S. Friedman, *op. cit.*, p. 98.

57. *CB*, May 12, 1939, p. 4.

58. The *Jewish Frontier* did speak up strongly and urge such a campaign, but it did so in its July issue, which reached its readers after the bill had died.

59. S. Friedman, *op. cit.*, p. 98.

60. Feingold, *Politics*, p. 151.

61. Barely a year later, in June 1940, as London suffered under German bombs, 58 percent of Americans polled by Gallup favored accepting English and French children in the United States for the duration of the war; 25 percent (meaning 5 to 7 million homes) were willing to take "one or more of these children" into their homes. *NYT*, June 26, 1940, p. 12. Of course, this arrangement was temporary while admitting Jewish children would have been permanent.

62. *NYT*, June 7, 1939, p. 11.

63. Bauer, *My Brother's Keeper*, p. 279. Bauer claims that President Bru wanted $450,000 in his pocket aside from the bond.

64. *JTA*, June 25, 1938, pp. 2–3; *CJR*, July–August 1939, pp. 98–100. Similar statements were issued by England and the Liaison Committee of the League of Nations High Commission of Refugees on June 13.

65. See editorials in *MJ*, June 2, 4, and 8, 1939, all of which express outrage at the refusal of the "Western World" to admit the refugees, but which avoid suggesting that the United States admit them.

66. A. Mokdony, "The Demoralized World Where Evil Is Right," *Forward*, June 11, 1939, p. 4.

67. S. Rosenfeld, *The Day*, June 8, 1939, p. 6.

68. Jacob Lestschinsky, "Where Do We Stand?" *CB*, June 16, 1939, p. 5.

69. Henry L. Feingold, "An Eccentric Founder," a review essay on Louis Lipsky's "Memoirs in Profile," *Midstream*, January 1977, p. 79. In 1940, the Jews were more successful with a refugee ship that had been turned away from Mexico and stopped for coal at Norfolk. A delegation of American Jews visited Hull, and with the help of Eleanor Roosevelt, the refugees were admitted. Morse, *op. cit.*, pp. 30–31.

70. Quoted in Morse, *op. cit.*, p. 288.

CHAPTER 4: THE FINAL SOLUTION

1. Dawidowicz, *War Against Jews,* pp. 129–39, indicates that the planning of the Final Solution began in the summer of 1941, "perhaps as early as May." Bauer places the decision around the ides of March 1941. See his *The Holocaust in Historical Perspective,* (Seattle: University of Washington Press, 1978), p. 14, and his *American Jewry and the Holocaust,* p. 20. The coordination of the work of the various agencies was requested by Hermann Goering of Reinhardt Heydrich, chief of Security Police, on July 31, 1941, and was effected at a conference called by Heydrich in a Berlin suburb, Am Grossen Wannsee, January 20, 1942. The plan began to operate on a small scale in March 1942, when the first Slovakian Jews arrived in Auschwitz. (Bauer suggests that the implementation of the policy began before the Wannsee meeting.)

2. *NYT,* December 18, 1942, pp. 1 and 10, and *JTA,* December 18, 1942, pp. 1–2, among many other papers and periodicals.

3. Henry Morgenthau, Jr., "The Morgenthau Diaries: 6: The Refugee Run-Around," *Colliers,* November 1, 1947, p. 23; Kubowitzki, *op. cit.,* p. 158; and Wise, *Challenging Years,* p. 274. The term "Final Solution" is an abbreviated form of "The Final Solution of the Jewish Question." This, according to Dawidowicz, was the code name assigned by the German bureaucracy to the annihilation of the Jews. *War Against Jews,* p. xiii.

4. See also Wyman, *Abandonment,* chapters 2 and 3, and p. 61 for a further analysis of when confirmation of the Final Solution reached Jewish leaders and the Jewish public. On the Bund report and its dissemination see Yehuda Bauer, "When Did They Know," *Midstream,* April, 1968, pp. 52–57. See also *JTA,* June 26, 1942, pp. 1–2. *NYT,* June 27, 1942, p. 5, and *The Day,* June 30, 1942, p. 1. See also Morse, *op. cit.,* p. 5, concerning Riegner's awareness of the Bund report.

5. Kubowitzki, *op. cit.,* p. 161; *NYT,* June 30, 1942, p. 7; *JTA,* June 30, 1942, p. 2.

6. *NYT,* July 22, 1942, p. 1; *JTA,* July 22, 1942, pp. 1–2; *AJYB,* 45(1943–1944), p. 191. For the role of the American Jewish Congress in organizing this rally see Kubowitzki, *op. cit.,* p. 161. The rally inspired a number of non-Jewish expressions of horror at the Nazis and sympathy for their victims. It also stimulated a day of fasting and prayer for Jews nationwide on August 12, 1942. See *JTA,* July 23, 1942, p. 3, and July 24, 1942, p. 4, and *The Day, MJ,* and *Forward,* August 12, 1942, p. 1.

7. Morse, *op. cit.,* p. 8, and Laqueur, *Terrible Secret,* p. 80.

8. Morse, *op. cit.,* p. 8; Laqueur, *Terrible Secret,* p. 77.

9. Morse, *op. cit.*, p. 97.

10. The decision to consult first with Welles before taking any action was made at a closed session of the American Jewish Congress' Executive Board. Friedman, *op. cit.*, p. 142. Isaac Lewin, however, in "Attempts at Rescuing," pp. 5–6, recalls that a meeting of Jewish leaders was held to evaluate the Riegner information and a report from Isaac Sternbuch in Switzerland on the extermination of Warsaw Jewry. The consensus of the leaders was to seek confirmation from American intelligence through Welles.

11. Wise, *Challenging Years*, p. 275. What Wise could not have known was that Welles not only knew of the cable before Wise's consultation with him, but that in fact Welles had initialed the decision to suppress it in the first place. Morse, *op. cit.*, p. 9.

12. Hilberg, *op. cit.*, p. 718.

13. See Voss, ed., *op. cit.*, pp. 248–51, and Polier and Wise, *op. cit.*, pp. 260–61.

14. Elie Wiesel, "Telling the Tale," *Dimensions in American Judaism*, 2 (Spring 1968), p. 11.

15. Isaac Lewin, "The Catastrophe of European Jewry and Its Reverberations in America," *Idisheh Shtimeh*, November 1942, reprinted in Lewin's *Hurban Eropah* (New York: Research Institute for Post-War Problems of Religious Jewry, 1948), pp. 32–35.

16. Henry Feingold, "Who Shall Bear the Guilt," p. 277.

17. Hilberg, *op. cit.*, p. 718.

18. Wise, *Challenging Years*, p. 276; Friedman, *op. cit.* p. 142, gives the date as November 4.

19. *NYT*, November 25, 1942, p. 10, and November 26, 1942, p. 16; *JTA*, November 25, 1942, p. 2; *The Day*, *MJ*, and *Forward*, November 25, 1942, p. 1.

20. *NYT*, November 25, 1942, p. 10, and November 26, 1942, p. 16; *JTA*, November 25, 1942, p. 1; and *The Day*, November 25, 1942, p. 1.

21. *JTA*, November 24, 1942, p. 1.

22. *NYT*, November 26, 1942, p. 1.

23. These figures were also reproduced in *JTA*, November 27, 1942, p. 2.

24. *Congress Weekly*, December 4, 1942, p. 16.

25. Roosevelt's statement about the mills of the gods was taken from a Longfellow translation of Friedrich von Logau's *Sinngedichte*. The President's reaction was extensively covered by the *NYT*, December 9, 1942, p. 20, and by all the Yiddish dailies on p. 1. Also see Margoshes in *The Day*, December 10, 1942, p. 1.

26. Morse, *op. cit.*, p. 29. See also a parenthetical remark of Hayim

Greenberg in "Bankrupt," *Yiddisher Kemfer,* February 12, 1943, translated in *Midstream,* March 1964, p. 7, and *JTA,* December 7, 1942, p. 1. Morse writes that "on the day that Rabbi Wise and his delegation visited the President, a first draft of this [eleven nation] declaration, written by the British, arrived at the State Department."

27. *JTA,* December 18, 1942, pp. 2–3.

28. By the end of 1942, the anti-Axis countries were known as the United Nations, even though no formal organization had yet been created. See N. Cohen, *op. cit.,* p. 241. See also Sol Bloom, *The Autobiography of Sol Bloom* (New York: G. P. Putnam's Sons, 1948), p. 275, for the United Nations' role at the time as a collectivity of nations pledged to fight the Axis powers.

29. Hilberg, *op. cit.,* p. 719.

30. *Ibid.* For corroboration of the Hilberg view, see Halperin, *op. cit.,* p. 31, Laqueur, *Terrible Secret,* p. 93, Dawidowicz, "American Jews and the Holocaust," *NYT Magazine,* April 18, 1982, pp. 102–107, and Wyman, *Abandonment,* p. 61.

31. *JTA,* November 29, 1942, p. 2; November 30, p. 1; December 2, pp. 1–2; and December 3, pp. 1–2. The Agudat Ha-Rabanim, which initiated the observance, followed the example of Chief Rabbi Herzog and the Palestinian community; *JTA,* November 27, 1942, p. 1.

32. *JTA,* December 8, 1942, p. 1, and December 9, p. 1.

33. *The Day,* November 28, 1942, p. 1; editorial, December 3, 1942, p. 4; December 16, 1942, p. 1, and editorial, December 23, 1942. *The Day* was one of the few Jewish organs that dared to advocate openly the admission of refugees from Nazi Europe into the United States. December 18, 1942, p. 4 (editorial), and December 22, p. 1: "We shall not have done our full duty to those of our kith and kin who have died and are about to die in Europe unless and until we shall have done everything possible . . . to persuade the United Nations, our own United States included, to lift the bars and keep the doors of hope open for those who can still escape. . . ."

34. Margoshes, "New and Views," *The Day,* December 16, 1942, p. 1.

35. *The Day,* December 4, 1942, p. 4, and December 19, 1942, p. 1.

36. *The Day,* November 25, 1942, p. 1. See also A. Glanz in *The Day,* two months later on February 28, 1943, p. 4, who saw the Jewish mood as one of despair.

37. Editorial, *The Day,* November 27, 1942, p. 4; B. Z. Goldberg, *The Day,* November 29, 1942, p. 4, and December 21, 1942, p. 1.

38. Editorial, *MJ,* March 1, 1943, p. 1. The same thought was repeated in its p. 4 editorial in the same issue. American Jewish leaders were criticized for not doing more at an earlier date.

39. Editorial, *Forward,* November 27, 29, and December 2, 1942, p. 4, and December 6, 1942, p. 6.

40. L. Fogelman, *Forward,* December 11, 1942, p. 4.

41. Editorial, *Forward,* December 15, 1942, p. 4, and December 22, 1942, p. 4.

42. *The Sentinel,* December 11, 1942, p. 6.

43. *The Sentinel,* March 12, 1943, p. 1.

44. *JA,* December 4, 1942, p. 1, two-column editorial entitled "Boston's Greatest Disaster."

45. *JA,* December 11, 1942, p. 1.

46. The event was described in *JA,* January 1, 1943, p. 2.

47. *JE,* December 4 and 11, 1942, p. 1.

48. *JE,* December 25, 1942, p. 4.

49. *JE,* February 19, 1943, p. 4.

50. *JE,* March 5, 1943, p. 4.

51. *Ibid.*

52. Editorial, *CW,* December 25, 1942, p. 3. See also a full-page editorial on January 22, 1943, p. 3, which argued the case for rescue more urgently.

53. *JR,* January 1943, pp. 3–4.

54. These excerpts are from editorials in *JS* in the January, February, and March issues of 1943. They are on page 4 in each issue. The lengthy excerpt that follows is also from the March editorial.

55. *Reconstructionist,* December 25, 1942, p. 4; January 8, 1943, p. 4; March 13, 1943, p. 8.

56. M. Shoshani, "On the Destruction in Poland," *Hadoar,* December 4, 1942, front page. The magazine continued to devote extensive news and editorial space every week to the ongoing crises.

57. *Hadoar,* December 25, 1942.

58. *Opinion,* February 1943, p. 12. Dr. Atkinson, general secretary of the Church Peace Union, had spelled out his rescue proposals in detail in an article in *CW,* January 8, 1943, p. 7.

59. *Ibid.,* p. 24.

60. Feingold, *Politics,* pp. 128–31. Wyman, *Paper Walls,* describes the security fear in the prewar period as well, pp. 185–91.

61. Feingold, *Politics,* pp. 173–74. When Harold Dodds, leader of the American delegation to the Bermuda Conference in April 1943, was confronted by the various rescue proposals, he said such a program "would not only be foolish, it would be criminal." *Ibid.,* p. 174.

62. Editorial signed by Edward E. Grusd, *NJM,* January 1943, p. 145.

63. *Ibid.,* January 1943, p. 164; February 1943, pp. 188 and 200; April 1943, p. 249.

64. *Ibid.*, April 1943, p. 250.

65. *NP*, December 4, and 18, 1942, p. 3; January 8, 1943, p. 2; December 4, 1942, p. 4, and January 22, 1943, p. 4.

66. *Hadassah Newsletter*, February 1943, p. 4, and March 1943, p. 3. The *Newsletter* also issued a call to the women of the world by Henrietta Szold to save children from the Nazis, February 1943, p. 5.

67. *Hadassah Newsletter*, April 1943, p. 4.

68. *Jewish Outlook*, February 1943, p. 4. The statement of twelve principles that emerged from the convention dealt entirely with the postwar period. There was nothing on "solving the bloody dilemma of Europe's Jewish population." That would be left for Palestine after the war. *Outlook*, April 1943, pp. 2–3. The most clearly exploitative use of the Holocaust in this period was found in a large advertisement in the *Times*, February 23, 1943, p. 13, placed by the New Zionist Organization of America and signed by Louis Germain, treasurer, and Col. Morris J. Mendelsohn, president. "Massacred by Foe, Ignored by Friend," the message began. It ended with an appeal for a $1 million political fund to place the Jewish question on the world agenda. The group that sponsored the advertisement was a Revisionist Zionist group, which went under various names. There will be more discussion about this group in Chapter 6.

69. Alan S. Green, "The Jewish Scene," *The Synagogue*, March 1943, pp. 17–18. Ely Pilchik, whose column offered items of interest on Jews and Judaism, cited two articles on the Holocaust in both the February and March issues.

70. Emanuel Gamoran in *The Synagogue*, March 1943, pp. 9–11.

71. Asher Isaacs, "Views on News," *Orthodox Union*, February 1943, p. 4.

72. *JTA*, March 10, 1943, p. 3.

73. "Press Comment," *Notes and News*, February 19, 1943, p. 3. The quote is from an editorial in the *Reconstructionist*, February 5, 1943.

74. The *JTA*, January 18–20, 1943, also mentioned no discussion of the plight of European Jewry.

75. Lionel Gelber, "American Jewry Bethink Ye!" the lead article in the *Menorah Journal*, 21 (Winter, January–March 1943).

76. Henry Hurwitz in a signed opening statement, *Menorah Journal*, 21 (Winter, January–March, 1943).

77. Baruch Braunstein, "Men and Events," *Opinion*, March 1943, p. 13.

78. A few examples are the following:

NYT, editorial, December 2, 1942, p. 24.
CJR, February 1943, p. 24; Zachariah Shuster, "The Passion of a

People: Anno MCMXLII." "Suddenly, during the summer of 1942, world public opinion was shocked out of its lethargy by the realization that the Nazis had decreed the complete extinction of six million Jews."

JS, April, 1943, pp. 25–27, reprinting an editorial from the *New Statesman and Nation* in London: "The pre-war Jewish population of Europe was about six million. It will take some time to kill them all. . . ."

Ibid., February 1943, pp. 25–27. Varian Fry, "The Massacre of the Jews," (reprinted from the *New Republic,* December 21, 1942, pp. 816–19).

New York Herald Tribune, editorial, December 6, 1942, ". . . millions dead, the extermination of countless others decreed."

Chicago Times, editorial, December 2, 1942.

Cleveland News, editorial, December 2, 1942 (the last three were reprinted in *Contemporary Jewish Record*).

CW, December 11, 1942, reprints of the editorials in the *Herald Tribune, Chicago Times,* and *Cleveland News.*

JTA, December 21, 1942, p. 1.

NYT, February 26, 1943, p. 14 (full page advertisement).

JF, January 1943, p. 3.

Opinion, "Ten Years of Hitler," February 1943, p. 12.

NJM, editorial, January, 1943, p. 145.

NP, December 4, 1942, p. 3.

Time, March 8, 1943, pp. 29–30.

The Sentinel, December 11, 1942, p. 1.

Ibid., March 12, 1943, p. 1.

The Day, February 25, 1943, p. 1.

Ibid., February 27, 1943, p. 1.

Ibid., February 28, 1943, p. 1.

MJ, February 25, 1943, p. 1.

Ibid., February 26, 1943, p. 1.

79. *JTA,* February 2, 1943, p. 1. *NYT,* February 26, 1943, p. 14, carried a full-page advertisement.

80. *Yiddisher Kemfer,* February 12, 1943, pp. 1–3. It is not clear why Greenberg, who was the editor of the *Jewish Frontier,* chose the Yiddish medium exclusively for this condemnation, unless perhaps he did not want the non-Jewish world to read his anguished criticism of fellow Jews. In any event, "Bankrupt" did not appear in English until 1964, when it was published by Shlomo Katz in *Midstream,* March 1964, pp. 3–14.

81. *Midstream,* March 1964, p. 8. *CW* quoted Greenberg in its issue of February 19, 1943, p. 3.

82. Stember, *op. cit.*, p. 141.

83. Laqueur, *Terrible Secret,* p. 3.

84. See also Feingold, *Politics,* pp. 298–99, for a review of the problems which had to be confronted in any rescue activity.

85. Polier and Wise, *op. cit.*, p. 263.

86. *JTA,* December 8, 1942, p. 2.

87. *NYT,* December 20, 1942, p. 17. Hyman J. Schachtel also spoke about "after the war" matters.

88. See also Boris Smolar, "Post-War Thoughts," *CJC,* January 1, 1943.

89. *JTA,* December 22, 1942, p. 2, and December 27, 1942, p. 3.

90. *NP,* January 22, 1943, p. 17.

91. *NJM,* March 1943, p. 221. See also the first two editorials in this issue (p. 232), which speak of the coming "dawn" and "the year of retribution" which is upon us. The magazine suggests that Hitler's punishment should be to live as an outcast, a wanderer. The speculation, unfortunately, was premature and distracting. See also Harry Kovner's article, "A Plan for Lasting Peace" in *JS,* January 1943, pp. 11–12, in which he suggests that the end of the war is approaching and the rivers of blood will soon dry up. He proposes that the peace conference be held at Mount Sinai.

92. *JTA,* February 1, 1943, p. 1, and *CJR,* February 1943, p. 3. The last words come from a Hull statement.

93. *JTA,* April 20, 1943, reported the change in name at the same time as it reported the American Jewish Committee's decision to join the new conference.

94. *JTA,* January 11, 1943, p. 3. See also Alexander S. Kohanski, ed., *The American Jewish Conference* (New York: American Jewish Conference, 1944), p. 15.

95. Halperin, *op. cit.*, pp. 220–22.

96. Kohanski, *op. cit.*, pp. 17–32.

97. The quote is from Lewin's elaboration of this theme in *MJ,* February 2, 1943, p. 5. See also Lewin, *Hurban Eropah,* pp. 43–46.

98. Kohanski, *op. cit.*, pp. 323–26.

99. *JTA,* January 25, 1943, p. 2.

100. Kohanski, *op. cit.*, p. 34; *JTA,* January 25, 1943, p. 2.

101. Pierre van Passen, "To the Conscience of America," *JS,* January 1943, p. 27. Edward E. Grusd, *B'nai B'rith* (New York: Appleton-Century, 1966), p. 231, asserts that the "one immediate goal" of the Pittsburgh meeting was "to save as many lives as possible." It is not clear where Grusd found this "goal." His assertion (which may be the source for other scholars who consider rescue to have been one of the purposes for the founding of the American Jewish Conference) is

somewhat misleading. The idea of rescue was actually a last-minute addition to the conference's program. Hilberg, *op. cit.*, p. 719, reflects surprise that Monsky seemed disinterested in rescue. "The Holocaust was unopposed," he writes. "The paralysis was complete."

102. *JTA*, November 30, 1942, p. 1; *CW*, December 18, 1942, p. 13; *The Day*, December 3, 1942, p. 1; Judah Piltch, *Hadoar*, January 5, 1943, p. 174; and *Reconstructionist*, March 5, 1943, p. 20.

103. *MJ*, December 17, 1942, p. 1. Judging from the *NYT* sermon reviews, there may have been little participation on the part of the rabbis.

104. Editorial, *MJ*, December 17, 1942, p. 4.

105. *Reconstructionist*, March 5, 1943, p. 20.

106. *CW*, December 11, 1942, p. 3.

107. *JTA*, December 20, 1942, p. 2, and the *Forward*, same date, p. 1.

108. *JTA*, December 20, 1942, p. 2.

109. It is strange that Monsky did not maintain his interest in rescue in planning the Pittsburgh meeting. What is also surprising is the lack of editorial support for rescue in the *National Jewish Monthly*, the official publication of B'nai B'rith, until March 1943.

110. *JTA*, December 24, 1942, p. 4. In preparation for this punishment, Isaac Lewin, *MJ*, January 11, 1943, p. 5, proposed a careful study of the Hague Conventions for the conduct of war in order to alert the world to the violation of these conventions in the treatment of Jews in occupied lands. He felt that this might have a deterrent effect on the Nazis in the same way that the conventions' prohibition of poison gas had deterred the Nazis from using it on the battlefield.

111. *JTA*, January 3, 1943, p. 4.

112. Stephen S. Wise, "United Nations vs. Mass Murder," *Opinion*, January 1943, p. 5. *The Day*, editorial, December 30, 1942, p. 4. An exception was Henry A. Atkinson, the Christian leader, writing in *CW*, January 8, 1943, p. 7.

113. *JF*, March 1943, p. 3. See also *MJ*, November 27, 1942, p. 3; *JTA*, January 8, 1943, p. 3; *JS*, February 1943, p. 4, and *Opinion*, January 1943, p. 5.

114. Feingold, *Politics*, p. 187.

115. *NYT*, December 7, 1942, p. 14. See also Hayim Greenberg, "Bankrupt," p. 7, and S. Friedman, *op. cit.*, p. 156.

116. For a full discussion of the possibilities for this rescue, see Morse, *op. cit.*, pp. 71–86. See also Dawidowicz, "American Jews and the Holocaust," p. 109.

117. Morgenthau, "Diaries," *Colliers*, November 1, 1947, p. 23, and Kubowitzki, *op. cit.*, pp. 178–80.

118. Wise's statement of February 23, was reported in *NP*, March 5, 1943, p. 4. His reaction is discussed by Ben Hecht in *Perfidy* (New York: Julian Messner, 1961), p. 192. It is noteworthy that Wise himself, in a letter to Holmes, defended the Ben Hecht group as having been fooled by the Romanians. Polier and Wise, *Wise Letters*, p. 265.

119. Editorial, *NP*, March 5, 1943, p. 4. Schlomo Grodzensky in *JF*, March 1943, p. 8, was similarly skeptical. "No one knows whether it [the Romanian rescue] is authentic, a feeler, or just a rumor," he wrote. "But there cannot be any doubt that our Revisionist friends are still in need of funds for their organization."

120. Morgenthau, *op cit.*, p. 62. To Americans, the choice of the expression "disposing of" somehow seems more appropriate for garbage than for human beings, although Chambers Dictionary, the English Webster's, does indicate that its normal meaning is "to arrange" or "to distribute."

121. *Ibid.* Robert E. Sherwood, *Roosevelt and Hopkins* (New York: Harper and Brothers, 1948), p. 717, describes a meeting in March 1943 that suggests an earlier example of this death sentence. Discussing with Roosevelt, Hopkins, Hull, and others the possibility of rescuing 60,000 to 70,000 Bulgarian Jews, Foreign Minister Anthony Eden expressed a negative view. He added that, if we made the effort for the Bulgarians, the Jews of the world would want us to make similar offers for Polish and German Jews, and even if Hitler agreed, there weren't enough ships to transport them.

122. See advertisements in *The Day*, December 21, 1942, p. 2, and *MJ*, December 22, 1942, p. 10.

123. The *Forward*, however, did promote aggressively "the Day of Protest and Mourning" called by the Workman's Circle and the Jewish Labor Committee on February 26, 1943. Editorial, *Forward*, February 25, 1943, p. 4, also February 26, p. 1, and February 28, p. 1.

124. *MJ*, December 23, 1942, p. 10. See also *AJYB*, 45 (1943–1944), p. 194, which described the meeting.

125. *JTA*, January 10, 1942, p. 2.

126. *Reconstructionist*, January 22, 1943, p. 6. The extent of the "shielding" may be evident from the comments of a young woman who was sixteen in 1943, an honor student, who lived in a communally active Jewish home: "I don't remember ever hearing a word about extermination camps or Jews being killed in Europe. . . . I thought of the war purely in American patriotic terms." Personal interview, November 25, 1976.

127. Morgenthau, *op. cit.*, p. 23. Morgenthau goes on to explain how the State Department, after this telegram, sent a cable to its minister to Switzerland, Leland Harrison, instructing him to stop relaying any

messages from Riegner, in order to prevent further demonstrations and protests. Joseph Tenenbaum, "They Might Have Been Rescued," *Congress Bi-Weekly,* February 2, 1953, pp. 3–7, accepts the Morgenthau interpretation of the stimulus for the rally as does Hilberg, *op. cit.,* p. 719. On the other hand, a *Hadoar* writer, February 19, 1943, p. 259, indicated that the rally was stimulated by a telegram from British Jewry, calling on American Jews to scream loudly for rescue before it was too late.

128. *MJ,* March 3, 1943, p. 1.

129. See *Opinion,* March 1943, p. 4.

130. For a full list of the cooperating groups see *CW,* February 19, 1943, back page.

131. *NYT,* February 26, 1943, p. 14.

132. *The Day,* February 25, 27, and 28, *MJ,* February 25 and 26.

133. *JTA,* March 2, 1943, pp. 1–2, and March 3, 1943, pp. 1–4, and all the Yiddish papers.

134. All the speeches were reproduced in *CW,* March 5, 1943, pp. 3–15.

135. The full text of the proposals appeared in the *NYT,* March 2, 1943, p. 4, and *CW,* March 5, 1943, p. 16. A synopsis was in *JTA* and other newspapers. It is noteworthy that the theme of retribution, which was the main thrust of the original presidential and United Nations reactions to the Wise revelations and which was applauded by Jews at the time, was now dropped to last place on the list. The priorities had clearly shifted to efforts for immediate succor.

136. *NYT,* March 3, 1943, p. 22. Other strong press reactions were reprinted in *CW,* March 12, 1943, pp. 12–13. See also *Time* Magazine's reaction in its issue of March 8, 1943, pp. 29–30.

137. The words are those of Anne O'Hare McCormick, *NYT,* March 3, 1943, p. 22.

138. See *JTA,* March 5, 1943, p. 3, March 10, 1943, p. 1, *AJYB,* 45 (1943–1944), p. 195, and *JTA,* March 12, 1943, p. 4.

139. Morse, *op. cit.,* p. 46, credits the rally with stimulating the Bermuda Conference while S. Friedman, *op. cit.,* p. 280, n. 12, disagrees. Both probably have a point. The idea for the conference originated in January with the British Foreign Office. Its implementation, however, seems to have been expedited by the rally and the public reaction to it.

140. Freda Kirchway, *op. cit.,* pp. 816–19. See also the same inference drawn by *CW,* March 12, 1943, p. 3. *JTA,* March 4, 1943, p. 1, reported that Welles linked the note to the resolutions from the rally. Great Britain, in turn, announced in Washington on March 4 its agreement with the Hull note, *JTA,* March 5, 1943, p. 2.

141. *CW*, April 30, 1943, *op. cit.*, pp. 11–12; *AJYB*, 45 (1943–1944), p. 196; Voss, *op. cit.*, pp. 258–59. Arieh Tartakower and Kurt R. Grossman, *The Jewish Refugee* (New York: Institute of Jewish Affairs, 1944), pp. 580–89, have a long memorandum submitted by the World Jewish Congress to the Bermuda Conference as an introduction to the Emergency Committee's proposals. The conference turned out to be a great disappointment. According to Feingold, *Politics*, p. 190, and Friedman, *op. cit.*, p. 173, it was orchestrated from the beginning to help the governments of the United States and Britain and not to provide aid to the victims of Nazi persecution.

142. This pageant was not covered in advance except by *The Day* and *MJ*, March 9, 1943, p. 1. It was reviewed fully by the *JTA*, March 10, p. 2, and the *Forward* of the same date, p. 1. *The Day* and *MJ* reviewed it partially on March 11, pp. 5 and 10, respectively.

143. The *Answer*, May 1943, pp. 8–9; Isaac Zaar, *Rescue and Liberation* (New York: Block Publishing Co., 1954), p. 40. For a fuller discussion of the pageant see Wyman, *Abandonment*, pp. 90–92.

144. Voss, *op. cit.*, p. 257, published a letter by Wise to his son saying that "Ben Hecht would like us to merge our meeting with theirs on the 9th [of March]. But we have decided against it." See also Feingold, *Politics*, pp. 174–75, on the Bergson group's popularity.

145. Stember, *op. cit.*, p. 121.

146. *Ibid.*, p. 79.

147. Gerhard Riegner, personal interview, April 24, 1975.

148. *JTA*, November 30, 1942, reporting on Wohl's address to a National Labor Committee for Palestine convention in New York.

CHAPTER 5: THE WARSAW GHETTO

1. Jacob Glatstein, Israel Knox, and Samuel Margoshes, *Anthology of Holocaust Literature* (Philadelphia: The Jewish Publication Society of America, 1969), Mordecai Anielewicz's last letter, pp. 334–35. Anielewicz was the leader of the ZOB, the Jewish Combat Organization in the ghetto. Dawidowicz, *War Against Jews*, p. 332, cites other examples of resistance but concludes that "only in the Warsaw ghetto did Jewish resistance attain its objectives."

2. Reitlinger, *op. cit.*, p. 293.

3. Philip Friedman, ed., *Martyrs and Fighters: The Epic of the Warsaw Ghetto* (New York: Frederick A. Praeger, 1954), p. 147.

4. *Ibid.*, pp. 219–25. See also Dawidowicz, *War Against Jews*, pp. 333–36.

5. *Ibid.*, p. 335. The message was sent to Stephen Wise of the

American Jewish Congress, Nahum Goldmann of the World Jewish Congress, and George Backer of the JDC. See Dawidowicz, *War Against Jews,* p. 434, n. 51. This note may have played a catalytic role in the organizing of the Madison Square Garden Rally. It does not deal specifically with the Warsaw ghetto but rather with Polish Jewry in general, and it contains no implication that resistance on the part of the victims was either carried out already or was contemplated in the future. A Bund message, which was sent to Zygelboym in London on February 7, did refer guardedly to the initial resistance, but obviously could not contain any implications of the large-scale revolt which was in the offing.

6. Dawidowicz, *War Against Jews,* p. 336, and Ber Mark, *Uprising in the Warsaw Ghetto,* translated by Gershon Friedlin (New York: Schocken Books, 1975), p. 17.

7. For critical analysis of the Bermuda Conference see Morse, *op. cit.,* pp. 37–64; Feingold, *Politics,* pp. 167–207; and S. Friedman, *op. cit.,* pp. 155–80, and Wyman, *Abandonment,* 104–23.

8. Dawidowicz' phrase. Her figures for the battle are generally agreed upon by other chroniclers. See, for example, Reitlinger, *op. cit.,* p. 298. Professor Dawidowicz' date for the conclusion of the battle is May 10 when about seventy-five ZOB fighters escaped to the "Aryan" side of the wall through the sewers. Ziviah Lubetkin, "Last Days of the Warsaw Ghetto," *Commentary,* May 1947, pp. 401–11, gives the date as May 12. Most observers, however, use the May 16 date. See P. Friedman, *op. cit.,* pp. 252–53; Reitlinger, *op. cit.,* p. 298; Hilberg, *op. cit.,* p. 326, Dan Kurzman, *The Bravest Battle* (New York: G. P. Putnam's Sons, 1976), p. 336, and Leon Poliakov, *Harvest of Hate* (Philadelphia: The Jewish Publication Society of America, 1954), p. 236. Poliakov cites an entry in Goebbels' diary for May 22, indicating that while there was still fighting going on, the "resistance is no longer dangerous and is virtually broken." Mark, *op. cit.,* cites serious sporadic fighting through June 3, which would mean that the struggle lasted six weeks, a figure that coincides with that of Jacob Apenszlak and Moshe Polakiewicz, *Armed Resistance of the Jews in Poland* (New York: American Federation for Polish Jews, 1944), pp. 39–45. Kurzman, perhaps basing his information on Ber Mark, in part, adds that "scattered bands of trapped Jewish fighters continued resisting for several more months. They were called the 'rubble resistance.' " Some escaped; most were killed. The last "survivor," a young girl, was discovered on December 13, 1943, badly burned and barely alive. Ultimately captured by the Nazis, she so awed the Gestapo by the miracle of her survival that they brought her back to health and fitted her out with a wardrobe. "After a few weeks, SS men tortured her and then shot her" in Pawiak prison.

9. Dawidowicz, *War Against Jews,* pp. 336–39. Her evaluation is supported by at least three primary sources. The first is a May 1 entry in Goebbels' diary:

> The extremely bitter fighting at Warsaw between our police forces, and the *Wehrmacht* itself, and the rebellious Jews should be noted. The Jews have succeeded in making the ghetto a kind of fortified position.
> Fierce fighting is in progress and the Jewish High Command even publishes daily communiqués. This joke isn't going to last long. But one sees what the Jews can do when they are armed.

The entry is found in Poliakov, *op. cit.,* p. 236, and P. Friedman, *op. cit.,* p. 258. The second primary source is a *JTA* report, May 26, 1943, p. 2, citing the death sentence for a Gestapo chief in Warsaw who had failed to prevent the uprising. The report notes a Stockholm press account of weeks of heroic fighting against "picked Nazi units." The Stockholm press "compares the battles in the ghetto with the battle for Stalingrad and emphasizes that the Jews fought for each street and for every house before giving ground before superior Nazi forces." The third source is *NYT,* May 22, 1943, p. 4, which gives the casualty count of 1,000. See also *JTA,* June 6, 1943, p. 1, which quotes a Polish radio count of 2,300.

10. Reitlinger, *op. cit.,* pp. 293–94 and Hilberg, *op. cit.,* p. 326.

11. See text of Anielewicz's farewell letter in Glatstein et al., *op. cit.,* pp. 334–35.

12. *JTA,* May 13, 1943, p. 2, originally reported it as a natural death. On May 18, p. 2, it was reported as a suicide. The *NYT* reported the suicide on May 22, p. 4.

13. These excerpts from the letter were published widely in the Jewish press and in the periodicals. They appeared initially in the *NYT,* June 4, 1943, p. 7, and the *JTA,* June 3, 1943, p. 2. I have used the translation from Glatstein et al., *op. cit.,* pp. 329–31. There was a poignant profile of Zygelboym in *Time,* May 31, 1943, p. 24.

14. *CW,* February 26, p. 6 (following February 19, 1943, pp. 3–4). *Hadoar,* February 12, 1943, also bewailed the deportation of the last Jews in Warsaw.

15. *CW,* March 26, p. 3, and *JTA,* April 4, 1943, from Stockholm sources.

16. *NYT,* April 23, 1943, p. 9. The last paragraph in the *Times* story was not true. The Jewish defenders pleaded for help but received nothing but a few pistols. See Kurzman, *op. cit.,* pp. 52–60.

17. *NYT,* May 15, 1943, p. 6.

18. *NYT,* May 22, and June 4, 1943, pp. 4 and 7 respectively.

19. The small report on the ghetto uprising was insignificant in comparison with a full-page report on atrocities in Lwow.

20. See Apenszlak and Polakiewicz, *op. cit.*, pp. 36 and 37, and P. Friedman, *op. cit.*, p. 269. Both books document the delay in receipt of cables from Warsaw. Friedman states that Ignacy Schwartzbart, Jewish representative on the Polish National Council in London, received his first two accounts of the battle from the Jewish underground in Warsaw on May 21 although they were dated April 28 and May 11. It appears that these were the cables released by Wise and Goldmann on May 31. Apenszlak and Polakiewicz report that Wise and Goldmann received the cables only on May 30 (p. 36). In any event, it was at least late May before American Jewish leaders received the kind of information that alerted them to the heroic nature of the resistance in Warsaw. By the time they received that information, they also knew that the battle was over.

21. *Forward,* May 11, 1943, p. 8.

22. S. Margoshes, *The Day,* "New and Views," May 12, 1943, p. 1.

23. Last news item in the foreign news section, May 14, 1943, p. 2.

24. *CW,* May 21, p. 3. *NP* also revealed a clear understanding of the uprising in its May 21 issue with a page 3 editorial entitled "Second Battle of the Warsaw Ghetto."

25. *CJR,* June 1943. "Chronicles, March–April," p. 297, and August 1943, pp. 409–11.

26. The *Ghetto Speaks,* No. 12 (June 1, 1943).

27. *The Day,* May 23 and 27, 1943, p. 4; *MJ,* May 24, 1943, p. 4; *Forward,* June 3, 1943, p. 4, and June 21, 1943, p. 1.

28. *CW,* June 25, 1943, p. 4.

29. Wise's speech at Carnegie Hall, June 19, 1943, was published in *CW,* June 25, 1943, pp. 10–11. Hurwitz' comment appeared in the *Menorah Journal,* 31 (July–September, 1943), lead page.

30. *JS,* June, 1943, pp. 4–5.

31. "Yizkor," *Hadoar,* May 28, 1943, p. 486. Only the *Hadassah Newsletter* and the *Jewish Outlook* failed to comment at all.

32. Covered by the *JTA* and the Yiddish press on June 21. The Yiddish papers featured it on p. 1, but the *JTA* placed it on p. 4.

33. *The Day,* June 3, 1943, p. 1, and *JTA,* same day, p. 3.

34. P. Friedman, *op. cit.,* p. 272.

35. *JF,* June 1943, p. 3.

36. Ainsztein, *op. cit.,* p. 38.

37. The *Reconstructionist,* June 25, 1943, p. 4.

38. *JF,* June 1943, p. 4.

39. *Menorah Journal,* 32 (Spring 1944), p. 19.

40. Address at Carnegie Hall, April 19, 1944, reproduced in *JF,* May 1944.

41. *Menorah Journal*, 32 (Spring 1944), p. 19.

42. Elie Wiesel, Introduction to Vladka Meed, *On Both Sides of the Wall* (Tel Aviv: Ghetto Fighters House and Hakibbutz Hameuchad Publishing House, 1972), p. 14.

CHAPTER 6: THE CAMPAIGN FOR A RESCUE AGENCY

1. For a full discussion of the WRB and its role, see Feingold, *Politics*, pp. 242–94, and S. Friedman, *op. cit.*, pp. 213–22. For further information on the campaign to create an agency for rescue and on the WRB itself, see Wyman, *Abandonment*, pp. 193–234.

2. See Morgenthau, *op. cit.*, pp. 22, 23, 62, 65.

3. Morse, *op. cit.*, pp. 88–92, and Feingold, *Politics*, pp. 239–41. The report was prepared by Randolph Paul, Joseph E. DuBois, and John Pehle, all of the Treasury Department.

4. Selig Adler, "The United States and the Holocaust," *AJHSQ*, 64 (September 1974), p. 20. He explains that Roosevelt saw the evidence in the Morgenthau report as a political catastrophe should it become public knowledge.

5. *CW*, April 30, 1943, p. 12. One of the first proposals for a separate governmental rescue agency was made to the British Government by Chief Rabbi Hertz in January 1943. See *JTA*, January 27, 1943, p. 2.

6. *JF*, August 1943, pp. 4–5. The writer pleaded that victory in the war would not be a solution for the Jews, because at the current rate of extermination, there would be no Jews left to take care of in the postwar period.

7. *JTA*, July 26, 1943, p. 2.

8. Ben Hecht, *Perfidy* (New York: Julian Messner, 1961), p. 189, corroborated by S. Friedman, *op. cit.*, p. 147, and *NYT* advertisements February 16, 1943, p. 11; April 13, 1943, p. 19, and May 4, 1943. p. 17. The Bergson groups were variously known as the American Friends of a Jewish Palestine, the Committee for an Army of Stateless and Palestinian Jews, and the American League for a Free Palestine, in addition to the Emergency Committee to Save the Jewish People of Europe, which became the group's new title following the July conference.

9. *JF*, August 1943, p. 4.

10. *JTA*, July 26, 1943, p. 2. The texts of all the messages were in print in the *Answer*, the publication of the Emergency Committee, August 1943, pp. 4–5. See also Zaar, *op. cit.*, pp. 44–45.

11. *JTA* and Zaar, *loc. cit.*

12. *NYT*, October 7, 1943, p. 14 (six-column story). The *JTA*, Oc-

tober 7, 1943, p. 4, reported only 300 rabbis. The 500 figure comes from the *Answer,* October 15, 1943, pp. 6–7.

13. Peter Bergson and his colleague, Samuel Merlin, had a tendency to think in grand terms. There is no evidence that the petition campaign resulted in even 10 percent of that figure.

14. The *Answer,* October 15, 1943, back page.

15. William D. Hassett, *Off the Record with F.D.R.: 1942–1945* (New Brunswick, N.J.: Rutgers University Press, 1958), p. 209.

16. Editorial, *JF,* September 1943, pp. 4–5.

17. See, for example, Halperin, *op. cit.,* pp. 220–21 and 245–46, Louis Lipsky, *Memoirs in Profile* (Philadelphia: The Jewish Publication Society of America, 1975), p. 606, Hilberg, *op. cit.,* pp. 721–22, and Kohanski, *op. cit.* They all confirm this main interest. Some also explain the different emphases of Abba Hillel Silver, on the one hand, who was interested solely in gaining communal approval of the Biltmore Platform (calling for a Jewish commonwealth in Palestine) and Lipsky and Wise, on the other, who were equally concerned with the establishment of an ongoing democratic organization. Isaiah Minkoff, who represented the JLC at the conference, confirmed this difference in the approaches of these Zionist leaders (personal interview, October 23, 1977). His recollection also corroborates the historians' conclusion that the issue of rescue was not the major concern of this conference.

18. Stephen S. Wise, "The American Jewish Conference: A Forecast by Stephen S. Wise," *Opinion,* August 1943, p. 5.

19. Editorial, *CW,* August 20, 1943, p. 4.

20. Kohanski, *op. cit.,* p. 56.

21. *JTA,* August 30, 1943, p. 1.

22. *Ibid.,* p. 2.

23. Kohanski, *op. cit.,* pp. 55 and 80. See also *JTA,* August 31, 1943, p. 2. An additional session on the plight of European Jewry was held on the third day of the conference, August 31. *JTA,* September 1, 1943, p. 1.

24. Kohanski, *op. cit.,* pp. 128–29.

25. Editorial, *Opinion,* October 1943, pp. 6–7.

26. Feingold, *Politics,* p. 219. Bergson's group was to take a different position on this point in November 1943.

27. Editorial, "After the Conference," *CW,* September 24, 1943, pp. 5–6.

28. Title of an editorial statement in *CW,* November 12, 1943, p. 12—a satirical reference to Joseph Davies' best-selling book on his experiences as United States ambassador in the U.S.S.R., *Mission to Moscow,* 1942.

29. *NYT,* November 2, 1943, p. 14. Stories about the different parts of this important joint communiqué were on pp. 1, 7, and 14. See also *JTA,* November 2, 1943, p. 2.

30. "Chronicle of Events," *CW,* November 5, 1943, p. 2.

31. *The Day:* S. Dingol, November 3, 1943, p. 4, S. Margoshes, November 5, 1943, p. 1, Ben Hecht, "My Uncle Abraham Admits," November 6, 1943, p. 1; *MJ:* A. Revuski, November 8, 1943, p. 4; editorial, *Forward,* November 3, 1943, p. 4. The *JA* in Boston also expressed its disappointment, November 11, 1943, p. 5.

32. Editorial, *NP,* November 12, 1943, p. 87.

33. *Jewish Outlook,* January 1944, p. 4; *Reconstructionist,* November 26, 1943, pp. 3–4.

34. *JS,* December 1943, p. 6.

35. *CW,* November 12, 1943, p. 12.

36. Kubowitzki, *op. cit.,* pp. 160–61.

37. See S. Friedman, *op. cit.,* pp. 226–27, and Feingold, *Politics,* p. 271. An unfortunate practical result of this tendency to evade mention of Jews came in a decision of the United Nations Relief and Rehabilitation Administration not to recommend "special and extraordinary measures" for dealing with the Jewish relief problem, as had been requested by Jewish groups. See *JTA,* November 23, 1943, p. 3.

38. *JTA,* November 7, 1943. *The Day,* November 11, 1943, p. 1.

39. *The Day,* November 11, 1943, p. 1. This was also a rare Jewish criticism of the President.

40. *JTA,* November 19, 1943, p. 1. The headline over this lead item in the bulletin was "MOSCOW CONFERENCE DECISIONS INCLUDE PUNISHMENT OF NAZIS FOR CRIMES AGAINST JEWS."

41. *JTA,* November 26, 1943, p. 4.

42. Editorial, *The Day,* November 19, 1943, p. 4. A. Glanz, November 21, 1943, p. 4, called it a "historic statement."

43. *Opinion,* December 1932, pp. 4–5.

44. *Answer,* December 5, 1943, p. 21.

45. *NYT,* November 5, 1943, p. 14, and *The Day,* November 6, 1943, p. 1.

46. *The Day,* November 7, 1943, p. 4, and *CW,* November 9, 1943, p. 5.

47. The *Answer,* December 5, 1943, p. 4.

48. *NYT,* March 25, 1944, p. 1.

49. *NYT,* November 10, 1943, p. 19, and *JTA,* November 10, 1943, p. 1.

50. *Forward,* November 10, 1943, p. 1. See also Feingold, *Politics,* p. 230 and the *Answer,* December 5, 1943, pp. 18–19. An indication of the persuasiveness of Bergson and his associates is found in Lucy

Dawidowicz' judgment that Gillette's legislative record of opposition to the Nazis had been particularly weak, "American Jews," p. 111.

51. Editorials, *MJ*, November 21, 1943, p. 4, and December 22, 1943, p. 4. Y. Fishman—who opposed Bergson personally—and D. Eidelsberg both supported the resolutions, December 3, 1943, p. 4, as did L. Kusman, December 9, 1943, p. 4.

52. December 3, 1943, pp. 1 and 4. The *Forward* reprinted that day the December 1 editorial from the *New York Herald Tribune* in support of the resolutions.

53. *The Day*, November 20, 1943, p. 1.

54. *The Day*, Margoshes' column, November 25, 1943, p. 1.

55. *The Day*, *loc. cit.*, and editorial, December 4, 1943, p. 4. See also Dr. I. Brutzkus, December 10, 1943, p. 4, who strongly criticized Wise for opposing Gillette-Rogers.

56. *The Day*, December 7, 1943, p. 1. The same view was expressed by S. Dingol on p. 4 of the same issue. He complained that Wise's criticism was too mild. "The resolution is worse than nothing."

57. *NYT*, December 3, 1943, p. 4.

58. Among the Jewish organizations only the Agudat Ha-Rabanim was reported to have openly urged the House to pass the Rogers resolution. *Morning Journal*, December 21, 1943, p. 7. It appears that the National Council of Jewish Women may also have expressed some support. See *JTA*, November 28, 1943, p. 4. Otherwise, no large Jewish organization seems to have supported the resolutions publicly. Non-Jewish groups, on the other hand, seem to have been less hesitant about their support, perhaps because of the public relations efforts of the Emergency Committee. See *NYT*, December 3, 1943, p. 4, and *JTA*, December 16, 1943, p. 4, and December 22, 1943, p. 2.

59. *JTA*, December 3, 1943, p. 1. See also the *Conference Record: A Bulletin of Activities of the American Jewish Conference*, 1:6 (January 15, 1944), p. 2.

60. *CW*, December 10, 1943, p. 3. The same point was made by *NJM*, January, 1944, p. 146.

61. Feingold, *Politics*, pp. 238–39.

62. "Chronicle of Events," *CW*, November 26, 1943, p. 2 and *NP*, January 7, 1944, pp. 174, 189–90.

63. *JTA*, November 24, 1943, p. 4.

64. This metaphor was used by Henry Feingold in considering the importance of the issues that divided American Jews during the Holocaust. "Roosevelt and the Holocaust." p. 267. See also E. Aurbach in *MJ*, January 4, 1944, p. 4, who bemoaned the public nature of the fight.

65. *Reconstructionist*, January 21, 1944, p. 3.

66. B. Z. Goldberg in *The Day*, November 16, 1943, p. 4.

67. See D. Eidelsberg, *MJ.* November 1943, p. 4; L. Kusman *MJ,* December 9, 1943, p. 4, and Y. Brutzkus, *The Day,* December 24, 1943, p. 6.

68. The text of the statement may be found in *NP,* June 7, 1944, pp. 174, 189–90.

69. The *MJ* also vacillated, but its editorial on January 11, 1943, p. 4, showed it backing away from its former support of the committee.

70. *JTA,* January 4, 1944, p. 3, January 21, 1944, p. 2, and *Forward,* January 20, 1944, p. 1. On January 22, Chief Rabbi Herzog issued a statement denying any ties with the committee and indicating that his rescue contacts were with the established Jewish agencies. *JTA,* January 23, 1944, p. 3; *The Day,* same date, p. 3.

71. Quoted in the *Answer,* June 15, 1944, p. 19.

72. The terrible dilemma faced by Zionists, when they were forced to choose between support of rescue or support of Palestine, is described by Henry Feingold in his review essay "An Eccentric Founder," on Lipsky's memoirs, pp. 79–80. See also Bauer, *My Brother's Keeper,* p. 135, who cites a similar dilemma for Zionists in the 1930s when avenues of escape other than Palestine presented themselves and were either minimized or ignored.

73. Isaac Lewin, "How Long Will We Play Politics with Jewish Blood?" *Idisheh Shtimeh,* January 1944, p. 5. See also Lewin, *Hurban Eropah,* pp. 78–83.

74. Zaar, *op cit.,* pp. 75–76.

75. Zivyon in the *Forward,* January 8, 1944, p. 6. "A dispute for the sake of heaven" is a reference to a dispute for noble purposes, as described in *Talmud Bavli, Avot,* 5:17.

76. Much of Hirschman's story can be read in his book *Life Line to a Promised Land* (New York: The Vanguard Press, 1946).

77. On January 24, Senator Gillette announced on the Senate floor that he was withdrawing his resolution, because the creation of the WRB made it superfluous. Representative Rogers indicated he would do the same. *JTA,* January 25, 1944, p. 1. The text of the executive order for the creation of the WRB was published in *JTA,* January 24, 1944, p. 2.

78. Strong praises of Roosevelt's action were expressed in the first editorials in the *MJ,* January 24, 1944, p 4, the *Forward,* January 25, 1944, p. 4, and *The Day,* January 25, 1944, p. 4. Similarly, the *NYT* and the *Herald Tribune* both greeted the WRB favorably in editorials on February 1, 1944. See also *JTA,* January 24, 1944, p. 3, January 25, 1944, pp. 1–2, January 26, 1944, p. 2, January 30, 1944, p. 2, and February 1, 1944, p. 3. See also Wyman, *The Abandonment of the Jews,* p. 214.

79. *Forward* and *MJ* on January 25, pp. 8 and 10 respectively. *The Day* on January 26, p. 6.

80. *MJ*, January 24, 1944, p. 4.

81. Cf. editorial, *JF*, February 1944, p. 3.

82. *Conference Record* 1:7 (February 15, 1944), pp. 6–7. *JA* made the same point in a front-page story, January 27, 1944.

83. *CW*, February 5, 1944, p. 3. Kubowitzki, *op. cit.*, p. 165, also gives credit to the established organizations for laying the groundwork for the WRB. He assigns no role to Bergson's group.

84. *NP*, February 4, 1944, p. 227.

85. *NJM*, March 1944, p. 224.

86. Celler to Roosevelt, January 25, 1944, Personal Correspondence File, Roosevelt Library, quoted by S. Friedman, *op. cit.*, p. 230.

87. Hirschman, *Life Line*, p. xv; Kubowitzki, *op. cit.*, pp. 166–67 and Morgenthau, *op. cit.*, p. 65. Feingold in *Politics*, p. 247, is the author of the phrase "indifference and inadvertent collusion with the Nazis." S. Friedman, *op. cit.*, pp. 221–22, estimates the number of lives saved as 50,000. The estimate of 200,000 is Wyman's in *Abandonment*, p. 285.

88. Feingold, *Politics*, p. 242.

89. *JTA*, January 31, 1944, p. 3; *Forward* and *The Day*, January 31, 1944, p. 1.

CHAPTER 7: THE TRAP SHUTS

1. Dawidowicz, *War Against Jews*, p. 38, gives the figure as 750,000, but the press accounts available to American Jews at the time put the figure at 900,000 (JTA, March 22, 1944, p. 1, and *NJM*, April 1944, p. 245), 1 million (*MJ*, March 22, 1944, p. 1), 1.05 million (*CJR*, June 1944, p. 291), and 800,000 (*NYT*, March 12, 1944, p. 4, and *CW*, March 31, 1944, p. 5). The *CJR*, *loc cit.*, estimated that 150,000 of the Jews in Hungary were refugees from other lands.

2. Dawidowicz, *War Against Jews*, pp. 379–81. See also Henry Feingold's analysis in "The Roosevelt Administration and the Effort to Save the Jews of Hungary," *Hungarian Jewish Studies*, Randolph L. Braham, ed. (New York: World Federation of Hungarian Jews, 1969), pp. 217–18. See also the Jewish press' analysis of the special character of preoccupation Hungary in *AJYB*, "Review of the Year 5704," 46 (5705; 1944–1945), pp. 254–57, plus *NJM*, April 1944, p. 245, *CW*, March 31, 1944, p. 5, and *JTA*, March 22, 1944, p. 1.

3. Editorial, *JF*, April 1944, p. 5.

4. *NYT*, November 2, 1943, p. 14, and *JTA*, November 2, 1943, p. 2.

5. *JTA*, March 21, 1944, p. 2.

6. *JTA*, March 16, 1944, p. 1.

7. *JTA*, January 28, 1944, p. 1, and February 2, 1944, p. 1, and throughout February and March.

8. *JTA*, March 6, 1944, p. 1.

9. Although it proved futile at the time, it is possible that this campaign helped to rally public support, which eventually proved useful in the establishment of Israel. One can see support for such a view in the report on Marshall's testimony, *JTA*, March 6, 1944, p. 1.

10. The same news, and its implications for Hungarian Jewry, appeared in the *Times* on March 21, 1944, pp. 1 and 4.

11. Editorial, *MJ*, March 22, 1944, p. 4.

12. The quote is from *JTA*, p. 1, but the reports were page 1 news in all the Yiddish papers. Similar reports were in *NYT*, March 22, 1944, p. 12, and March 23, 1944, p. 7.

13. *NYT*, March 24, 1944, p. 4.

14. *JTA*, April 5, 1944, p. 1.

15. *JTA*. April 2, 1944, p. 1.

16. *MJ*, March 22, 1944, p. 1, and *JTA*, March 23, 1944, p. 2.

17. Editorial, *The Day*, April 3, 1944, p. 6.

18. *JTA*, April 14, 1944, p. 2, and *The Day* and *Forward* same day, p. 1.

19. *NYT*, April 16, 1944, p. 17, and *JTA*, next day, p. 1. This occurred over several days and was reported through April 24.

20. *The Day* and *Forward*, April 17, 1944, p. 1. "Confirmed" in *JTA*, April 19, 1944, p. 1. It is not clear from Dawidowicz, *War Against Jews*, when the deportations actually began. Hilberg, *op. cit.*, cites mid-May as the beginning of mass deportations and suggests that trial deportations were held on April 27 and 28. In any event, what is of concern for this study is not when they began but when American Jews thought they began.

21. *JTA*, April 18, 1944, p. 3.

22. *JTA*, April 24, 1944, p. 2.

23. *NYT*, April 28, 1944, p. 5; *JTA*, same date, p. 2.

24. *JTA*, May 4, 1944, p. 2.

25. *NYT*, May 18, 1944, p. 5. This was repeated by *CW*, May 26, 1944, p. 10. The same magazine, in its April 28 issue, had parenthetically noted in a page 3 editorial, that "trainloads of Hungarian Jews are already on the way to extermination camps in Poland."

26. *JTA*, May 28, 1944, p. 1.

27. Reitlinger, *op. cit.*, pp. 459–61; Dawidowicz, *War Against Jews*, p. 382. According to S. Friedman, *op. cit.*, pp. 220–21, John Pehle, head of the WRB, first wrote to Roosevelt on June 5, informing him that 300,000 Jews were about to be deported. By July 7, Dawidowicz records that over 437,000 had been deported.

28. *JTA*, June 15, 1944, p. 2. A similar story appeared that day on p. 1 in *MJ*. For the earlier reports see *MJ*, June 6, 1944, p. 7, *The Day*, June 10, 1944, p. 2, *MJ*, advertisement, June 12, 1944, p. 2.

29. *JTA*, July 5, 1944, p. 1. See also *NYT*, July 2, 1944, p. 12.

30. *JTA*, June 30, 1944, p. 2. This report in *JTA* was one of the first to use the name "Auschwitz."

31. *NYT*, July 19, 1944, p. 5, and *JTA*, July 31, 1944, p. 1. See also *NYT*, June 22, 1944, p. 9, June 27, 1944, p. 6, Anne O'Hare McCormick, July 15, 1944, p. 12, *JTA* and Yiddish press, June 5, 1944, p. 1, with respect to the King of Sweden's intercession, and Reitlinger, *op. cit.*, p. 468, and Kubowitzki, *op. cit.*, p. 184.

32. *NYT*, March 25, 1944, pp. 1 and 4; *The Day* and *Forward*, same day; *JTA* and *MJ*, March 26.

33. Margoshes in *The Day*, March 28, 1944, p. 1, was the only observer to take note of this at the time.

34. *JTA*, March 27, 1944, p. 4, and *The Day*, March 26, 1944, p. 2.

35. It is unlikely that this call had anything to do with the issuance of Roosevelt's statement. The President's public act was probably the result of WRB strategy, which saw the overwhelming problems involved in attempting to rescue Jews from Hungary and which therefore adopted the strategy of impeding the extermination effort by encouraging the Hungarian bureaucracy to disengage itself from it. The President's warning was designed to stimulate that disengagement. Feingold, *Politics*, p. 251. That this kind of warning had some effect can be judged in part from reports that deportations were often carried out at night in order to avoid interference by the local populace (*JTA*, July 10, 1944, p. 1) and attempts by Hungarian authorities to deny any involvement in the deportations (*JTA*, July 17, 1944, p. 1).

36. The call (see above) was in *JTA*, March 24, 1944, p. 1, and the *Forward*, p. 12. The Proskauer statement of thanks appeared in *JTA*, March 31, 1944, p. 3.

37. Editorial, "The President Speaks Out," *Opinion*, April 1944, p. 7. Glatstein's article in *The Day* appeared on March 26, 1944, p. 4.

38. *JTA*, March 27, 1944, p. 3, quoting the editorial reaction in the *Manchester Guardian*. The *NYT* took a similar position in its editorial, March 25, 1944, p. 14. See also editorial, *The Day*, March 25, 1944, p. 4, and *CW*, "Jewish Commentary," April 7, 1944, p. 12. Theodore N. Lewis in *Opinion*, April 1944, p. 14, described Roosevelt's warning as a "futile undertaking," adding that if the Nazis were really clever they would embarrass the United Nations by offering to free Hungarian Jews on condition that havens be provided for them.

39. *JTA*, April 5, 1944, reported that only 23,775 aliens entered the United States as immigrants in 1943, the lowest figure in eighty years. Obviously wartime restrictions on travel and the dangers of crossing a submarine-infested ocean were at work here, but so was Hitler's extermination program—the people who most needed to come were now dead.

40. *Hadoar,* March 31, 1944, p. 370.

41. Editorial, *JS,* April 1944, p. 5. See also Morse, *op. cit.,* pp. 337–39.

42. *JS, loc. cit., CW,* March 31, 1944, p. 6; *MJ,* April 11, 1944, p. 5.

43. *NYT,* April 19, 1944, p. 1. The *Times* also supported the idea editorially on May 3, 1944, p. 18. See also Feingold, *Politics,* p. 260. For the text of the Grafton proposal see *CJR,* August 1944, and *Opinion,* July 1944, p. 15.

44. Editorials: *The Day,* May 13 and 27 and June 2; the *Forward,* May 6 and 8, and June 2; *CW,* April 28, 1944, pp. 3–4, and May 26, 1944, p. 10; *JE,* June 16, 1944, p. 6; and *JA,* June 1, 1944, p. 1.

45. Editorial, *Forward,* May 6, 1944, p. 4; *JTA,* May 7, 1944, p. 4, and May 11, 1944, p. 3.

46. *JTA,* June 12, 1944, p. 3. What is somewhat surprising about this optimistic appraisal is that it was made right after Roosevelt announced his decision for one Free Port, which would accommodate 1,000 refugees among whom there would only be some Jews. See also *JF,* May 1944, pp. 3–4.

47. June 15, 1944, p. 4. This was also after the June 9 announcement of the Free Port by Roosevelt. Other endorsement came from the Independent Order of Brith Abraham (*JTA,* June 20, p. 4), United Rumanian Jews (*JTA,* May 15, p. 4), the Union of American Hebrew Congregations, and the National Committee Against Persecution of the Jews, headed by Judge Murphy (*JTA,* May 29, p. 3). See the *CJR,* August 1944, p. 401, for other organizations, Jewish and non-Jewish.

48. Editorial, *JS,* June 1944, p. 5, and Murray Frank, "WRB and Free Ports," *NP,* May 19, 1944, pp. 400 and 410.

49. See Feingold, *Politics,* pp. 264–65.

50. *JTA,* June 11, 1944, p. 3. See also *JTA,* June 4 and 11, 1944, p. 1, and *NYT,* June 10, 1944, p. 1. See also S. Friedman, *op. cit.,* p. 220.

51. *JTA,* June 23, 1944, p. 3. See also *JTA,* June 12, 1944, p. 2, and June 14, 1944, p. 3.

52. *Hadoar,* June 16, 1944, p. 589. Ribalow had earlier expressed the hope that the United States, which until then had had room only for camps for "degenerate butchers," that is, German POWs, would now establish camps for refuge for the victims. April 28, 1944, p. 430.

53. Editorial, "Who Will Be the Lucky Thousand?" *JS,* July 1944, p. 4.

54. *JF,* July 1944, p. 6–8. The polls were a matter of concern, for in November Roosevelt was to run for his fourth term.

55. *Ibid.*

56. Hilberg, *op. cit.,* p. 723 and 771.

57. *The Day* and *MJ,* April 4, 1944, p. 1.

58. *JTA,* May 15, 1944, p. 2.

59. Feingold, *Politics,* p. 292.

60. Editorial, "Saving the Last Million," *CW,* May 19, 1944, pp. 3–4. See also *Jewish Forum,* May 1944, p. 96.

61. Hilberg, *op. cit.,* p. 723.

62. *JTA,* July 2, 1944, p. 1.

63. Personal interview with two Hungarian survivors of Auschwitz, February 24, 1977. Ben Hecht, *Perfidy,* p. 264, quoting Rabbi Michael Dov Weissmandle, who rescued many Jews from Eastern Europe, reports that when the Germans intercepted a message to the Allies calling on them to bomb certain railroad bridges leading from Hungary to Auschwitz, they then felt free to use those bridges for troop movements because they were sure the bridges would be immune from attack.

64. Isaac Lewin, "Attempts at Rescuing Jews," p. 14.

65. *JTA,* July 20, 1944, p. 1.

66. Editorial, "Last Chance for Rescue," *JF,* August 1944, p. 4.

67. Herbert Druks, "Why the Death Camps Were Not Bombed," *American Zionist,* December 1976, p. 18. Fishman's article is in *MJ,* June 27, 1944, p. 1.

68. Kubowitzki, *op. cit.,* p. 167. For an analysis of Allied capabilities for such missions see S. Friedman, *op. cit.,* p. 228, and Louis Tursky, "Could the Death Camps Have Been Bombed?" *JS,* September 1964, pp. 19–24. Hecht, *Perfidy,* p. 264, quoting the transcript of the Rudolf Kastner trial, reports that a survivor testified at the trial that the industrial plants and the military targets in Auschwitz were bombed but the gas chambers and crematoria were not. The most comprehensive discussion of the pleas for bombing the rail junctions and the camps appears in David S. Wyman, "Why Auschwitz Was Never Bombed," *Commentary,* May 1978, pp. 37–46. He concludes that bombing the junctions would not have been effective, but that bombing the camps might have saved tens of thousands of lives. See also Wyman, *Abandonment,* pp. 288–307. The full text of the McCloy letter is on p. 296.

69. *MJ,* March 23, 1944, p. 1.

70. Y. Fishman, *ibid.,* May 19, 1944, p. 1.

71. Editorial, *MJ,* June 28, 1944, p. 4.

72. *Forward,* March 22, 23, April 19, 1944, p. 4, and May 12, 1944, p. 1.; *The Day,* March 22, 1944, p. 4; Margoshes in *The Day,* March 23, 1944, p. 1; editorial, *The Day,* April 3, 1944, p. 6.

73. *Reconstructionist,* April 13, 1944, p. 7. It was a brief comment. On June 23 there was an editorial in support of Free Ports without mention of Hungarian Jewry.

74. *NJM,* April 1944, p. 245.

75. *Opinion,* June 1944, p. 5. Theodore Lewis in the same magazine urged a more active and constructive response, but the editorial policy remained one of resignation. See April 1944, p. 5, and May 1944, p. 4.

76. *JS,* May 1944, p. 4.

77. *JS,* May and July 1944, p. 6.

78. Murray Frank, "WRB and Free Ports," *NP,* May 19, 1944, p. 400. See also *NP,* April 21, 1944, p. 347. The editorial accused the world of treating the Hungarian crisis "with sloth of heart, with frivolity of mind, with a bad conscience, to be sure, but with a bad conscience which prefers its own discomfort and its own gnawing to any redeeming or liberating act." See also *JF,* April 1944, pp. 5–6.

79. *Jewish Outlook,* June 1944, p. 4. See also editorials, April 1944, pp. 4–5, June, 1944, p. 4, and Gedaliah Bublick's "The Year 5705," September 1944, pp. 5–6.

80. Editorial, "The Critical Tasks Ahead," *CW,* June 30, 1944, p. 4.

81. Pehle cited both of these organizations for their rescue and rehabilitation work. *JTA,* May 15, 1944, p. 3.

82. See N. Cohen, *op. cit.,* pp. 247–48, on its role during this period.

83. *JTA,* July 12, 1944, p. 3.

84. See Dingol, *The Day,* May 13, 1944, p. 7, and *Conference Record,* June 1944, p. 8.

85. See advertisements in *MJ,* April 19, 1944, p. 10, May 5, 1944, p. 3, May 10, 1944, p. 3, and June 23, 1944, p. 12. Articles appeared May 5, 1944, p. 1 and 4, and June 10, 1944, p. 10. Rabbi Silver's support was reported May 8, 1944, p. 2, and May 10, 1944, p. 1.

86. *NYT,* April 20, 1944, p. 10. *The Day,* April 20, 1944, p. 1, did not indicate that the American Jewish Conference program in Carnegie Hall called for action to save European Jewry.

87. *Forward,* June 24, 1944, p. 12. *JTA,* June 27, 1944, p. 4, and following days. *Liberal Judaism* devoted thirteen pages to the CCAR Convention in its issue of July 1944. The Hungarian Jewish plight was not even mentioned. It was as if it did not exist. The Conference of Jewish Social Workers met for five days in May. *JTA* reported no mention of the Hungarian situation, May 18, 1944, p. 3, and May 21 and 22.

88. This was the implication in the American Jewish Congress' decision to cancel its biennial convention in late June. *JTA,* June 16, 1944, p. 4. See also *JTA,* June 27, 1944, p. 4, on the Rabbinical Assembly Convention, and *JTA,* May 18, 1944, p. 3, on the Social Workers Conference. That conference took place before June 6 but the mood of looking toward the future was probably already well established.

89. Full-page ads appeared in *The Day* (April 10, p. 3), the *Forward*

(April 11, p. 3), and the *MJ* (April 11, p. 10), and again in *The Day*, June 2, p. 3, and July 12, p. 7.

90. The *Answer*, May 1, 1944, p. 30; *MJ*, April 3, 1944, p. 1.

91. *The Day*, May 1, 1944, p. 3. *The Day* and *MJ* carried ads for the rally and printed page 1 news stories about it in advance. *JTA* did not cover it.

92. *The Day*, July 20, 1944, p. 1. Full-page ads had appeared in all three Yiddish dailies for two weeks before the rally. Again the *JTA* did not report on the rally.

93. *Conference Record*, August 1944, p. 7.

94. Editorials, July 21 and 31, 1944, p. 4.

95. *MJ* cited the lower figure, *The Day* the higher one, while the *Forward* estimated 75,000. All stories were on page 1 on August 1, 1944. See also *NYT*, same date, p. 17.

96. *JTA*, August 1, 1944, p. 2.

97. *NJM*, September 1944, p. 2.

98. *CW*, August 11, 1944, p. 3.

CHAPTER 8: WERE WE OUR BROTHERS' KEEPERS?

1. See Jacob Katz, "Was the Holocaust Predictable?" *Commentary*, May 1975, pp. 41–48.

2. Stember, *op. cit.*, p. 110.

3. Wyman, *Paper Walls*, p. 69.

4. *Ibid.*, pp. 23–25.

5. *CW*, May 26, 1944, p. 10; *Opinion*, July 1944, p. 15.

6. See Ben Halpern, "We and the European Jews," *JF*, August 1943, p. 15.

7. Halperin, *op. cit.*, p. 21.

8. *Ibid.*, p. 381, n. 62.

9. Bauer, *The Holocaust in Historical Perspective*, p. 22.

10. Louis De Jong, "The Netherlands and Auschwitz," *Yad Vashem Studies*, 8, p. 78.

11. Kubowitzki, *op. cit.*, p. 195.

12. Menachem Rosensaft's phrase in "The Holocaust," p. 55.

13. Stember, *op. cit.*, p. 141.

14. One rabbi, who was in his early twenties in 1938, recalled in a personal interview (December 24, 1977) that when he first heard the reports his instinctive reaction was: "These must be more atrocity stories like those that were created in World War I to inspire hatred of

the enemy." One wonders how many others were affected by this recollection, which was reinforced by historians writing about World War I in the 1930s.

15. This explanation was offered by Mortimer Ostow, M.D., in a personal letter, July 12, 1978. It has since been documented by Walter Laqueur in his "Jewish Denial and the Holocaust," *Commentary*, December 1979, pp. 44–55, and in *Terrible Secret*.

16. See Dawidowicz, "American Jews," pp. 101–102. This explanation has been offered by many American Jews in recollecting what their major concerns were during the Holocaust years. It is probably an accurate reflection of what was transpiring in their lives.

17. Daniel J. Elazar, "Jews and American Political Ideas," *Congress bi-Weekly*, January 3, 1969, p. 5.

18. Wise's letter to Roosevelt, December 2, 1942, asking him to meet with the Joint Emergency Committee for Jewish Affairs with reference to the reports about the Final Solution. Voss, *op. cit.*, p. 253.

19. *Ibid.*

20. Elie Wiesel, "Telling the Tale," *Dimensions in American Judaism*, Spring 1968, p. 11.

21. See S. Friedman, *op. cit.*, pp. 152–54. He suggests that an attack on the President would have been condemned as seditious.

22. Marie Syrkin, personal letter, January 18, 1978.

23. For a review of what was known in the period from the beginning of the war until the Wise disclosures, see Alex Grobman, "What Did They Know? The American Jewish Press and the Holocaust, 1 September 1939–17 December 1942," *AJH*, 68 (March 1979), pp. 327–52, and Laqueur, *Terrible Secret*.

24. See Feingold, *Politics*, pp. 299–301.

25. See B. Shelvin, "American Jewry's Indifference," *JS*, November 1940, p. 21, and Jacob Lestchinsky, "Where Do We Stand?" *CB*, June 16, 1939, p. 5, among others.

26. See S. Friedman, *op. cit.*, pp. 68–69, for additional options. See also Feingold, *Politics*, pp. 127 and 305, and Wyman, *Abandonment*, pp. 331–35.

27. Feingold, *Politics*, p. 307.

28. Elie Wiesel, *Zalman, or the Madness of God* (New York: Random House, 1974), p. 169. David S. Wyman, *Abandonment*, p. 329, comes to the same conclusion about American Jewish leaders who were unable to break out of a business-as-usual pattern during the Holocaust. Few schedules were rearranged; vacations were seldom sacrificed, and few projects of lesser significance were put aside. A unique sense of urgency was not forthcoming.

29. March 22, 1944, p. 4.

30. Allan G. Field, "And for the Sin of Callous Indifference," *JS*, September 1945, pp. 16–17.

31. *Menorah Journal*, Spring 1944, p. 3.

32. Judah Piltch, "A Day of Mourning for Children," *Hadoar*, January 15, 1943, p. 174. The "49 levels" is a literary reference from Jewish lore concerning a state of spiritual defilement and impurity.

33. *Reconstructionist*, March 5, 1943, p. 20.

SELECTED
BIBLIOGRAPHY

PRIMARY SOURCES

The newspapers and periodicals that have been read for the periods under review are listed in Chapter 1.

Adamic, Louis. *America and the Refugees,* Public Affairs Pamphlets No. 29. New York: Public Affairs Committee, 1939.

Alderman, Harry. Oral interview, August 4, 1975. Mr. Alderman was an editor of the *American Jewish Year Book* during the Holocaust and was serving as director of the Blaustein Library of the American Jewish Committee at the time of the interview.

Apenszlak, Jacob, and Moshe Polakiewicz. *Armed Resistance of the Jews in Poland.* New York: American Federation for Polish Jews, 1944.

Benedict, Libby. "After Germany Is Liberated," *Congress Weekly,* November 14, 1941, pp. 8–10.

Bloom, Sol. *The Autobiography of Sol Bloom.* New York: G. P. Putnam's Sons, 1948.

Cohen, Morris R. "Jewish Studies of Peace and Post-War Problems," *Contemporary Jewish Record,* April 1941, pp. 110–25.

Engelbrecht, H. C., Joshua Trachtenberg, et al. *How to Combat Anti-Semitism in America.* New York: Jewish Opinion Publishing Corp., 1937.

Field, Allan G. "And for the Sin of Callous Indifference," *Jewish Spectator,* September 1945, pp. 16–17.

Fortune Survey XX. *Fortune,* April 1939, pp. 86–87.

General Jewish Council. Minutes of meetings on November 13, 1938, and December 18, 1938. Available in Blaustein Library, American Jewish Committee, New York, N.Y.

The Ghetto Speaks. Nos. 11 (May 1, 1943), 12 (June 1, 1943), 15 (September 1, 1943). Press releases issued by the American Representation of the General Jewish Workers' Union of Poland. New York.

Goldberg, Nathan. "Decline of the Yiddish Press," *Chicago Jewish Forum,* Fall 1944, pp. 15–21.

Greenberg, Hayim. "Bankrupt," *Yiddisher Kemfer,* February 12, 1943, pp. 1–3. Translated into English by Shlomo Katz.

———. "6,000,000 and 5,000,000: Notes in Midstream." *Midstream,* March 1964, pp. 3–14.

Halpern, Ben. "We and the European Jews," *Jewish Frontier,* August 1943, pp. 15–18.

Hirschman, Ira A. *Life Line to a Promised Land.* New York: The Vanguard Press, 1946.

———. Taped interview, New York, April 12, 1977.

Hull, Cordell. *The Memoirs of Cordell Hull.* 2 vols. New York: The Macmillan Co., 1948.

Ickes, Harold L. *The Secret Diary of Harold L. Ickes.* Vol. II, *The Inside Struggle 1936–1939.* New York: Simon and Schuster, 1954.

Joint Emergency Committee for European Jewish Affairs. "Program for the Rescue of Jews from Nazi Occupied Europe. Submitted April 14, 1943, to the Bermuda Refugee Conference," *Congress Weekly,* April 30, 1943, pp. 11–12.

Kaplan, Mordecai M. "What the American Jewish Conference Should Ask For," The *Reconstructionist,* June 25, 1943, pp. 7–13.

Karski, Jan. *Story of a Secret State.* Boston: Houghton Mifflin Co., 1944.

Kohanski, Alexander S., ed. *The American Jewish Conference: Its Organization and Proceedings of the First Session, August 20 to September 2, 1943.* New York: American Jewish Conference, 1944.

Lewin, Isaac. *Hurban Eropah: A Collection of Essays.* New York: Research Institute for Post-War Problems of Religious Jewry, 1948.

Linfield, H. S. "Jewish Communities of the United States: Number and Distribution of Jews of the United States in Urban Places and in Rural Territory," *American Jewish Year Book,* 42 (5701, 1940–1941). Philadelphia: The Jewish Publication Society of America, 1940, pp. 215–65.

Lubetkin, Zivia. "Last Days of the Warsaw Ghetto." *Commentary,* May 1947, pp. 401–11.

Minkoff, Isaiah. Personal interview, October 23, 1977.

Morgenthau, Henry, Jr. "The Morgenthau Diaries. No. VI. The Refugee Run-Around," *Colliers,* November 1, 1947, pp. 22, 23, 62, 65.

Netanyahu, B. "Our Post-War Problems," *Congress Weekly,* March 14, 1941, pp. 7–9.

Neustadt, Aaron M. "An Orchid for the Jewish Press," *National Jewish Monthly,* November 1946, pp. 94–95, 108–109.

Park, Robert E. *The Immigrant Press and Its Control.* New York and London: Harper and Brothers, 1922.

Riegner, Gerhard. Taped interview, April 24, 1975, New York, New York.

Ringelblum, Emmanuel. *Notes from the Warsaw Ghetto: The Journal of Emmanuel Ringelblum.* Edited and translated by Jacob Sloan. New York: McGraw-Hill Book Co., 1958.

Rothschild, Richard C. "Are American Jews Falling into the Nazi Trap?" *Contemporary Jewish Record,* 3 (January–February 1940), pp. 9–17.

Sachar, Abram Leon. *Suffering Is the Badge.* New York: Alfred A. Knopf, 1939.

Shelvin, B. "American Jewry's Indifference," *Jewish Spectator,* November 1940, pp. 21–22.

Soltes, Mordecai. *The Yiddish Press: An Americanizing Agency.* New York: Teachers College, Columbia University, 1924.

Strong, Donald S. *Organized Anti-Semitism in America: The Rise of Group Prejudice During the Decade 1930–40.* Washington, D.C.: American Council on Public Affairs, 1941.

Tartakower, Arieh, and Kurt R. Grossman. *The Jewish Refugee.* New York: Institute of Jewish Affairs of the American Jewish Congress and World Jewish Congress, 1944.

Wechsler, James. "Coughlin Terror," *The Nation,* July 22, 1939, pp. 92–97.

Weizmann, Chaim. *Trial and Error: The Autobiography of Chaim Weizmann.* New York: Harper and Brothers, 1949.

Wise, Stephen S. *As I See It.* New York: Jewish Opinion Publishing House, 1944.

———. *Challenging Years: The Autobiography of Stephen Wise.* New York: G. P. Putnam's Sons, 1949.

Secondary Sources

Abella, Irving, and Harold Troper. *None Is Too Many: Canada and the Jews of Europe, 1933–1948.* New York: Random House, 1982.

Adler, Selig. "America's Moment of Failure," Review of *While Six Million Died,* by Arthur D. Morse. *Midstream,* May 1968, pp. 66–72.

———. "The United States and the Holocaust," *American Jewish Historical Quarterly,* 64 (September 1974), pp. 14–23.

Agar, Herbert. *The Saving Remnant: An Account of Jewish Survival.* New York: The Viking Press, 1960.

Ainsztein, Reuben. "Facing the Truth," *The Jewish Quarterly,* 16 (Spring 1968), pp. 35–39.

Arendt, Hannah. *Eichmann in Jerusalem: A Report on the Banality of Evil.* New York: The Viking Press, 1963.

Bailey, Thomas A. *The Man in the Street: The Impact of American Public Opinion on Foreign Policy.* New York: The Macmillan Co., 1948.

Bauer, Yehuda. *American Jewry and the Holocaust: The American Jewish Joint Distribution Committee 1929–1939.* Detroit: Wayne State University Press, 1981.

———. *From Diplomacy to Resistance: A History of Jewish Palestine 1939–1945.* Translated by Alton M. Winters. Philadelphia: The Jewish Publication Society of America, 1970.

———. *The Holocaust in Historical Perspective.* Seattle: University of Washington Press, 1978.

———. *My Brother's Keeper: A History of the American Jewish Joint Distribution Committee 1929–1939.* Philadelphia: The Jewish Publication Society of America, 1974.

———. Reply to letter of Marie Syrkin, *Midstream,* May 1968, pp. 63–54.

———. "When Did They Know?" *Midstream,* April 1968, pp. 51–58.

Berger, Meyer. *History of the Times: The Story of the New York Times 1851–1951.* New York: Simon and Schuster, 1951.

Berman, Aaron. "American Zionism and the Rescue of European Jewry: An Ideological Perspective," *American Jewish History*, 70:3 (March 1981), pp. 310–30.

Black, Edwin. *The Transfer Agreement: The Untold Story of the Secret Pact Between the Third Reich and Jewish Palestine.* New York: Macmillan Publishing Company, 1984.

Brody, David. "American Jewry, the Refugees and Immigration Restriction (1932–1942)," *Publication of the American Jewish Historical Society*, 45 (June 1956), pp. 219–47.

Cohen, Noami W. *Not Free to Desist: The American Jewish Committee 1906–1966.* Philadelphia: The Jewish Publication Society of America, 1972.

Dawidowicz, Lucy S. *The War Against the Jews 1933–1945.* New York: Holt, Rinehart and Winston, 1975.

Diamond, Sander A. "The Kristallnacht and the Reaction in America," *YIVO Annual of Jewish Social Science*, 14 (1969), pp. 196–208.

Druks, Herbert. "The Allies and Jewish Leadership on the Question of Bombing Auschwitz," *Tradition*, 19:1 (Spring, 1981), pp. 28–34.

———. *The Failure to Rescue.* New York: Robert Speller and Sons, 1977.

———. "Why the Death Camps Were Not Bombed," *The American Zionist*, December 1976, pp. 18–21.

Elazar, Daniel J. "Jews and American Political Ideas," *Congress bi-Weekly*, January 13, 1969, pp. 3–7.

Emery, Edwin. *The Press and America: An Interpretive History of Journalism.* Englewood Cliffs, N.J.: Prentice-Hall, 1954.

Feingold, Henry L. "An Eccentric Founder," review essay on *Memoirs in Profile*, by Louis Lipsky. *Midstream*, January, 1977, pp. 77–80.

———. *The Politics of Rescue: The Roosevelt Administration and the Holocaust, 1938–1945.* New Brunswick, N.J.: Rutgers University Press, 1970.

———. Review essay on *No Haven for the Oppressed: United States Policy Toward Jewish Refugees, 1938–1945*, by Saul S. Friedman, *American Jewish Historical Quarterly*, 64 (December 1974), pp. 161–66.

———. Review essay of *While Six Million Died*, by Arthur D. Morse, *American Jewish Historical Quarterly*, 58 (September 1968), pp. 150–55.

————. "Roosevelt and the Holocaust: Reflections on New Deal Humanitarianism," *Judaism*, 18 (Summer 1969), pp. 259–76.

————. "The Roosevelt Administration and the Effort to Save the Jews of Hungary," *Hungarian Jewish Studies*. Randolph L. Braham, ed. New York: World Federation of Hungarian Jews, 1969, pp. 211–44.

————. "Who Shall Bear the Guilt for the Holocaust?" *American Jewish History*, 68:3 (March 1979), pp. 261–82.

————. *Zion in America: The Jewish Experience from Colonial Times to the Present*. New York: Hippocrene Books, 1974.

Friedman, Philip, ed. *Martyrs and Fighters: The Epic of the Warsaw Ghetto*. New York: Frederick A. Praeger, 1954.

Friedman, Saul S. *No Haven for the Oppressed: United States Policy Toward Jewish Refugees, 1938–1945*. Detroit: Wayne State University Press, 1973.

Fuchs, Laurence H. *The Political Behavior of American Jews*. Glencoe, Ill.: The Free Press, 1956.

Gilbert, Martin. *Auschwitz and the Allies*. New York: Holt, Rinehart and Winston, 1981.

Glatstein, Jacob, Israel Knox, and Samuel Margoshes, eds., *Anthology of Holocaust Literature*. Philadelphia: The Jewish Publication Society of America, 1969.

Goldberg, B. Z. "The American Yiddish Press at Its Centennial," *Judaism*, Spring 1971, pp. 223–28.

————. "The Passing of the Day—Jewish Morning Journal," *Midstream*, April, 1972, pp. 12–29.

Goldin, Milton. *Why They Give: American Jews and Their Philanthropies*. New York: Macmillan Publishing Co., 1976.

Goldmann, Nahum. *The Autobiography of Nahum Goldmann: Sixty Years of Jewish Life*. New York: Holt, Rinehart and Winston, 1969.

Gottlieb, Moshe. "The Anti-Nazi Boycott Movement in the American Jewish Community, 1933–1941." Ph.D. dissertation, Brandeis University, 1967.

————. "The First of April Boycott and the Reaction of the American Jewish Community," *American Jewish Historical Quarterly*, 57 (June 1968), pp. 516–56.

Grinstein, Hyman B. *The Rise of the Jewish Community of New York 1654–1860*. Philadelphia: The Jewish Publication Society of America, 1945.

Grobman, Alex. "What Did They Know? The American Jewish Press and the Holocaust, 1 September 1939–17 December 1942." *American Jewish History*, 68:3 (March, 1979), pp. 327–52.

———. "The Warsaw Ghetto Uprising in the American Jewish Press," *Wiener Library Bulletin*, 29 (1976), New Series Nos. 37/38.

Grossman, Kurt R. "Refugees, DP's and Migrants," *The Institute Anniversary Volume 1941–1961*. New York: Institute of Jewish Affairs, World Jewish Congress, 1962.

Gruber, Ruth. *Haven: The Unknown Story of 1000 World War II Refugees*. New York: Coward-McCann, Inc., 1983.

Grusd, Edward E. *B'nai B'rith: The Story of a Covenant*. New York: Appleton-Century, 1966.

Halperin, Samuel. *The Political World of American Zionism*. Detroit: Wayne State University Press, 1961.

Handlin, Oscar. *Adventure in Freedom: Three Hundred Years of Jewish Life in America*. New York: McGraw-Hill Book Co., 1954.

———. *A Continuing Task: The American Jewish Joint Distribution Committee 1914–1964*. New York: Random House, 1964.

Hecht, Ben. *Perfidy*. New York: Julian Messner, 1961.

Hilberg, Raul. *The Destruction of the European Jews*. Chicago: Quadrangle Books, 1961.

Hochhuth, Rolf. *The Deputy*. Translated by Richard and Clara Winston. New York: Grove Press, 1964.

Katz, Jacob. "Was the Holocaust Predictable?" *Commentary*, May 1975, pp. 41–48.

Katz, Shlomo, translator, "6,000,000 and 5,000,000: Notes in Midstream," *Midstream*, March 1964, pp. 3–14.

Kochan, Lionel. *Pogrom, 10 November 1938*. London: Andre Deutsch, 1957.

Kubowitzki, A. Leon, et al., eds. *Unity in Dispersion: A History of the World Jewish Congress*. New York: World Jewish Congress, 1948.

Kurzman, Dan. *The Bravest Battle: The Twenty-Eight Days of the Warsaw Ghetto Uprising*. New York: Putnam, 1976.

Laqueur, Walter. *A History of Zionism*. New York: Holt, Rinehart and Winston, 1972.

———. "Jewish Denial and the Holocaust." *Commentary*, December 1979, pp. 44–55.

————. *The Terrible Secret: Suppression of the Truth About Hitler's 'Final Solution.'* Boston, Toronto: Little, Brown and Company, 1980.

Laub, Morris. "A Lament for the Tog." *Conservative Judaism*, 26:4, pp. 63–66.

Lazin, Frederick A. "The Response of the American Jewish Committee to the Crisis of German Jewry, 1933–1939." *American Jewish History*, 68:3 (March 1979), pp. 283–304.

Levin, Nora. *The Holocaust: The Destruction of European Jewry 1933–1945.* New York: Schocken Books, 1973.

Lewin, Isaac. "Attempts at Rescuing European Jews with the Help of Polish Diplomatic Missions during World War II." *The Polish Review*, 22:4, pp. 3–23.

Lipsky, Louis. *Memoirs in Profile.* Philadelphia: Jewish Publication Society of America, 1975.

Lowenheim, Francis L., Harold D. Langley, Manfred Jonas, eds. *Roosevelt and Churchill: Their Secret Wartime Correspondence.* New York: Saturday Review Press/E. P. Dutton and Co., 1975.

Lowenstein, Sharon. "A New Deal for Refugees: The Promise and Reality of Oswego," *American Jewish History*, 71:3 (March 1982), pp. 325–41.

MacLeish, Archibald. "Poetry and Journalism," *A Continuing Journey.* Boston: Houghton Mifflin Co., 1967.

Mark, Ber. *Uprising in the Warsaw Ghetto.* Originally published in Polish in 1959. Translated into Yiddish and then into English, the latter by Gershon Friedlin. New York: Schocken Books, 1975.

Meed, Vladka. *On Both Sides of the Wall: Memoirs from the Warsaw Ghetto.* Translated by Moshe Spiegel and Steven Meed. Tel Aviv: Ghetto Fighters House and Hakibbutz Hameuchad Publishing House, 1972.

Monsky, Daisy (Mrs. Henry), and Maurice Bisgyer. *Henry Monsky: The Man and His Work.* New York: Crown Publishing, 1947.

Morse, Arthur D. *While Six Million Died: A Chronicle of American Apathy.* New York: Random House, 1967.

Penkower, Monty Noam. "In Dramatic Dissent: The Bergson Boys," *American Jewish History*, 70:3 (March 1981), pp. 281–309.

————. *The Jews Were Expendable: Free World Diplomacy and the*

Holocaust. Urbana and Chicago: University of Illinois Press, 1983.

Poliakov, Leon. *Harvest of Hate: The Nazi Program for the Destruction of the Jews of Europe.* Philadelphia: The Jewish Publication Society of America, 1954.

Polier, Justine Wise, and James Waterman Wise, eds. *The Personal Letters of Stephen Wise.* Boston: The Beacon Press, 1956.

Postal, Bernard. "The English-Jewish Press," *Dimensions in American Judaism,* Fall 1969, pp. 30–34.

Rapaport, Joseph. "Jewish Immigrants and World War I: A Study of American Yiddish Press Reactions." Unpublished Ph.D. dissertation, Columbia University (12/01, 00–03112).

Reitlinger, Gerald. *The Final Solution: The Attempt to Exterminate the Jews of Europe 1939–1945.* 2d rev. ed. New York: Thomas Yoseloff, 1961.

Rosensaft, Menachem. "The Holocaust: History as Aberration," *Midstream,* May 1977, pp. 53–55.

Sanders, Ronald. "The *Jewish Daily Forward,*" *Midstream,* December 1962, pp. 79–94.

Schachner, Nathan. *The Price of Liberty: A History of The American Jewish Committee.* New York: The American Jewish Committee, 1948.

Schoenberg, Philip Ernest. "The American Reaction to the Kishinev Pogrom of 1903," *American Jewish Historical Quarterly,* 42 (March 1974), pp. 262–83.

Sharf, Andrew. *The British Press and Jews Under Nazi Rule.* London: Oxford University Press, 1964.

Sherwood, Robert E. *Roosevelt and Hopkins: An Intimate History.* New York: Harper and Brothers, 1948.

Silverman, David Wolf. "The Jewish Press: A Quadrilingual Phenomenon," in Martin E. Marty et al. *The Religious Press in America.* New York: Holt, Rinehart and Winston, 1963, pp. 125–72.

Stember, Charles Herbert et al., *Jews in the Mind of America.* New York: Basic Books, 1966.

Syrkin, Marie. Letter to the Editor, *Midstream,* May 1968, pp. 62–63.

———. "Perfidy and Stale Venom" (a review of Ben Hecht's *Perfidy*), *Jewish Frontier,* January 1962, pp. 13–17

Szonyi, David M. "The Holocaust: Prelude and Postscript." *Jewish Currents,* June 1966, pp. 33–35.

Talese, Gay. *The Kingdom and the Power*. New York and Cleveland: The World Publishing Company, 1969.

Tenenbaum, Joseph. "The Anti-Nazi Boycott Movement in the United States," *Yad Vashem Studies*, 3 (1959), pp. 141–59.

———. "They Might Have Been Rescued," *Congress bi-Weekly*, February 2, 1953, pp. 3–7.

Thalmann, Rita, and Emmanuel Feinermann. *Crystal Night: 9–10 November 1938*. Translated by Gilles Cremonesi. New York: Coward, McCann and Geoghegan, 1974.

Thomas, Gordon, and Max Morgan Witts. *Voyage of the Damned*. Greenwich, Conn.: Fawcett Publications, 1975.

Tursky, Louis. "Could the Death Camps Have Been Bombed?" *Jewish Frontier*, September 1964, pp. 19–24.

Voss, Carl Herman, ed. *Stephen S. Wise: Servant of the People; Selected Letters*. Philadelphia: The Jewish Publication Society of America, 1969.

Wiesel, Elie. "Telling the Tale," *Dimensions in American Judaism*. Spring 1968, pp. 9–12.

———. *Zalman, or The Madness of God*. New York: Random House, 1974.

Wischnitzer, Mark. *To Dwell in Safety: The Story of Jewish Migration Since 1800*. Philadelphia: The Jewish Publication Society of America, 1948.

———. *Visas to Freedom: The History of HIAS*. Cleveland: The World Publishing Co., 1956.

Wyman, David S. *The Abandonment of the Jews: America and the Holocaust, 1941–1945*. New York: Pantheon Books, 1984.

———. *Paper Walls: America and the Refugee Crisis 1938–1941*. Boston: University of Massachusetts Press, 1968.

———. "Why Auschwitz Was Never Bombed," *Commentary*, May 1978, pp. 37–46.

Zaar, Isaac. *Rescue and Liberation: America's Part in the Birth of Israel*. New York: Bloch Publishing Co., 1954.

Zuroff, Efraim. "Rescue Priority and Fund Raising as Issues During the Holocaust: A Case Study of the Relations Between the Vaad Ha-Hatzala and the Joint," *American Jewish History*, 68:3 (March 1979), pp. 305–26.

INDEX

A

Abandonment of the Jews, The, 22
Adamic, Louis, on refugees, 545
Advisory Committee on Refugees, 69
Agudat Ha-Rabonim, 70
  Final Solution news and, 110
  fund-raising appeal of, 74
  Kristallnacht reaction of, 72
Agudat Israel
  action call of, 133
  day of prayer and, 135
  Final Solution news and, 109
  in Joint Emergency Committee, 143
  on rescue, 20
Alfange, Dean
  American Jewish Conference attack rebuttal by, 178
  on Gillette-Rogers Resolutions, 174
America and the Refugees, 55
American Emergency Committee for Zionist Affairs
  in Joint Emergency Committee, 143
American Federation for Jews in Poland, rally by, 138
American Federation of Labor, rally sponsorship by, 140
American Friends Service Committee and Wagner-Rogers Act, 98
American Institute on Judaism and a Just and Enduring Peace, 132

American Jewish Assembly. *See* American Jewish Conference.
American Jewish Committee
  appeal to Roosevelt by, 112
  condemnation of, 130
  day of prayer and, 135
  Final Solution news and, 110
  on Free Ports proposal, 193
  in General Jewish Council, 57
  Hungarian activities, 201
  mass rally nonparticipation by, 140
  postwar concerns, 132
  reaction to Roosevelt appeal, 191
  silence policy of, 60
American Jewish Conference
  agenda of, 167
  attacks on Gillette-Rogers Resolutions, 177
  convening of, 166
  formation of, 133
  on Free Ports proposal, 194
  Hungarian activities, 201
  on Palestine, 175
  postwar concerns of, 133
  reaction to Roosevelt appeal, 191
  Rescue Commission on Hungarian deportations, 202
American Jewish Congress
  anti-Nazi activity of, 76
  boycott movement and, 76
  day of prayer and, 135

American Jewish Congress (*continued*)
  Final Solution news and, 110
  in General Jewish Council, 57
  on immigration, 96
  in Joint Emergency Committee, 143
  and mass rallies, 107, 140
  and *St. Louis,* 88
  silence policy of, 60
American Jewish Joint Distribution Committee. *See* Joint Distribution Committee.
American Jewish Labor Committee and Final Solution news, 110
American Jewish leaders, role of, 210
American Jewish response, analysis of, 205
American Jewish Year Book, 26
  on immigration, 94
American League for Defenses of Human Rights, 76
  See also Non-Sectarian Anti-Nazi League.
American League for Peace and Democracy, 63
Angell, Sir Norman, 141
Anielewicz, Mordecai, death of, 148
Answer, 26
  credit to Emergency Committee by, 181
  on Free Ports, 193
Atkinson, Henry A.
  at mass rally, 141
  and rescue call, 123
Atlanta Journal on *Kristallnacht,* 36
Auschwitz and the Allies, 22

B

Baldwin, Joseph Clark, 173
Baruch, Bernard M., 30
  on refugees, 69
Batista, Fulgencio
  Jewish friends of, 88
  and *St. Louis,* 83
Bauer, Yehuda, analysis of American Jewry by, 209
Ben-Gurion, David, on Bergson Group, 163
Benites, Manuel, and Cuban visas, 82
Berenson, Lawrence, and *St. Louis,* 83
Bergson, Peter
  anti-American Jewish Conference action of, 178

and Emergency Conference to Save the Jews of Europe, 163
  and Jewish Legion proposal, 1376
  petition to Roosevelt, 164
  See also Bergson Group; Emergency Committee.
Bergson Group
  actions of, 163
  support for, 163
  See also Bergson, Peter; Emergency Committee.
Berlin, Meir, on Emergency Committee, 179
Bermuda Conference
  effects of, 161
  implications of, 145
  organization of, 143
  and War Refugee Board, 181
Bermuda Refugee Conference. *See* Bermuda Confernce.
Bernstein, Philip S., food relief proposal of, 136
Beveridge, Sir William, 141
Black Thursday. *See Kristallnacht.*
Bloom, Sol, 30, 33
  attacks on Bergson by, 176
  and Gillette-Rogers Resolutions, 176
Bloomingdale's, refugee policies of, 95
B'nai B'rith
  American Jewish Conference and, 133
  appeal to Roosevelt and, 112
  caution of, 124
  and day of prayer, 135
  Final Solution news and, 110
  in General Jewish Council, 57
  in Joint Emergency Committee, 143
  mass rallies and, 107, 140
  rescue proposals of, 136
  and *St. Louis,* 88
  silence policy of, 60
  See also Monsky, Henry.
Boston Advocate and *St. Louis,* 86
Boycott movement, 76
Brandeis, Louis D., 79
Bremen, demonstration at, 63
British Foreign Office, Romanian rescue obstruction by, 138
British policies on Palestine, campaign against, 187
British White Paper on Palestinian immigration, 81, 186

campaign against, 102
psychological effect of, 204
Broun, Heywood, 79
Bru, Federico Laredo, and Cuban immigration, 84
Buchenwald, 36
Buck, Pearl S., and Final Solution news, 122
Budapest, bombing of, 195
Bund, and Polish Jewry extermination, 106

C

Cannon, James Jr., and *St. Louis,* 84
Canterbury, Archibishop of, on Warsaw Ghetto Uprising, 156
Carey, James B., at Carnegie Hall meeting, 156
Carnegie Hall rally on Warsaw Ghetto Uprising, 156
Carnegie Institute of Washington, 95
Catholic Church reaction to Final Solution news, 114
Celler, Emanuel, 30
on immigration, 97, 182
rally support by, 139
Central Conference of American Rabbis
postwar concerns of, 132
on rescue, 201
and *St. Louis,* 87
Central Jewish Council, Hungarian, 189
Chamberlain, Neville, and Palestine, 51
Chase National Bank and *St. Louis,* 83
Chicago Jewish Chronicle, 27
on Final Solution news, 116
and *Kristallnacht,* 73
on refugee problem, 90
and *St. Louis,* 86, 90
Christian Front Organization, activities of, 91
Christian Science Monitor on War Refugee Board, 181
Church Peace Union, mass rally sponsorship by, 140
Churchill, Winston
and Moscow Declaration, 169
on refugee policy, 28
Ciechanowski, Jan, at Carnegie Hall meeting, 156
CIO, mass rally sponsorship by, 140

Cohen, Benjamin V., on refugee policy, 29, 30
Committee for a Jewish Army of Stateless and Palestinian Jews, 137
actions of, 143
Committee for the Rescue of European Jewry, 168
Conference Record, 27
on Hungarian Jews, 201
on War Refugee Board, 181
Congress Bulletin, 26
on American immigration, 207
and collective discipline, 60
on immigration, 96, 99
Kristallnacht reaction of, 49
and *St. Louis,* 86, 89
Congress of Industrial Organizations. *See* CIO.
Congress Weekly
on American Jewish Conference, 167
on American Jewish Conference rally, 204
American Jewry analysis by, 203, 207
on day of prayer, 135
on Final Solution news, 119
on Free Ports proposal, 193
on Gillette-Rogers Resolutions, 176
on Hecht advertisement, 173
on Hungarian bombing, 195
on Moscow Declaration, 171
on Palestine issue, 175
on rescue efforts, 200
on Warsaw Ghetto,150
on Warsaw Ghetto Uprising, 155
on War Refugee Board,
See also Wise, Stephen S.
Conquest by Immigration, 95
Contemporary Jewish Record, 26
and *Kristallnacht,* 50
and *St. Louis,* 87
on Warsaw Ghetto Uprising, 155
Coughlin, Charles E.
anti-Semitism of, 31, 62, 91
audience for, 78
influence of, 91
Council of Churches plea to Roosevelt, 143
Council of Jewish Federations and Welfare Funds
on Final Solution, 127
and *Kristallnacht,* 54
Cuba as refugee host country, 82

D

Dachau, 36
Daily Express (London) on immigration policy, 44
Das Schwartze Korps, threats of, 49
Das, Taraknath, and *Kristallnacht,* 51
Dawidowicz, Lucy S., 23
Day, The, 25, 70, 71
  on American Jewish Conference, 201
  on American Jewish Conference rally for Hungarians, 202
  on day of prayer, 155
  on Emergency Committee, 177
  on Final Solution news, 114
  on Free Ports proposal, 193
  on Gillette-Rogers Resolutions, 174
  on Hecht advertisement, 173
  on Hungarian atrocities, 188, 189
  on Hull statement, 172
  on Jewish silence, 65
  and *Kristallnacht,* 45, 46
  on *Kristallnacht* meeting, 72
  and mass rallies, 63, 139, 140
  on Moscow Declaration, 170, 172
  on rescue operations, 198
  on Roosevelt, 171
  on Roosevelt appeal, 191
  and *St. Louis,* 86, 88
  on Warsaw Ghetto Uprising, 152, 154
Death camps, proposal to bomb, 196
Defender Magazine, immigration policies of, 95
Deutscher, Isaac, advice to S. Zygelboym of, 157
Dewey, Thomas E.
  Final Solution news and, 122
  and *Kristallnacht,* 39
  at mass rally, 141
Dickstein, Samuel, 30
  Free Ports appeal by, 114
  on immigration, 97
Dies, Martin, alien phobias of, 96
Douglas, William O., at mass rally, 14
Down-town Dry Goods Jobbers Association, boycott by, 63
Dubinsky, David, fundraising by, 64

E

Eden, Anthony, and pleas to bomb camps, 197

Edman, Irvin, and Final Solution news, 122
Emergncy Conference to Save the Jewish People of Europe, 163
Emergency Committee on Free Ports, 193
Emergency Committee on Palestine, 175
  ish People of Europe
  Gillettee-Rogers Resolutions as effect of, 174
  on Moscow Declaration, 172
  rabbinic rally by, 164
  reaction to Roosevelt appeal, 191
  rescue activities of, 202
  results of actions by, 179
  support for, 177
  and War Refugee Board, 180
  work for, 173
  See also Bergson, Peter.
Emergency Committee on Palestine, 175
Epstein, Judith K., and *Kristallnacht,* 53
Eugenics Record Office, 95
Evening News (London) on immigration policy, 44
Evian Conference, 54
  action at, 162

F

Federal Council of Churches of Christ in America
  appeal on Hungarian Jews, 190
  Kristallnacht reaction of, 40
  prayer day of, 58
Federation of Polish Jews, on prayer and mourning, 135
Feingold, Henry L., 22
Final Solution, the, 105
  incomprehensibility of, 208
Fishman, Y.
  on bombing camps, 197
  fears for Hungarian Jews, 198
  on mass rally, 140
Flandre and Cuba, 83
Ford, Henry, on refugee policy, 44
Foreign Policy Association on Nazi blackmail, 61
Fort Ontario as emergency refugee shelter, 194. *See also* Free Ports.
Fortune on immigration, 97, 103
Forward
  on Final Solution news, 116

on Free Ports Proposal, 193
on Gillette-Rogers Resolutions, 174
on Hungarian deportations, 190
immigration advice, 97
and *Kristallnacht*, 45, 47
and mass rallies, 64, 139, 141, 170
on rescue operations, 198
and *St. Louis*, 86
on Warsaw Ghetto Uprising, 152, 154
Frankfurter, Felix, 30
and Final Solution news, 108, 131
Free Ports, 193, 194
Free World Association, mass rally sponsorship by, 141
Freiheit, The, 26
and *Kristallnacht*, 26
and rallies, 63, 139
and *St. Louis*, 86, 88
Friedman, Solomon M.
at rabbinic prayer conference, 164
on Roosevelt appeal, 193

G

General Jewish Council
creation of, 57
demonstration policy of, 59
LaGuardia protest and, 63
policies of, 60, 64
protest policy of, 46
reactions to, 79
and *St. Louis*, 88
General Jewish Workers' Committee of Poland, on Warsaw Ghetto Uprising, 155
German-American Bund, 92
Gilbert, Martin, 22
Gillette, Guy M., 173
effect of Jewish split on, 179
Gillette-Rogers Resolutions, 173
Jewish community split on, 176
Zionist positions on, 176
Ghetto Speaks, The, on Warsaw Ghetto Uprising, 155
Glatstein, Jacob
on Jewish silence, 65
on Roosevelt appeal, 191
Goebbels, Josef, threats of, 61
Golinkin, Noah, on rescue plans, 129
Gold, Wolf, at rabbinic prayer conference, 164

Goldberg, B. Z.
on Emergency Committee, 177
on Jewish silence, 65
Goldman, Solomon, and *Kristallnacht*, 53
Goldmann, Nahum
fears for Hungary of, 186
on guilt, 205
Goldstein, Israel
at American Jewish Conference, 168
appeal to Roosevelt, 112
Hungarian rescue plea of, 188
on rescue, 123
Grafton, Samuel, Free Ports proposal of, 1983
Great Britain
Kristallnacht reaction of Jews of, 71
resettlement plan of, 43
See also British.
Green, William, at mass rally, 141
Greenberg, Hayim
condemnation of American Jewry by, 129
and food relief proposal, 136
and *Kristallnacht*, 51
Grodzinski, Chaim Ozer, *Kristallnacht* reaction of, 72
Grynszpan, Heischel, vom Rath assassination by, 35
Grynszpan, Zindel, and vom Rath assassination, 35
Gustaf V of Sweden, appeal to Horthy by, 190

H

Hadassah, 34
Kristallnacht reaction of, 73
Hadassah Newsletter, 27
on Final Solution, 125
on *Kristallnacht*, 53
Hadoar
on day of prayer, 135
on Final Solution news, 121
on Jewish accountability, 214
and *Kristallnacht*, 55
on refugee rescue, 192
on Roosevelt gesture, 194
and *St. Louis*, 90
on Warsaw Ghetto Uprising, 156
Halifax, Lord, and refugee conference, 143

Halperin, Samuel, American Jewry analysis by, 208

Hecht, Ben
  on Moscow Declaration, 172
  pageant of, 143
  and Romanian Jews rescue idea, 137

Held, Adolph
  at American Jewish Hungarian Conference, 202
  appeal to Roosevelt, 112
  at Carnegie Hall meeting, 156
  and public demonstrations, 59

Heller, James G., action call of, 134

Hertz, Joseph H.
  Bergson Group support by, 163
  Kristallnacht, reaction of, 72

Herzog, Isaac Halevi
  Bergson group support by, 163
  Emergency Committee support by, 177

Hebrew Immigrant Aid Society, contribution to War Refugee Board by, 180

Hilberg, Raul
  American Jewry analysis by, 196
  and Final Solution news, 113
  and Jewish reactions, 31

Hillman, Sidney, 30

Hirschman, Ira, and War Refugee Board, 180

Holmnan, Rufus, alien phobias of, 96

Holmes, John Haynes
  and Final Solution news, 108, 122
  and *Kristallnacht*, 51, 61

Hoover, Herbert C.
  Bergson Group support by, 164
  immigration policies of, 94
  on Wagner-Rogers Act, 98

Horthy, Nicholas
  appeals to, 190
  and Nazi occupation of Hungary, 184

Houghtelling, James L., on immigration, 99

House Foreign Affairs Committee on Hungarian atrocities, 190

Hull, Cordell
  on ambassador recall, 41
  Bergson Group support by, 163
  on Hungarian atrocities, 172, 190
  Jewish attitude toward, 33
  and refugee conference, 143
  and War Refugee Board, 180

Hungarian deportations, American Jewish reactions to, 190, 212
  See also Hungary.

Hungary
  atrocities in, 187
  bombing proposal for, 195
  Central Jewish Council of, 1898
  Final Solution in, 189
  Nazi occupation of, 24, 184
  See also Hungarian.

Hurwitz, Henry
  on Final Solution, 127
  and Hungarian crisis, 214
  on Warsaw Ghetto Uprising, 155

Hyman, Joseph C., and Joint Distribution Committee position on refugees, 101

I

Ickes, Harold
  Kristallnacht, reaction of, 40
  pro-Jewish attitude of, 79
  on Wagner-Rogers Act, 98
  on War Refugee Board, 181

Intergovernmental Committee for Political Refugees, 69, 162

International Jewish Colonization Society, 75

International Ladies Garment Workers' Union, fundraising by, 64

J

Jewish Advocate, 27
  on Final Solution news, 110, 117
  and *Kristallnacht*, 73

Jewish Agency for Palestine, postwar concerns of, 132

Jewish Center and *Kristallnacht*, 55

Jewish community, divisions within, 179, 212

Jewish Combat Organization. *See* ZOB.

Jewish Daily Foward, 25. *See also* Forward.

"Jewish Day," proposal for, 156

Jewish Exponent, 27
  on Final Solution news, 118
  and *St. Louis*, 86, 90

Jewish Forum on Hungarian bombing, 195

Jewish Frontier, 26, 71, 77
  on Bergson Group, 163
  bombing proposals of, 196
  on Final Solution news, 120
  and food relief proposal, 136
  on Free Ports proposal, 193

on Gillette-Rogers Resolutions, 176
on Hungarian atrocities, 185
and *Kristallnacht,* 51
on rescue efforts, 200
on Warsaw Ghetto Uprising, 156, 158
on Zygelboym suicide, 156, 157
Jewish Legion, proposal for, 137
Jewish National Committee *See* ZKN.
Jewish Labor Committee
    action appeal of, 136
    and appeal to Roosevelt, 112
    boycott by, 76
    condemnation of, 130
    and day of prayer, 135
    on Free Ports Proposal, 193
    in General Jewish Council, 57
    in Joint Emergency Committee, 143
    and mass rallies, 59, 64, 107, 140, 141
    and *St. Louis,* 88
    and Warsaw Ghetto Uprising, 151, 156
Jewish National Fund
    on Final Solution, 124
    Kristallnacht reaction of, 73
Jewish Outlook, 27
    on Final Solution, 125
    and *Kristallnacht,* 54
    on Moscow Declaration, 170
    on rescue efforts, 200
Jewish People's Committee, 66
    and *Kristallnacht,* 40
    public policy of, 62, 63
    rally by, 138
Jewish Socialist Party of Poland. *See* Bund.
Jewish Spectator, The, 21, 26, 34
    American Jewry criticism by, 214
    on Final Solution news, 120
    and food relief proposal, 136
    on Free Ports proposal, 193
    on Gillette-Rogers Resolutions, 176
    on Jewish policy, 29
    on Moscow Declaration, 170
    on Roosevelt appeal, 192
    on Roosevelt gesture, 194
    on Warsaw Ghetto Uprising, 155
JTA
    Budapest bombing report, 195
    on Final Solution, 113
    on Gillette-Rogers Resolutions, 176
    Hungarian bombing report, 196
    on Hungarian atrocities, 187, 188, 189
    and *Kristallnacht,* 48
    and mass rally, 140
    news role of, 25, 49

on protest, 63
on Warsaw Ghetto, 150
on Warsaw Ghetto Uprising, 152
Jewish Telegraphic Agency Daily News Bulletin. See JTA.
Jewish Theological Seminary students
    on American Jewry, 128
    on day of prayer, 135
Jewish War Veterans boycott movement, 76
Johnson, Edwin C., Bergson Group support by, 164
Johnson Immigration Act of 1924, 67, 94
Joint Boycott Council, 76
Joint Distribution Committee
    Hungarian activities, 201
    Kristallnacht, reaction of, 73
    and *St. Louis,* 83, 100
    and War Refugee Board, financial contribution to, 180
Joint Emergency Committee for European Jewish Affairs
    and Bermuda Conference, 162, 163
    creation of, 143
Junior Hadassah and *Kristallnacht,* 54

K

Kallay, Miklos, Hungarian policies of, 184
Kapov-Kagen, Ben Zion, at American Jewish Conference, 167
Karshi, Jan, and Final Solution news, 131
Katz, Shlomo, on American Jewry, 34
Kerstein, Louis E., death of, 117
Kirchway, Freda
    rally comments of, 143
    on United States policy, 28
    See also Spectator, The.
Kotler, Aaron, food relief proposal of, 136
Krensky, Rosemary, 93
Kristallnacht, 23, 35
Kubowitzki, A. Leon, on bombing death camps, 197
Kuhn, Fritz, and German-American Bund

L

LaGuardia, Fiorello, and rallies, 63, 141
Landon, Alfred, on Wagner-Rogers Act, 98
Laqueur, Walter
    on Final Solution perception, 131
    on Jewish leaders, 34

Laughlin, Harry, on immigration, 95
Lehman, Herbert H., 30
  and Final Solution news, 122
Leiper, Henry Smith, and *Kristallnacht*, 51
Lerner, Max
  on Bergson conference, 164
  and Final Solution news, 122
  on Intergovernmental Agency, 164
Levinthal, Bernard L., at rabbinic prayer
  meeting, 164
Levick, H., on Warsaw Ghetto Uprising,
  158
Levin, Isaac
  action call of, 133
  and Final Solution news, 109
  on Jewish community split, 179
Liberal Judaism, 26
  on Warsaw Ghetto Uprising, 156
Liberty Magazine, 79
Lincoln (Nebraska) *Journal* on refugee
  policy, 42
Lipnick, Jerome, on rescue plans, 129
London Evening Standard proposals for
  "Jewish Day," 156
Long, Breckinridge
  Jewish Frontier attack on, 176
  Morgenthau condemnation of, 161
  Romanian rescue obstruction by, 138
  visa policy of, 28
Lookstein, Joseph H., rally support by,
  139

M

MacIntyre, Marvin H., Bergson petition
  to Roosevelt through, 164
Macy's
  German boycott by, 76
  refugee hiring policy of, 95
Manchester Guardian on Warsaw Ghetto
  Uprising, 155
Mann, Thomas, and Final Solution news,
  122
Margoshes, Samuel, 70
  on Final Solution news, 114
  on Gillette-Rogers Resolutions, 175
  Kristallnacht articles by, 45
  on rescue operations, 198
  Roosevelt comments of, 1;71
  on Warsaw Ghetto Uprising, 154
Marshall, George C., on American-Brit-
  ish relationships, 186

McCloy, John J., on bombing death
  camps, 197
McCormick, Anne O'Hare
  on immigration, 142
  on *Kristallnacht*, 39
Menorah Journal
  on anti-Semitism, 55
  on Final Solution, 127
  Hungarian crisis disregard by, 214
Messersmitt, George, in State Department, 41
Mexico as refugee haven, 89
Miller, Irving, on Warsaw Ghetto, 151
Mizrachi Organization of America
  on Final Solution, 125
  and *Kristallnacht*, 54
Modzitser Rabbi, *Kristallnacht* appeal of,
  75
Monsky, Henry
  action proposals of, 58
  at American Jewish Conference, 167
  at American Jewish Conference Hun-
    garian rally, 202
  postwar concerns of, 133
  rescue proposal of, 136
  Roosevelt appeals by, 112
  See also B'nai B'rith.
Morgenthau, Henry, Jr., 30
  Bergson Group support by, 163
  and Final Solution news, 109
  Long condemnation by, 161
  and mass rally, 140
  on Romanian rescue obstruction, 138
  and War Refugee Board, 161, 180, 183
Morning Journal, 25, 76
  on American Jewish Conference rally
    for Hungarians, 202
  anti-Semitism concerns of, 93
  on bombing death camps, 197
  criticism of American Jewry, 214
  on demonstrations, 65
  credit for Emergency Committee by,
    181
  on Final Solution news, 115
  on Gillette-Rogers Resolutions, 174
  on Hungarian atrocities, 187, 198
  and *Kristallnacht*, 45, 47, 49, 72
  and mass rallies, 139, 140
  on Moscow Declaration, 170
  on prayer and mourning, 135
  on rescue operations, 198, 201
  and *St. Louis*, 86, 89

on Warsaw Ghetto Uprising, 152, 153, 154
Morse, Arthur D., 21, 22
Moscow Declaration, 169, 185
Murphy, Frank, support for Jews by, 183
"My Uncle Abraham Reports . . ." 172

N

Nathan, Edgar J., Jr., postwar concerns of, 132
Nation, The
  and food relief proposal, 136
  and rescue plans, 129
  and United States policy, 28
National Conference of Jews and Christians prayer day, 58
National Committee Against Nazi Persecution and Extermination of the Jews of Europe, 183
National Coordinating Committee *Kristallnacht* response, 74
National Jewish Monthly, 26
  on American immigration, 182, 207
  attitude to refugees of, 68
  on death statistics, 124
  on Hungarian Jewry, 199
  and *Kristallnacht,* 52
  on protest efficacy, 203
  on War Refugee Board, 182
National Jewish Welfare Board and *Kristallnacht,* 55
National Refugee Service activities with Hungarians, 201
New Palestine, 27, 89
  and Committee for a Jewish Army, 138
  on Final Solution, 124, 125
  on Free Ports Proposal, 194
  on Gillette-Rogers Resolutions, 176
  and *Kristallnacht,* 52
  on Moscow Declaration, 170
  on rescue efforts, 200
  and *St. Louis,* 88
  on War Refugee Board, 182
New Republic
  on refugee policy, 44
  and rescue plans, 129
New Statesman and Nation on Jewish policy, 29
New York State Chamber of Commerce, immigration ideas of, 95

New York Daily News on immigration laws, 44
New York Post on War Refugee Board, 181
New York Times, The, 25
  on American Jewish Conference attack on Emergency Committee, 178
  on day of prayer, 111
  death statistics summary by, 162
  on Final Solution, 105, 112, 116
  on Free Ports proposal, 193, 194
  on Gillette-Rogers Resolutions, 176
  Hadassah letter to, 34
  on Hungarian Jewry, 187, 188, 198, 201
  on immigration, 142
  Jewish Legion advertisement in, 137
  on Jewish People's Committee rally, 63
  Kristallnacht description by, 36
  Kristallnacht reaction by, 39
  mass rally advertisement in, 140
  on Moscow Declaration, 172
  on Nazi brutality, 37
  Rabbi Pool prayer text in, 40
  on rabbinic prayer meeting, 164, 165
  on refugee resettlement, 43
  report on Roosevelt after *Kristallnacht,* 41
  on Sachsenhausen brutality, 49
  and *St. Louis,* 84, 90, 93, 100
  sermon summaries on Final Solution, 129
  on War Refugee Board, 160
  on Warsaw Ghetto Uprising, 150
  on Warsaw Ghetto Uprising Anniversary, 201
  on Zygelboym suicide, 149
News Chronicle on Sachsenhausen, 38
Night of the Broken Glass. *See Kristallnacht.*
Niles, David K., 30
No Haven for the Oppressed, 22
  on Roosevelt appeal, 193
Non-Sectarian Anti-Nazi League, 70, 76
Nonsectarian Committee for German Refugee Children, 98
Notes and News, 27
  on Final Solution, 127
  and *Kristallnacht,* 54

O

Opinion, 26
  action urged by, 93

Opinion (continued)
  on American immigration, 207
  on American Jewry, 128
  on Final Solution news, 122
  on General Jewish Council, 62
  on Gillette-Rogers Resolutions, 176
  on Hull statement, 172
  on Hungarian Jewry, 199
  and *Kristallnacht,* 51
  on Roosevelt appeal, 191
  See also Wise, Stephen S.
Orduna and Cuba, 83
Orthodox Union, The, 26
  on Final Solution, 126
  and *Kristallnacht,* 54
Oswego Free Port, Jewish press reaction
  to, 207. *See also* Fort Ontario; Free
  Ports.

P

Palestine
  Hadassah emphasis on, 125
  as Jewry issue, 175
Paper Walls, 22
Pehle, John, as War Refugee Board Di-
  rector, 193
Perkins, Frances
  anti-refugee attitude of, 68
  on immigration, 96
  on Wagner-Rogers Act, 98
Philadelphia Jewish Exponent and *Kristall-
  nacht,* 73
Picket, Clarence, on Wagner-Rogers Act,
  98
Piltch, Judah, on Jewish accountability,
  214
Pittsburgh Assembly, proceedings of, 166
Poland
  annihilation of Jewish remnant in, 186
  anti-Semitism in, 68
  Jews of, 50
  See also Polish.
Polish Government in Exile and Final So-
  lution news, 109, 110
Polish National Council and Polish Jewry
  extermination, 106
Polish Union of Rabbis, *Kristallnacht* re-
  action by, 72
Pool, David De Sola, and *Kristallnacht,* 40
Pope Pius XII appeal to Horthy, 190

Proskauer, Joseph M., on Roosevelt appeal, 191
"Protocols of the Elders of Zion," 78

Q

Quill, Michael, rally support by, 139

R

Rabbinic prayer meeting, petition of, 165
Rabbinical Assembly on rescue efforts, 201
Rabinical Council of America
  rally support by, 139
  on rescue, 201
Rankin, John, alien phobias of, 96
Reconstructionist, 26
  on American Jewry, 128
  anti-General Jewish Council statements
    of, 65
  comments on children's activism, 139
  on Emergency Committee, 176
  on Final Solution news, 121
  on Hungarian Jewry, 199
  and *Kristallnacht,* 52
  on Moscow Declaration, 170
  on Warsaw Ghetto Uprising, 155
  on Zygelboym suicide, 157
Reform Jewish movement
  on Final Solution, 126
  and *Kristallnacht,* 54
Reitlinger, Gerald, 23
  on Warsaw Ghetto Uprising, 146
Resolution on Rescue of European Jewry
  of American Jewish Conference, 168
Revisionist Zionists and Jewish Legion
  proposal, 137
Revel, Bernard, on *Kristallnacht,* 72
Reynolds, Robert, alien phobias of, 96
Reynolds-Starnes bill, 97
Ribalow, Menachem
  on *Kristallnacht,* 55
  on refugee rescue, 192
  and *St. Louis,* 90
  See also Hadoar.
Riegner, Gerhard
  on American Jewry, 145
  and Final Solution announcement, 106,
    107
  message as mass rally stimulus, 139

Riff, Naftaly, at American Jewish Conference, 167
Ringelbaum, Emanuel, on Warsaw Ghetto attitudes, 61
Rogers, Edith, on immigration, 98
Rogers, Will Jr., 173
  Bergson Group support by, 164
  purpose of action by, 179
Romania
  anti-Semitism in, 68
  Jews of, 50
  rescue idea for Jews of, 137
Roosevelt, Eleanor
  support for Bergson Group by, 163
  on Wagner-Rogers Act, 98
Roosevelt, Franklin Delano, 70
  action proposals to, 142, 143
  anti-Semitic remarks of, 79
  appeals to, 112, 140, 191
  Bergson Group support by, 163
  Bergson petition to, 164
  Free Ports establishment by, 194
  Holocaust information avoidance by, 171
  immigration policies of, 94
  Jewish perception of, 51, 210
  Kristallnacht reaction of, 41
  and Moscow Declaration, 169
  nonreception of rabbis by, 165
  promises regarding Nazis of, 107
  and public opinion, 32
  and quotas on immigration, 67
  refugee attitude of, 28
  refugee policies of, 69
  shortcomings of, 213
  and War Refugee Board, 160, 180
  War Refugee Board proclamation, Jewish omission in, 182
  warning to Nazis, 173
Rosenberg, Israel
  appeal to Roosevelt, 112
  at rabbinic prayer meeting, 164
Rosenberg, James N.
  as anti-Zionist, 74
  and *St. Louis*, 84
Rosenman, Samuel, 30, 69
  advice to Roosevelt on rabbinic meeting, 165
Rosmarin, Trude Weiss
  editorials on Hungary, 199
  on Final Solution news, 120
  on Roosevelt appeal, 192
  See also Jewish Spectator.

S

Sachs, N. Bertram, on rescue plans, 129
Sachsenhausen, 36, 38
  reportage on, 49
St. James Conference, actions of, 171
St. Louis
  immigration policy effects on, 93
  Jewish response to, 90
  psychological effect of, 102
  voyage of, 23, 81
Saltsonstall, Leverett, support for Jews by, 183
Sandler, Bernard H., and *St. Louis*, 100
Schacht, Hjalmar, proposal of, 77
Schroeder, Gustav, as *St. Louis* captain, 82
Schwartzbart, Ignacy, and Polish Jewry, 107
Schwellenbach, Lewis B., on anti-alien bias, 207
Shoshani, M., *See* Ribalow, Menachem.
Shuster, George, at mass rally, 141
Sikorski, Wladyslaw
  World Jewish Congress reply from, 171
  Zygleboym letter to, 149
Silver, Abba Hillel, on Palestine, 74
Silver, Eliezer
  appeal for rescue funds, 201
  rebuttal of American Jewish Conference charges, 178
Silverman, Sidney, Final Solution information to, 108
Sizoo, Joseph R., and *Kristallnacht*, 40
Smith, Alfred E.
  and Final Solution news, 122
  and *Kristallnacht*, 39
Social Justice, anti-Semitism of, 78
Soloveitchik, Joseph B., and *Kristallnacht*, 73
Springfield Republican on *Kristallnacht*, 38
State Department, United States
  Final Solution policy of, 123
  Morgenthau condemnation of, 161
  obstructionism of, 144
  policies of, 131
  on rescue, 123
  Romanian rescue interference by, 138
  suppression of Final Solution news, 108

Stalin, Josef, and Moscow Declaration, 169

Starnes, Joe, alien phobias of, 96

Stern Brothers Department Store, refugee policies of, 95

Sternbuch, Isaac, report on Hungarian atrocities, 196

Stimson, Henry L.
  on British-American relationships, 186
  and War Refugee Board, 180

Sweden, appeal to Horthy by, 109

Synagogue, The, 26
  on Final Solution, 126
  and Kristallnacht, 54

Synagogue Council of America
  and appeal to Roosevelt, 112
  and day of prayer, 135
  and Final Solution news, 110
  in Joint Emergency Committee, 143
  and Kristallnacht, 40

Syrkin, Marie, appeal to Roosevelt by, 195

Szotjay, Dome, as Hungarian Nazi leader, 185

T

Taylor, Myron C., 69, 70

Terrible Secret, The, on perception of Final Solution, 131

Thackrey, Ted O., on War Refugee Board, 181

Thompson, Dorothy, and German-American Bund, 92

Time on Sachsenhausen brutality, 38, 47

Transit Workers' Union, rally support by, 139

Troper, Morris, and St. Louis, 85

Tucker, George, at mass rally, 141

U

Ukraine, Jewish population of, 50

Union of Grand Rabbis of the United States and Canada, and rabbinic prayer meeting, 164

Union of Orthodox Jewish Congregations of America and Kristallnacht, 54

Union of Orthodox Rabbis
  at American Jewish Conference, 167
  appeal for rescue funds, 201
  appeal to Roosevelt, 112
  and day of prayer, 135

and rabbinic prayer meeting, 164
  rebuttal of American Jewish Conference charges, 178

United Jewish Appeal for Refugee and Overseas Needs, Kristallnacht response of, 74

United Nations, condemnation of, 130

United Palestine Appeal, Kristallnacht reaction of, 73, 74

United States
  immigration restrictions, 93
  State Department. See State Department, United States.

United Wholesale and Warehouse Workers' Union, and boycott, 63

V

Va'ad Ha-Hatzala
  rescue activities of, 201
  and War Refugee Board, financial contribution to, 180

vom Rath, Ernst, assassination of, 35

van Passen, Pierre, warnings of, 134

W

Wagner, Robert F.
  on immigration, 98
  at mass rally, 141

Wagner-Rogers Act on immigration, 98

Wallace, Henry A.
  and Final Solution news, 122
  rabbinic plea to, 164
  support for Jews by, 183

War Refugee Board
  acceptance for, 180
  creation of, 23, 160, 180
  financial contributions to, 180
  food parcel program of, 137
  functions of, 180
  futility of, 200
  Jewish disunity as cause for creation delay, 183
  and Hungarian rescue plans, 203
  as policy shift of government, 182
  proclamation, Jewish omission from, 182
  recognition for, 198
  on refugee immigration, 193

Warsaw Ghetto, conditions in, 150

Warsaw Ghetto Uprising, 23, 146
  Jewish press on, 149

news of, 151
start of, 147
Washington Post
  on *Kristallnacht,* 38
  on War Refugee Board, 181
We Will Never Die, performance of, 143
Weizmann, Chaim
  at mass rally, 141
  on public policy, 33
  proposal to bomb death camps, 197
Welles, Sumner, 69
  and Bermuda Conference, 143
  and Final Solution report, 108, 110
Wells, H. G., anti-Semitism of, 79
Wertheim, Maurice, appeal to Roosevelt
  by, 112
While Six Million Died, 21
Wiesel, Elie, 23
  on Jewish perception of Roosevelt, 211
  on Warsaw Ghetto Uprising, 158
Willkie, Wendell L.
  on Gillette-Rogers Resolutions, 174
  support for Jews by, 183
  on War Refugee Board, 181
Wilson, Hugh R., 70
  recall from Germany of, 41, 51
Wise, Jonah, as anti-Zionist, 74
Wise, Stephen S.
  on American Jewish Conference, 167
  at American Jewish Conference Hun-
    garian rally, 202
  on Americanism, 31
  on anti-Semitism, 92
  appeal to Roosevelt, 112
  Bergson action against, 178
  at Carnegie Hall meeting, 156
  and collective discipline, 60
  and Committee for a Jewish Army, 138
  and Final Solution news, 108, 110, 144
  and food relief proposal, 136
  on Gillette-Rogers Resolutions, 175
  and House Foreign Affairs Commit-
    tee, 175
  on Hungarian Jewry, 199
  and *Kristallnacht,* 51
  at mass rally, 141

and *Opinion* magazine, 122
on Palestinian immigration, 175
perceptions of, 131
public silence on immigration, 99
on Warsaw Ghetto uprising, 155
See also Congress Bulletin; Congress Weekly.
Wohl Matthew, on American Jewry, 145
Workman's Circle, rally by, 141
World Council of Churches on Hungarian atrocities, 190
World Jewish Congress
  and Final Solution announcement, 106,
    107, 110
  on Hungary, 186
  reaction to Roosevelt appeal, 191
  on St. James Conference, 171
  Rescue Division, on bombing camps,
    197
World Mizrachi Organization, on Emergency Committee, 179
Wyman, David S., 22
  on anti-Semitism, 91

Y

Yeshiva College and *Kristallnacht,* 72
Yiddish press, 25
  on War Refugee board, 180

Z

Zaar, Isaac, and Committee for a Jewish
  Army, 143
Zionist Organization of America
  at American Jewish Conference, 168
  and *Kristallnacht,* 52
  and Polish Jewry, 107
Zionist position on rescue, 175
ZKN, 147
ZOB, 147
  appeal by, 157
Zuckerman, William on Warsaw Ghetto
  Uprising, 153
Zygelboym, Samuel
  and Polish Jewry, 106
  suicide by, 149
  suicide, results of, 156

ABOUT THE AUTHOR

Haskel Lookstein comes to this subject from a life of concern for the well-being of Jews everywhere. Reared in a rabbinic home, he and his wife have visited the Soviet Union twice in order to bring strength and support to refuseniks there. Rabbi of Congregation Kehilath Jeshurun and Principal of the Ramaz School in New York, his congregation and school have been leaders in responding to the needs and sruggles of the Jewish people. Rabbi Lookstein is Chairman of the National Rabbinic Cabinet of the United Jewish Appeal and President of the New York Board of Rabbis. He is a Vice Chairman of The Coalition to Free Soviet Jews, formerly the Greater New York Conference on Soviet Jewry. Dr. Lookstein is also Joseph H. Lookstein Professor of Homiletics at Yeshiva University's Rabbi Isaac Elchanan Theological Seminary.

TITLES OF RELATED INTEREST FROM VINTAGE BOOKS

75525-1   Adler, Renata   RECKLESS DISREGARD: Westmoreland *vs.* CBS et al. Sharon *vs.* TIME
75288-0   Bialer, Seweryn   THE SOVIET PARADOX: *External Expansion, Internal Decline*
75538-3   Bonner, Elena   ALONE TOGETHER
72379-1   Cockburn, Andrew   THE THREAT: *Inside the Soviet Military Machine*
74308-3   Draper, Theodore   AMERICAN COMMUNISM AND SOVIET RUSSIA
75533-2   Eisenhower, David   EISENHOWER: *At War 1943–1945*
70390-1   Ellul, Jacques   THE TECHNOLOGICAL SOCIETY
72023-7   Fest, Joachim C.   HITLER
72767-3   Foucault, Michel   DISCIPLINE AND PUNISH: *The Birth of the Prison*
71914-X   Foucault, Michel   MADNESS AND CIVILIZATION
71935-2   Foucault, Michel   THE ORDER OF THINGS
75715-7   Gervasi, Tom   SOVIET MILITARY POWER: *The Pentagon's Propaganda Document, Annotated and Corrected*
70183-6   Goldman, Eric F.   THE CRUCIAL DECADE—AND AFTER: *America, 1945–1960*
72727-4   Grose, Peter   A CHANGING ISRAEL
70815-6   Grosser, Alfred   THE WESTERN ALLIANCE: *European-American Relations Since 1945*
75590-1   Gubaryev, Vladimir   SARCOPHAGUS: *A Tragedy*
75527-8   Hersh, Seymour M.   "THE TARGET IS DESTROYED": *What Really Happened to Flight 007 and What America Knew About It*
71746-5   Herzog, Chaim   THE ARAB-ISRAELI WARS: *War and Peace in the Middle East, from the War of Independence through Lebanon*
74721-6   Mandelbaum, Michael, and Strobe Talbott   REAGAN AND GORBACHEV
74724-0   Milosz, Czeslaw   THE CAPTIVE MIND
71195-5   Naipaul, V. S.   AMONG THE BELIEVERS
72728-2   Oz, Amos   IN THE LAND OF ISRAEL
74188-5   Ross, Bill   IWO JIMA: *Legacy of Valor*
74670-8   Sagan, Eli   AT THE DAWN OF TYRANNY: *The Origins of Individualism, Political Oppression, and the State*
74067-X   Said, Edward   ORIENTALISM
74478-0   Schorske, Carl E.   FIN-DE-SIECLE VIENNA: *Politics and Culture*
74655-4   Sennett, Richard   AUTHORITY
72420-8   Sennett, Richard   THE FALL OF PUBLIC MAN: *The Social Psychology of Capitalism*
71035-5   Sereny, Gitta   INTO THAT DARKNESS: *An Examination of Conscience*
75204-X   Sherwin, Martin   A WORLD DESTROYED: *Hiroshima and the Origins of the Arms Race*
71658-2   Smith, Denis Mack   MUSSOLINI: *A Biography*
72901-3   Spector, Leonard S.   NUCLEAR PROLIFERATION TODAY: *The Spread of Nuclear Weapons 1984*
74189-7   Spector, Leonard S.   THE NEW NUCLEAR NATIONS: *The Spread of Nuclear Weapons 1985*

74101-3	Spector, Ronald H. EAGLE AGAINST THE SUN: *The American War With Japan*
74731-3	Steel, Ronald WALTER LIPPMANN AND THE AMERICAN CENTURY
71962-X	Stern, Fritz THE VARIETIES OF HISTORY
70387-1	Stern, Fritz GOLD AND IRON: *Bismarck, Bleichroder, and the Building of the German Empire*
74009-2	Talbott, Strobe DEADLY GAMBITS
72635-9	Talbott, Strobe THE RUSSIANS AND REAGAN
70387-1	Taylor, A. J. P. BISMARCK: *The Man and the Statesman*
74482-9	Taylor, Telford MUNICH: *The Price of Peace*
75131-0	Timerman, Jacobo PRISONER WITHOUT A NAME, CELL WITHOUT A NUMBER
71471-7	Timerman, Jacobo THE LONGEST WAR: *Israel in Lebanon*
74057-2	Wiesel, Elie A JEW TODAY
74456-X	Wright, Jaime TORTURE IN BRAZIL
75445-X	Zuckerman, Lord STAR WARS IN A NUCLEAR WORLD